TRAITOR
TO THE
CROWN

TRAITOR
TO THE
CROWN

*The Untold Story of the Popish Plot
and the Conspiracy Against Samuel
Pepys*

JAMES LONG & BEN LONG

THE OVERLOOK PRESS
New York

This edition first published in paperback the United States in 2009 by
The Overlook Press, Peter Mayer Publishers, Inc.
141 Wooster Street
New York, NY 10012

Cataloging-in-Publication Data is available from the Library of Congress

Manufactured in the United States of America
ISBN 978-1-59020-264-7
10 9 8 7 6 5 4 3 2 1

For Annie, Harry and Matilda

Contents

List of Illustrations

Authors' Note

Seventeenth-century dates can be confusing. Legally, the new year did not begin until 25 March (Lady Day). However, in common practice it began on 1 January. As a result, both dates were given in the form '1 January 1678/79'. We have followed common practice in beginning the new year on 1 January.

Until 1752, British ('Old Style') dates were ten days behind their European ('New Style') equivalents. Dates in this book are generally Old Style unless otherwise stated.

In the interests of clarity, we have modernised spellings.

Acknowledgements

The authors would like to thank the master and fellows of Magdalene College, Cambridge, for access to Pepys's manuscripts. Dr Richard Luckett, Pepys Librarian, and Mrs Aude Fitzsimons generously lent their support, enthusiasm and knowledge. We are greatly indebted to them.

Our thanks to the librarians at the British Library, the Duke Humfrey's Library, Oxford, and the National Archives, and to the staff at the Institute of Historical Research. We are grateful to the Comptroller of Longleat for permission to use material from the Henry Coventry archive, and to Dr Kate Harris, curator of Longleat Historic Collections.

Dr C. S. Knighton and Guy de la Bédoyère were kind enough to answer our questions. J. H. L. Puxley generously shared his portraits with us, as did James P. S. Thomson, the Master of Charterhouse. James Rhys provided an informative tour of the Houses of Parliament. Thanks also to David Burnett, Will Hutton and Pete and Liz Strange.

Victoria Hobbs at A. M. Heath, the best possible agent and friend, saw the point straight away. Thanks to Henry Volans and to our editor at Faber, Julian Loose, who have steered us with patience and a deft touch.

The rest of the Long family, in putting up with arcane mealtime debates, a house overwhelmed by papers and our reading them numerous drafts, have proved themselves a tolerant and fine-spirited lot, and this book is dedicated to them.

ILLUSTRATION CREDITS

1: © The British Library; 2: © National Portrait Gallery, London; 3: © National Portrait Gallery, London; 4: © National Maritime Museum, London; 5: © National Portrait Gallery, London; 6: © National Portrait Gallery, London; 7: © The Trustees of the British Museum; 8: Charterhouse, London; 9: Charterhouse, London; 10: © Marquess of Bath, Longleat; 11: Mornamont, Volume 1, Pepys Library, Magdalene College, Cambridge; 12: © The Trustees of the British Museum; 13: Private Collection; 14 and 15: © Bodleian Library, University of Oxford; 16: © National Maritime Museum, London.

I

Into the Tower

He was led outside, the heat of their wrath at his back. As he emerged through the stone archway, fat drops of spring rain were falling from a dark sky.[1]

His eyes suggested a judicious mind and he carried authority, but his fleshy lower lip and extra chin told a more sensuous story of good food, wine and women. The inquisitive little frown was permanent though deepened at this moment, perhaps, by indignation. His colleague arrived beside him and, under guard, they began the journey away from their old lives. His name was Samuel Pepys. He was an MP. He had just been accused of treason in the whitewashed chamber of the House of Commons.

The heavy sky rumbled. They were led away from the seething Commons, through the houses that spilled down to the steps on the bank of the Thames and into a boat. Nearby, Pepys's luxurious private barge, decorated with paintings of 'little seas', lay ignored at its mooring.[2] They pulled out into the tide and got a last view of Westminster. The Commons' House – St Stephen's Chapel – rose in medieval splendour. Once Henry VIII's private place of worship (and lined with squirrel tails and peacock feathers), its stripped walls now contained the turbulent MPs who had taken it for themselves.[3] Beside it were Westminster Abbey and Westminster Hall, and beyond them, parkland and open fields. A hundred yards further on, they passed the Admiralty Office in Derby House with Pepys's comfortable lodgings over it, now entirely beyond his reach.

The modern world knows Pepys's loves, ambition, anxieties and transgressions through his Diary, but at this moment it remained his secret, closed ten years earlier and protected from prying eyes by his neat shorthand.

The men who had condemned him in the Commons knew him only for his public work as Secretary to the Admiralty; a short man who cut a mighty figure in King Charles II's administration.* The knowledge necessary to qualify a man for that position, as Pepys himself was aware, unavoidably carried with it the ability to deliver up his country (if, like this, an island) to any neighbour furnished with even a moderately powerful navy.[4] Nonetheless, it had come as an immense surprise to be accused of having sold England to her oldest enemy.

The King's ramshackle palace of Whitehall sprawled along the bank, then gave way to the gardens of the Strand mansions running down to the river. As the boat rounded the bend, the quiet, upstream world of governmental and judicial power dropped out of sight and London stretched ahead. At its western outskirts St James's church was under construction in the opulent new courtier area around Piccadilly, and the garden of the Earl of Leicester's mansion had recently been developed and renamed Leicester Square.[5] Their boat picked a line through the river bustle, and the mansions gave way to quays and wharves. In the aftermath of the Great Fire thirteen years before, the entire river frontage of the city had been cleared and the first buildings now stood forty feet back, making a space to collect water should the city burn again.[6] Behind these, the anarchic patchwork of timber-framed houses had gone. Londoners had pushed stakes into the charred ground to claim back the land their homes had stood on and medieval London had risen again, fast and

---

* Ten years before, Pepys had confided to his Diary that he could stand easily under the arms of 'the great tall woman . . . in Holborn'. When he went back to measure the giantess he found her to be six feet five inches tall without her shoes. By a process of deduction, it has been estimated that Pepys stood around five feet one inch tall. Walter H. Whitear, *More Pepysiana* (1927), p. 108.

bland, in brick and stone.[7] The buildings no longer reached over the streets at their upper storeys, and the sky seemed bigger.

Against the black clouds, the city was a sorry sight. Most of the spires – ornamental extras in a rebuilding effort born of pressing necessity – were not yet raised above the new churches.[8] Only the blackened skeleton of old St Paul's drew Pepys's eye upwards. When London burned, the lead had come pouring off the cathedral's high roof and its stones had burst like grenades.[9] All that was left were the high columns and soaring arches, and the sky was visible through the glassless windows. As the prisoners passed by, a host of labourers was scaling the heights to swing pickaxes into the scorched mortar. They detonated explosives under the taller structures, which rose a few feet before falling ponderously in a cloud of dust.[10] Tucked low, out of the prisoners' sight, were the beginnings of a new cathedral, gleaming in clean Portland stone.*

The city was familiar to Pepys and his serious-faced fellow MP, prisoner and companion on this journey, Sir Anthony Deane. They knew the towering Monument to the Fire, its walls filled with the rubble of old St Paul's.[11] They were familiar with the motion of the vessel on the water from years of travelling between the rural quiet of Westminster and this part of the city, a short boat-ride and a world away. Here was buzzing business and, beyond London Bridge, a clutter of tall masts. The bridge, the only crossing point for land traffic, acted as a giant sieve, allowing smaller craft through but forcing the larger ships to offload at the docks downriver. If the tide was wrong, even the smaller boats had to stop and their passengers disembark and walk since the narrow arches formed a sluice, through which the running tide poured in dangerous torrents. On the far side, blocks of white stone, wrapped against irreparable salt water staining, were being unloaded on to the dock and dragged by teams of

---

* More men were killed demolishing Old Paul's than died in the Great Fire. Some thirty-one or thirty-two people were killed in the demolition. Only five were killed directly by the Great Fire although that does not include those who may have died due to their living conditions in its aftermath.

straining horses off towards St Paul's churchyard.[12]

The tall buildings right across London Bridge blocked their view downstream. The barge rocked on the tide through the archway and rushed out into the port of London. There ahead, dominating the north bank, was William the Conqueror's grim bastion, the Tower of London. The barge came alongside and the two men were escorted ashore and taken into captivity by officials of the Tower. Samuel Pepys found himself a prisoner in the medieval building which formed the final eastern marker, the end of the city, on contemporary maps. It had been protected from the Fire by the good fortune of an easterly wind. From here, Pepys had watched medieval London, the London of Shakespeare – whose powerful kings could keep their servants safe under royal wings – burn and disappear.[13] Alone, with no hope of protection from King Charles, he faced a trial it would be almost impossible to win. If he lost, he would be executed.

2

Toys for King Louis

In May 1660, nineteen years before Samuel Pepys's imprisonment in the Tower of London, Charles Stuart came down in triumph to the beach at The Hague. After nine years as an exile on the Continent he was preparing to sail for England and sit as king on the throne that had been denied him. The white sands of the Dutch coast were black with the people who came to watch his departure. When the King's presence on the shore was made known to the English fleet waiting to collect him, its commander fired his ship's guns. The rhythmic explosions of the salute fell out of time as the fleet joined in, a disordered cacophony of celebration.[1] Pepys, who at that time was a young clerk, was on board one of the ships by virtue of his family links to Edward Montagu who commanded the fleet sent to bring Charles home. Pepys fired one of the guns himself, but leaned too far over, and the flash from the touchhole hurt his right eye.[2] All day the guns fired; England had a king again.

When Pepys woke the next morning, his eye was red and sore but his spirits were high, for a new age was being born. Everywhere the old regime was coming to an end. The ships' crews had been busy painting the royal coat of arms over the Commonwealth harp, and the King and his brother, the Duke of York, set to at a table on the *Naseby*'s quarterdeck to make changes. Having no wish to travel back to England in a ship named after the Cromwellian Civil War victory which finished his father, Charles renamed her the *Royal Charles*, while the *Richard,* accompanying her, became the *Royal James.* On deck Pepys watched as 'we weighed anchor, and with a fresh gale and most happy weather we set sail for England'.[3]

He set these events down in a book he had bought at the end of the previous year. Its pages were white, and he had ruled neat red margins on to them. On 1 January he had begun his record. It was the diary of a poor man at the beginning of his career.

As the wind filled the sails to return the fleet and its precious royal cargo to England, a series of little events marked the turn in the fortunes of Samuel Pepys. First, he discovered that he quite liked the new king. Pepys had been sufficiently republican to watch the execution of Charles I with interest, but there was a note of admiration in his description of the dead king's son. 'All the afternoon,' he observed, 'the King walked here and there, up and down (quite contrary to what I thought him to have been) very active and stirring.' Industrious Pepys admired the display of energy. The King could also tell a good story, relating what happened to him after the battle that drove him abroad.

Upon the quarterdeck he fell into discourse of his escape from Worcester, where it made me ready to weep to hear the stories that he told of his difficulties that he had passed through, as his travelling four days and three nights on foot, every step up to his knees in dirt, with nothing but a green coat and a pair of country breeches on, and a pair of country shoes, that made him so sore all over his feet, that he could scarce stir.[4]

In the years to come, Pepys was to hear this many times as Charles told it to courtiers at every opportunity. On that quarterdeck at that moment though, he was privy to the first telling of the most exciting adventure in the life of the most famous Englishman. It would be the talk of the alehouses the length and breadth of the country, a poignant tale with the happiest of endings.

Charles's dog defecated in the boat, to Pepys and his companions' huge delight. A king, Pepys concluded privately, is just as others are. The discovery was both mundane and momentous. At the heart of royal power there was a human being – fallible, powerful and accessible; Pepys was in the right place at the right time. As the fleet approached the English shore, he went to Charles's royal brother James, Duke of York, about some business, and the Duke delighted Pepys by showing that he already knew his name. Pepys plucked up the courage to ingratiate himself and the Duke's response was encouraging. In his diary that night the little clerk recorded the moment with typical brevity; the Duke, wrote Pepys, 'upon my desire did promise me his future favour'.[5] When the fleet completed its Channel crossing, great crowds greeted the royal brothers at Dover. 'The shouting and joy expressed by all is past imagination,' wrote Pepys.[6] Four days later, on 29 May, King Charles II entered London and the old city – Shakespeare's London, a city of tightly packed timber-framed houses whose upper levels still reached out over the streets and shrank the sky – welcomed him and his brother with celebration and open arms.

For his part in the Restoration, Pepys's patron Montagu was made Earl of Sandwich. Sharing Montagu's good fortune, Pepys was helped to the post of Clerk of the Acts – an administrative post with secretarial duties – in the Navy Office later that summer. It was a lucrative job. The Navy Office ran the supply side of the navy, providing it with men, materials and ships. Pepys was officially the most junior of the four officials in charge of it and his Diary shows that his enthusiasm was initially for the comforts of his new life.[7] The navy was disorganised and run on a hand-to-mouth basis. The new Clerk of the Acts did his job well enough but no better.

His life changed at the beginning of 1662 when new instructions from the Duke of York as Lord High Admiral arrived at the Navy Office. Pepys recognised in them the Duke's determined appetite for reform. He saw that he would do well to follow that lead and began to employ a vigorous precision in his work. As he wrote in his Diary the next day: 'and so to the office, where I begin to be exact in my duty there and exacting my privileges – and shall continue to do so.'[8] From then, he had an increasingly high regard for the Duke as a clear-sighted champion of proper resourcing for the beleaguered, cash-strapped navy. The Duke was a stiffer and less intelligent man than his subtle brother, the King, but he was an expert on this subject. The favour that he had promised Pepys on the ship came naturally. Pepys and the Duke stood together against frequent outbursts of obstruction, suspicion and criticism from the House of Commons and Pepys became the Duke's advocate and public protector in that forum. He was a man on the make, seizing the opportunities the job offered to raise his own status among his Navy Office colleagues and to swell his own income in the process.

Through the rest of the 1660s, as that first Diary was filled and succeeded by five slightly larger volumes, a million and a quarter words in Pepys's neat shorthand tell the story of his increasing status and the growing royal dependency on his bureaucratic and presentational skills. In the foreground of the Diary stand the dramatic events of that decade, the Plague and the Great Fire, woven in with Pepys's sharp observations on all around him and all within him – few diarists have been so honest about their own frailties and peccadilloes. He confessed everything on the page: his jealousy of his wife's flirtations, his own extramarital sexual encounters and, memorably, one unsuccessful search for any woman in a 'hot humour' which ended with him going to bed alone to fantasise about the Queen.[9] The Diary ended abruptly in sadness on 31 May 1669 when Pepys's eye troubles persuaded him he would go blind if he continued to write. It was a low point in his private life. His passionate French wife Elizabeth had caught him in a compromising position with their maid. A deep frost had glazed their marriage. Far more sadness followed. Soon after the Diary ended, Pepys took Elizabeth to Paris, perhaps to restore their joy. On the way home she caught typhoid fever and died.

In 1674, five years after her death, Pepys was made Secretary to the Admiralty. Political events had removed James, Duke of York from the post of Lord High Admiral the previous year. James, unwilling to take the anti-Catholic Test Act oath, had been replaced by a weak 'commission' of fifteen men supposedly running the Admiralty, leaving King Charles effectively in charge. Pepys, whose idea this may have been, was able to use the situation to redefine the role of Secretary, gathering new powers to himself and keeping the Duke well informed on key naval matters.[10] On 25 July of that year Pepys sent a letter to Anthony Deane, the man who was destined to accompany him on the grim journey from the House of Commons to the Tower. The letter instructed Deane to hurry up from Portsmouth 'to receive the King's commands touching the building of 2 yachts which the King of France desires to have built for him here'.[11]

Anthony Deane was a master shipwright, a status he had attained at the age of only twenty-six. He had designed a string of highly regarded ships and when he received Pepys's letter he was at the peak of his profession. He and Pepys had first encountered each other shortly after Pepys had discovered his new zeal for naval order in 1662. Pepys had been on his way to dinner with a new navy commissioner, a man of a similar mind.* As they approached the Ship tavern in Lombard Street, they bumped into the captain of the *Rosebush*, which was meant to be on its way to Jamaica. This kind of disorder infected the navy, and Pepys and his companion were trying to stamp it out. Pepys's companion had become enraged, threatening the errant captain with dismissal. After lunch, united by their indignation, the two men took a boat downriver to Woolwich where they boarded the *Rosebush* and told its officers to prepare for sea. Then they turned their attentions to the Navy Yard ashore, where they interrupted a half-hearted inspection and stocktaking 'so poor and unlike a survey of the Navy, that I am ashamed of it,' as Pepys declared. As they set out to find as much fault as possible with the way the yard was run, a young man came over to offer his help. He showed them how the navy was being overcharged by a fraudulent method of measuring the timber it was buying. Pepys recorded his

---

* Dinner in this case refers to the meal we would now term lunch. 'Luncheon' was used, as in Pepys's recording of Charles's flight after the battle of Worcester, to mean a daytime snack.

comments in that day's Diary but got his name wrong. In the first of his many appearances in that document, the young Anthony Deane is recorded as 'Mr. Day'.[12]

Soon, Deane was up in town to tell Pepys more about timber measuring and to offer an irresistible gift. 'He promises me also a model of a ship,' Pepys recorded, 'which will please me exceedingly, for I do want one of my own.'[13] Their relationship grew closer, and although Pepys was often aware of an underlying vanity in Deane, they shared a keen interest in building the up-to-date ships that the navy desperately needed. Deane was not always easy to deal with. He had an arrogant streak, sometimes put down to a need to compensate for his humble origins. A captain who fell foul of him in 1666 accused him of 'having an uncivil tongue' because he was a tradesman.[14]

Of his shipbuilding talent and loyalty to his king, however, there was no doubt, and when, through Pepys, the King's command came to build the two little yachts, he obeyed to the letter. They were to adorn King Louis XIV's lake at his palace of Versailles. Eleven months passed and they were ready – two neat examples of elegant design and Deane's superiority in international shipbuilding; a piece of English dexterity to sail on placid French waters. One was put in the water at Deane's yard at Portsmouth, where it showed off its excellent sailing properties. Pepys, taking his chance to sail in it, was delighted with it.[15]

The little yacht was not the only boat to go in the water that day, 29 June 1675. A brand-new 100-gun battleship named *Royal James* slid down the Portsmouth slipway. The ship was a replacement; three years earlier, the previous *Royal James* had been caught napping and found itself surrounded by an entire squadron of Dutch ships. Fighting desperately within sight of appalled spectators on the Suffolk shore, the *Royal James* had finally lost the battle when the Dutch sent a fireship alongside, igniting its powder magazine and blowing it to pieces. Edward Montagu, Earl of Sandwich, Pepys's patron, had made the *James* his flagship during the battle. Days later, Sandwich's remains were picked up out of the sea, identified only by the insignia of the Order of the Garter still pinned to his uniform.

This was the breadth of Deane's skill on display in Portsmouth that day. On the one hand were the toys for King Louis; on the other, one of the most powerful weapons of the time. Deane's ships were fast and seaworthy, and able to sail closer to the wind than most. They could carry heavy guns on their upper decks without compromising their sailing – an advantage in battle. Up there (unlike down below), the wind would blow the thick clouds of powder smoke away and give the gunners a clear view of their target, and the gunports could be opened safely even in a heavy sea. Such technical know-how was coveted, and a great gift to the country.

King Charles arrived in Portsmouth late, having encountered a violent storm on his journey from Gravesend which forced him ashore on the Isle of Wight. He missed the launch of the *Royal James*, but when he saw it, he immediately knighted its designer, who found himself designated 'Sir Anthony Deane'.[16]

The delivery of the two little yachts to the lake at Versailles had been sanctioned by Charles as a friendly gesture to his French cousin, King Louis. Deane was to accompany the yachts and see them safely put in place. Pepys was later to insist that he had warned Deane that mischief might be made of this.[17] But the wish of a monarch is not easily resisted. As the summer peaked, Deane departed.

He did not go alone. His companion on the journey was Pepys's chief clerk, Will Hewer. Now thirty-three, he had been in Pepys's service since he was eighteen, in both the Navy Office and Pepys's private household. After a shaky start when Pepys had to counter young Will's fondness for late nights and bad company, he became Pepys's closest ally at work and also at home. He even acted as an intermediary to Samuel and Elizabeth at fraught moments in their tempestuous marriage. He was the nephew of the secretary to the powerful East India Company and was independently wealthy, lending his own money to the navy to finance shipbuilding.[18]

Hewer was not used to overseas travel and it worried him. He arranged safe-keeping for his chests full of gold and silver, totalling

£8,500, wrote his will and asked Pepys to keep an eye on his elderly mother.[19] His concern was reasonable. England's third war with the Dutch had ended the year before, but France was still at war with the Dutch and therefore no Channel crossing was completely safe. The Channel was a hunting ground for French and Dutch privateers – the private men-of-war operated under government licences, out to snatch ships or cargo belonging to the enemy.

Deane and Hewer sailed from Portsmouth for France on 9 August 1675 on the royal yacht *Cleveland*, another Deane design.[20] The *Cleveland* arrived safely at Le Havre and the yachts, which had already sailed across, were taken up the Seine. A letter from Deane to Pepys described the task. For a man who could draw precise designs for ships, something seemed to come to pieces when he used those same hands for writing. His spidery words are remarkably ill formed. The yachts had to be carried overland from the Seine to the Versailles canal, he told Pepys. The roads were bad and the route ran up and down hill for several miles. It took one hundred and sixteen horses to haul the first of the yachts to the palace.* By the time it arrived, the boat was filthy and the trolley they carried it on had broken.[21] Hewer also wrote about the incident, praising Deane for his efficiency in 'doing that in a day which the French were four days about'.[22]

Versailles had once been a small sandy knoll in the middle of a marsh. Louis XIV's father had had a twenty-room hunting lodge here; Louis had extended it enormously. He had enveloped it in a vast array of new wings, buildings and gardens, forbidding his architects, despite their pleas, to alter any part of the original. The labourers, mostly soldiers, who had struggled to make canals, aqueducts and a firm, level platform for the building, died in their thousands of malaria. Their bodies were taken away on carts at night to avoid

---

* The two yachts are described as weighing 40 tons each, making them surprisingly large vessels for a canal that, according to Sir Anthony Deane, was only some three and a half feet deep. The number of horses required to draw them supports that size. They were apparently built in the original Dutch yacht style with a flat bottom and lee-boards instead of a deep keel.

upsetting the rest of the workforce.[23] The water supply had to be brought miles from the river Eure. The King's adviser tried to persuade him that the Louvre would make a better and more convenient palace but Louis did not want to be in the heart of Paris. Like Charles II, he had seen anti-monarchical violence as a child; he would not tolerate any challenge to supreme royal power, nor even reasoned criticism. Versailles was to be his refuge and eventually his seat of government. He went to Paris increasingly rarely after it was completed. Louis's France, with a vast standing army at his beck and call, was the superpower of Europe, funded by heavy taxation. Versailles was the excessively luxurious haven built to keep him away from the people who paid for it.

The sight of this Catholic king's palace would have made the average Protestant Englishman deeply uneasy. This, after all, was the concrete manifestation of a king who disdained the values of parliament and who denied his subjects a representative voice. But Will Hewer was rather taken with it. He was hugely impressed by the grandeur around him. He wrote to Pepys,

We have as yet seen only the King's house and garden at the Versailles, the place called the Goblings where the King employs the year round . . . painters, stone cutters, makers of hangings, silver smiths and a hundred more sort of artificers . . . I do believe there cannot in the whole world be anything that is finer.[24]

By 16 August the delivery of the yachts was complete and Deane and Hewer had arrived in Paris and gone sightseeing, visiting 'the gardens at the Lover and St Jermins but not the houses in regard we could not then get tickets'.[25] The French, delighted with Deane's work, made sure that he was well looked after. 'Sir Anthony', Hewer wrote home to Pepys, 'has been nobly and extraordinarily treated.' The French even provided him with an attendant to pay his bills and cover his expenses during his stay. The treasurer general of the French navy himself was instructed to accompany Deane and Hewer to Fontainebleau 'where it is said we shall see a very stately house and garden'.[26]

Such treatment was exactly what was required of the French. It was their duty as loyal subjects of their king to celebrate the shipwright, and Deane's diplomatic duty to enjoy the hospitality on behalf of his own king. But there was a bit of delicate diplomatic footwork going on in Deane's tourist gawping and in the French garlanding of him, for Deane's intentions were shadier. He was trying to do a little quiet research into the state of the French navy. However friendly the relations between the two kings might be, there were men in parliament who would be glad to learn of any deficiencies in the French defences – just in case. In return, the French were suspicious of Deane's intentions. Hewer, seeing through the façade of hospitality, realised that the French attendant who diligently leapt to pay any bills and was always at Deane's elbow made it difficult for Deane to see anything he should not or to travel independently to the great naval bases in the south. 'I confess,' Hewer wrote to Pepys, 'I am of opinion that they do defray his charges here on purpose to prevent his going.'[27] But if Deane could make the journey, Hewer would go too, for he thought he would never have such an opportunity again. The nervous traveller had become an enthusiastic explorer.

Deane and Hewer went to a grand dinner with the French navy minister, the Marquis de Seignelay.[28] After de Seignelay's feast, the entertainment continued. On 31 August, they were invited to dinner by navy treasurer Georges Pellissary at his house in the rue Cléry. The floors were paved with black and white marble, and the gardens contained myrtles and orange trees.[29] Pellissary had five of his friends there, senior men in the French administration. Deane spoke no French and Pellissary no English but fortunately Deane's son was on hand, brought along to act as an interpreter. After the meal, the men went to the rooms of Pellissary's wife, Magdalen Bibaud, who had been dining separately with her sister. There they heard her play the harpsichord and they danced to the 'Tambour de Basques of the Bohemians'.[30]

Deane never got far beyond Paris but he did procure enough information to compile a report on the state of the French navy. He had been ordered to do so. After his return to England, he wrote to

Secretary of State and spymaster Sir Joseph Williamson to say, 'I must take 12 or 14 days to complete what I have observed in my journey, which I hope is little less than a full satisfaction to what you gave me in command at my departure.'[31]

The elements of the plot against Pepys were all in place. His increasingly close relationship with James, Duke of York, was the first, the trip to France with the two little yachts was the second and the dinner at a French navy minister's house was the third. All innocent enough – patriotic even – but lethal when England flared.

3

A Single Hair

It began with an anxiety that moved under the skin of England. The average seventeenth-century English subject thought of him or herself as Protestant; even to those, like Samuel Pepys, whose commitment to religion was social rather than zealous, Protestantism was 'our religion'. But where there was a Protestant 'us' there was also an opposing 'them' to be feared and mistrusted: the Catholics in their midst. The Protestant Englishman entertained the suspicion that the Catholics' real desire, the dream they whispered to each other, was to finish new St Paul's in the gaudy colouring of a Catholic cathedral and take England back for the Pope. The Protestant Englishman quaked at the prospect for, to him, Catholicism was a superstition of fire and revenge, of Queen Mary's bonfires which had consumed good Protestants bound to the stake, of the Gunpowder Treason and perhaps (it was widely believed) even the Great Fire itself.*

This anxiety surfaced from time to time: here, as a piece of anti-Catholic legislation; there, in a rumour that a priest had been seen with an incendiary device to start another great fire. Such stories provoked a flurry of fear and gossip, which dissipated reluctantly when proof failed to appear, for in reality practising Catholics amounted to less than five per cent of the population.[1] Catholicism

---

* In 1681 an addition was made to the inscription on the Monument about the Great Fire: '... but Popish frenzy, which wrought such horrors, is not yet quenched'.

was a religion on the retreat, sustained in isolated pockets in the country seats of the remaining Catholic aristocracy – the last vestige of pre-Reformation English social structures. The beleaguered Catholics were financially broken by the penalties that following their religion incurred, and scorned for their beliefs. One MP called Catholicism 'a ridiculous and nonsensical religion. A piece of wafer, broken betwixt a priest's fingers, to be our Saviour! And what becomes of it when eaten, and taken down, you know.'[2]

When King Charles arrived in London, his Restoration had been all that mattered, and the English had poured out sentiment expressing their royalist credentials. 'That Monarchy is the best of governments is a matter so pre-eminently above all question,' wrote an enthusiast, 'that one penfull of ink spent on the subject cannot but be esteemed waste.'[3] Such loyalty might have continued if the English had been a Protestant people under an unambiguously Protestant king, but Charles's private inclinations lay elsewhere.

In 1662, Pepys watched Charles descend from his closet in Whitehall chapel, go down on his knees and receive the Protestant sacrament.[4] Increasingly, however, the court began to display a liking for cooking, dress and music that looked distastefully like what went on in Versailles. At the end of 1662, Charles tried to lessen the burden on Catholics by granting them liberty of conscience. The Commons put a stop to this, a defeat the King brushed off cheerily, saying he believed no prince had ever been happier in a House of Commons than he was.[5] In fact, as Pepys found out, Charles was incensed by the defeat. The growing realisation of the King's Catholic sympathies saddened Pepys, and he feared that if they were made known, there would be great general discontent.[6] The Protestant sacrament had lost its power to reassure. When, in 1666, Pepys again watched the King receive the sacrament, he shared the unease of other Protestants who found it disquietingly similar to the Catholic ceremony.[7]

It was true that Charles felt a strong affinity for Catholic France. His beloved sister had married into the French royal family. Until her death in 1670 at the age of twenty-six, she served as go-between to

King Louis, cementing the bond between the English and French crowns in the Treaty of Dover. The politicking between Whitehall Palace and Versailles, however, would never have been accepted on the London streets, where the ordinary people saw the Protestant Dutch as England's natural allies. The violence of this feeling among the English was so strong that a central part of Charles and Louis's treaty had to be kept secret from the common people; Charles had promised, in exchange for French money, that he would declare himself a Catholic as soon as circumstances permitted.[8]

The belligerence of English Protestantism meant that circumstances were never going to permit such a declaration. Nonetheless, Charles made pro-Catholic gestures to keep Louis's money coming in. In 1672 he again tried to enforce religious tolerance on his people with a Declaration of Indulgence, suspending penal laws against the Catholics. Just as it had ten years before, this proved only that his subjects were neither tolerant nor indulgent. A fearful society could not allow the objects of its fear more rights; the Commons snapped its wallet closed and so blocked the Declaration with the most effective weapon in its arsenal – the refusal to fund the Crown.

King Charles, caught between the need to rule a simmering Protestant nation and the need to please a foreign Catholic king, walked the finest line. His father had paid with his head for his disdain for the representatives of the people in the Commons; Charles was determined not to make the same mistake. But his situation was a strain, and the thin veneer of acceptable Protestantism which covered his unacceptable fondness for Catholic France began to crack. Suspicions grew in England's streets that Charles was in league with the hated Catholic king.

It might have gone badly for Charles but, although he sailed dangerously close to the wind, he kept his true sympathies hidden and the majority of his people were convinced he was indeed a Protestant king. Even some of his closest servants could not be certain with which religion his affections lay. Much later, after his death, a man who had served the Crown long and faithfully plucked up the courage to discover in which religion Charles had died. He was told in confidence that Charles lived and died a Roman Catholic, and he was shown a paper the late king had written charging the Church of England with heresy.[9]

The King's brother, James, Duke of York, was incapable of such prudent ambiguity. This was the man who had promised Pepys his future favour as they crossed the Channel at the Restoration, and to whom Pepys grew increasingly close through the 1660s and 1670s. Where the King was dextrous and flexible in politics, the Duke was rigid and unsubtle. He saw no need to grovel before England's prejudice, and some time in the ten years up to 1671 he converted to the Catholic faith. In 1672 he ceased to attend Anglican Communion and in 1673, when Parliament passed the first Test Act preventing those outside the Church of England holding public office, his resignation as Lord High Admiral was the most spectacular result. In the same year he married a fifteen-year-old Italian Catholic princess. The furious House of Commons voted to try to force a Protestant marriage. The poor princess, a girl 'of fine stature, brown, and her face promises a reasonable share of beauty as she grows a little older', learnt about the vote while she was on her way to England for her wedding and, distraught, took herself to bed without supper.[10]

James's conversion presented England with the prospect of a Catholic king, for since Charles had no legitimate children, his brother was the heir. The idea of the arrogant Duke succeeding to the throne was appalling. The last Catholic monarch had been the brutal Mary. Across the Channel, in the terrible splendour of Versailles, King Louis epitomised everything that was wrong with Catholic rule. If the Duke came to the throne, it began to be whispered, he would dispense with Parliament. At present the relationship between Crown and Parliament was reducible to the simplest form: the King's need for money forced him to summon a Parliament that demanded things of him in return for their cash. Parliament was the hand that restrained the King. The fearful whispers said that, as king, James would replace Parliament with a standing army and collect taxes by force. Since that army would have to be paid, taxes would soar. The people would suffer but would have no parliamentary voice to express their suffering. This was royal absolutism and at the moment the Duke became a Catholic it rose like a spectre to haunt the English.

Until 1678 this was just a possibility – nightmarish, but unlikely to come about when the King was robust and might well outlive his brother. But that August, as a result of a man named Titus Oates, everything changed.

Oates had a startling physical appearance. He had a dished face with his mouth right at the centre of it, the space below taken up by an enormous chin. His eyes were small and sunken, his cheeks prominent and ruddy. His voice left a strong and unpleasant impression on all who heard it; it was harsh, high-pitched and braying. He had left his Cambridge college under a cloud without a degree and been dismissed as chaplain of a naval frigate for homosexual practices. He moved easily in Catholic circles, befriended by priests. Through the patronage of the head of the English Jesuits (the Society of Jesus, a Catholic order), he was regarded as a potential recruit, sent first to the Jesuit college at Valladolid in Spain and then to their school at St Omers in France. His age, behaviour, lack of Latin, and sexual tastes did not fit and he was expelled.[11]

Returning to England in June 1678 desperately poor, he had taken up with an old acquaintance, a half-mad ex-Puritan, Israel Tonge, who suffered from powerful delusional beliefs centred on the Jesuits who, he thought, were responsible for the English revolution, the execution of Charles I and the Great Fire of London. Tonge had believed in a popish – that is, Catholic – plot for years and was anxious to extract anything Oates knew about the Jesuits. Oates, depending on Tonge for his subsistence, saw advantage in feeding that paranoia. He equipped himself with a bogus doctorate of divinity from Salamanca, the Spanish equivalent of Oxford University, a Catholic distinction which lent him credibility as one who knew the darker secrets of the Catholic Church.

Oates now invented a plot to kill the King and replace him by his

Catholic brother, laid out in forty-three numbered 'articles'. Through a like-minded friend the King was told of a plot to shoot him or, if that failed, for the Queen's doctor to poison him.

The King took a personal part in the cross-examination of Oates and soon caught him out on some of his facts. When Oates claimed to the Privy Council that he had seen Don John of Austria at a meeting of the plotters, Charles asked him to describe Don John's appearance. With no hesitation Oates said he was tall, lean and dark. Charles laughed. He said Don John, whom he knew well, was fat, short and fair.[12] Given such transparent incompetence, the 'plot' should have stumbled to a halt straight away. But then Oates produced the name of Edward Coleman. On Sunday, 29 September 1678, Oates told the Privy Council that if they read Coleman's letters they would find material that 'might cost him his neck'.

Coleman had been secretary to the Duke of York but he had been demoted to work for the Duchess instead, partly on account of the alarmingly unrestrained vigour of his Catholicism. From 1673 when changes in the law introduced a new intolerance of Catholics, Coleman kept up a busy correspondence with contacts in the French court, looking for ways to bring England and France closer together and cleanse England of its Anglican shame. He was a pawn convinced he was a knight, but sufficiently useful for Louis XIV to send him money to bribe key members of the English Parliament to French purposes.

Coleman's name was suspect before Oates denounced him. Two years previously, one of the two Secretaries of State (who combined the roles of Home Secretary, Foreign Secretary and spymaster), Henry Coventry, had received an unsigned order from the King to discover what correspondence Coleman had both at home and abroad, 'by intercepting letters'.[13] Coventry, anxious about interfering with the letters of a royal servant, asked the King to sign the order. Charles breezily replied that there was no need, since the matter was to be kept secret. Coventry persisted, concerned that the King might forget having given the order. Charles promised he would remember well enough, and so shifted responsibility to his long-suffering Secretary of State with a smile.[14]

Coventry had duly ordered officials at the Post Office to intercept Coleman's letters.[15] Such orders were not uncommon. The post went up and down the major roads radiating from London three times a week, so that most mail passed through the General Letter Office in Lombard Street. Those writing sensitive letters took precautions, delivering them just before the post so any interference would show up in their late delivery, or using intricate sealing techniques to detect tampering. Some apparently miraculous machines existed in the seventeenth century to defeat such precautions. A letter of 1695 says they could open a sealed letter without leaving a trace, copy a seal, imitate any writing or take a copy of an entire letter in a minute.* The benefits were obvious; by such means, 'the King may discover the true temper of his subjects.'[16]

Although the Secretary of State knew of Coleman's correspondence with the French, he certainly would not have passed such information on to Titus Oates. But there were men who realised how Oates's story might usefully inflame England's hatred of Catholicism and harden the country's resolve to stand united against a Catholic successor. These men saw the value of giving Oates credibility. Sir George Savile, Marquess of Halifax, was one of the King's inner circle, having become a Privy Councillor in 1672. By the time of Oates's accusations he, like others, had thrown himself into securing England against Catholicism, and worked closely with those men who had an interest in fanning the flames of Oates's story. Savile makes a possible suspect for getting the story of Coleman's betrayal to Oates.

When Oates gave Coleman's name, Coventry was aghast, saying of Oates, 'If he be a liar he is the greatest and adroitest I ever saw.'[17] Coleman destroyed most of his papers before his house was searched but forgot an old wooden box hidden in a fireplace. He was held

---

* The original machines were apparently destroyed in the Great Fire, but re-created by the republican, Major John Wildman, who served later as Postmaster General. He is said to have destroyed them when he left that position, to prevent anyone else using them.

while a Secret Committee of the Privy Council grappled with the letters hidden there, some written in cipher, some using vague and elusive terms. Coventry sent a progress report to the King who had gone horse racing at Newmarket: 'Mr. Coleman's letters have given us much more trouble, though most we have yet found are of an old date, very few of this year but the matters treated in those papers are of very high consequence.'[18] Coventry had them sealed up to prevent their details being leaked by committee members to stir up the public – but many details got out regardless. When the deciphering was done, the King was informed that the letters were treasonable. Coleman was found guilty on 27 November 1678 and executed six days later.

Oates's revelations – now seemingly backed by proven fact – put the match to the old powder-keg of suspicion and anxiety. Charles's death, Oates declared, would be followed by a Catholic revolution. Contemporary writers felt compelled to wake the 'drowsy subjects' of England to the threat. They spooled wildly through images of horror. 'Imagine you see the whole town in flame', urged a tract coming off the presses in 1679. 'You behold troops of papists ravishing your wives and daughters, dashing your little children's brains out against the walls, plundering your houses and cutting your own throats, by the name heretic dogs. Then represent to yourselves the Tower playing off its cannon, and battering down your houses about your ears.'[19] The images were potent. London's destruction by fire could be remembered by everyone in their late teens and upwards; the battered landscape was not long rebuilt.

'Casting your eyes towards Smithfield, imagine you see your father, or your mother, or some of your nearest and dearest relations, tied to a stake in the midst of flames, when with hands and eyes lifted up to heaven they scream and cry out to that God for whose cause they die.'[20] Everywhere, people came forward to support Oates's claims, and England's prejudice spoke with many voices. One pamphlet listed recent London fires begun, the writer claimed, by papists. Their tactics included 'fire-balls, put in with poles or otherwise through holes . . . into houses', 'hard fire-balls thrown through glass windows', creeping into empty houses and setting them alight or even 'firing their own lodging, as the French man did in Shoe Lane, in the time of the Great Fire'.[21] Vast French armies were said to be approaching the coasts. The Dorset militia was roused to oppose a rank of marauding invaders who turned out, in daylight, to be a hedgerow. Night riders were spotted everywhere, passing messages between secret Catholic strongholds.

Oates's 'discovery' of the Plot was fuel on the fire of the Duke of York's Catholicism but there was a third factor which put the blaze beyond control. The nation's suspicions that behind closed doors Charles was sympathetic towards Catholics at best, or at worst a practising Catholic himself, had been held at bay largely thanks to the work of the Earl of Danby, his first minister. Danby had followed a policy of placating the Commons with nationalist, anti-Catholic and anti-French policies. His open attempts to steer the King towards an alliance with the Protestant Dutch were popular in Parliament and the country, and reassured the Commons that he was restraining Charles.

At the end of 1678, that façade collapsed. Danby was demolished by an alliance of the former English ambassador to France and the French ambassador in England. Each had their reason for disliking him. The Englishman was driven by thwarted ambition and a thirst for revenge; Danby had blocked his promotion. The French ambassador in London hated Danby for his anti-French policy. Together they concocted a plan.[22] The Frenchman provided the Englishman with a letter that Danby had sent to the French. In it was a demand for six million pounds from the French, in return for which Danby would silence the English Parliament and guarantee peace between England and France. The letter was read in the Commons, who listened in horror. Every popular policy that Danby had pursued had been a sham – a smokescreen to distract England from his true intention: to get enough money from the French to allow Charles to rule without Parliament.

Nothing could have torn down the Lord Treasurer's pretence of a Protestant, anti-French policy more completely. The House voted that there was sufficient ground for impeachment.

Danby's exposure confirmed the nation's fears; the first moves towards absolutism were already in place. Catholicism loomed over England like a sword 'supported by no stronger force than that of a single hair, his Majesty's life'.[23] Samuel Pepys's patron, Catholic James, Duke of York, was waiting. The assassin's stroke would make him king. England had to act.

4

Gravesend

For a month after Titus Oates first made his wild claims, he might or might not have been believed by the people of London. Then, on 17 October 1678, a day of freezing rain and violent winds, three men found a body in a ditch.[1]

Edmund Berry Godfrey had been a wealthy London merchant selling coal and timber, and a Justice of the Peace, which combined the roles of magistrate, policeman and prosecutor. A tall, stooping man fond of wearing black, he showed signs of family melancholy; his father had died mad and suicidal. He was deaf and was said to walk the streets staring at the ground, wiping his mouth. He was also brave. During the Plague, he had stayed in London to help keep order. Chasing a grave-robber who, it was claimed, had dug up a thousand corpses to strip them of their winding-sheets, he entered the man's house when his constables baulked at the health risk and dragged him out into the street to face justice.

On 6 September, Titus Oates, accompanying Israel Tonge, had gone before Godfrey to swear his account of the Catholic plot to kill the King. As the spotlight of celebrity urged Oates on to invent more details he vastly expanded his story. He moved beyond naming the would-be assassins (mostly Jesuits and others against whom he had some personal grudge) and began to name the men who – he claimed – were ready to take over the government and the military after the King's death, among them some Catholic lords. On 27 September he returned to Godfrey with Tonge and another and swore to this expanded story.

Two weeks passed. On the morning of Saturday, 12 October, Godfrey left his house in Hartshorn Lane, close by the Thames. He was seen walking in the fields to the north of Oxford Street and then failed to turn up for an important lunch appointment. For no logical reason, rumours immediately spread that he had been done away with by papists. At two o'clock on the following Thursday afternoon, two men, a farrier and a baker, were heading for the White House Tavern at what is now Chalk Farm. Walking along the edge of a field on Primrose Hill they noticed gloves, a belt and a cane on the ground and, thinking the owner was possibly relieving himself, walked on. The landlord of the White House thought this was odd, but by now it was raining, so they stayed in the tavern drinking. When the rain stopped, the three men went back to the spot. Nearby, lying face down in a ditch, was Godfrey's body.

His own sword had been driven right through him and the tip was sticking out of his back. Despite the deep surrounding mud, the shoes on the corpse were absolutely clean. Investigators soon decided Godfrey had been killed elsewhere and brought to the spot possibly in the back of a cart, covered in hay.

There are several curiosities connected with the case: the candle wax smears on the clothes of his corpse, which suggested Catholic ritual; the man who announced in a barber's shop that Godfrey had killed himself on Primrose Hill two days before the corpse was found and another who proclaimed its discovery with the sword run through it but several hours too early and naming the wrong field. It had the hallmarks of a carefully staged production around the finding of the corpse in which some of the inflammatory publicity was mistimed.

It worked. The news of Godfrey's murder was instantly sensational and chilling. His name was on everyone's lips and in everyone's thoughts in a spreading wave of fearful apprehension that this was the first of the onslaught of Catholic terrorist murders. The hunt began for the murderer. Attention focused on the Jesuits, seen as the extreme end of the Catholic spectrum and believed to owe allegiance to neither king nor country, but only to spreading Catholicism by any means. Orders went out to the ports to watch for a fleeing Jesuit assassin. A report from Gravesend came back, admitting the escape of a man who fitted the bill perfectly. The report landed on Samuel Pepys's desk.[2]

Gravesend was a likely exit point for a fugitive. It had grown around a spur of chalk sticking out of the miles of marshland that lined the Thames estuary, a port of departure and a sailors' town. The streets and quays were lined with taverns and chandlers. Boatmen ferried passengers out to the larger vessels and local officials called 'searchers' investigated the goods and passengers coming in and out. The East India Company had a large base to provision its ships there. It was a busy place, and once a year it became even busier when crowds filled its streets for the Gravesend fair.[3]

In the early afternoon of Saturday, 19 October, two days after Godfrey's body was discovered, a boot- and shoe-seller named Constable was riding to the fair when he found himself with unwelcome company. He was joined a little short of the town by a stranger, a well-built man with a rough face, bushy eyebrows and a slight squint. The man was dressed expensively, almost flashily, with a bulky pale wig under his black hat and a jacket trimmed with lace. He was displaying a pair of holstered pistols and his black horse had clearly been ridden hard. Constable did not like the look of him. He took him for a highwayman.[4]

The rough-faced stranger left his lathered horse on the outskirts of the town at a house belonging to John Skelton and his wife. When the fair was on, the Skeltons made their house an inn, but it had no proper stables, only a small outbuilding. The stranger wiped the sweat from the horse's flanks, told the ostler to look after it and went in for a meal of pork and sausages. The busy fairground covered forty acres to the west of the town. After his meal, the stranger walked in and bought himself a heavy campaign coat. That purchase was significant in three ways. It undermined the account he was soon to give of having spent several days on the road; the previous day had been cold and wet and yet his quite unsuitable clothes seemed clean and dry. It was a heavy travelling coat, showing he had a journey ahead of him. But most importantly, and by the slenderest of chances, the stall-holder, one of the many who came from London to the fair, recognised him.

An eclipse of the moon made it an unusually dark evening. The new arrival decided not to lodge at the Skeltons' but left the horse, his pistols and holsters with them. He took the ostler into town to the Horns Tavern, where he took a room. In the kitchen, he plied the ostler with drink. Two men asked his name. He told them it was Godfrey.

It was a lie. It was also the most inappropriate pseudonym he could have conjured up. Everything he had done until that point had been designed to preserve his anonymity: he had arrived in the town when it was busy with strangers; he walked rather than rode in to merge with the crowd; and the campaign coat covered his distinctive lace-trimmed jacket. Now, at the first interview, he had blurted out the name of the murdered London Justice of the Peace. It was his misfortune that the two men who asked him, Mr Skarr and Henry Gals, worked for the port authorities. The name and his demeanour alerted them. They 'took more than ordinary notice of him there and resolved to watch him the next day'.

The attempt to discover whether Godfrey was the wanted assassin began. Early the following morning, Henry Gals set himself to watch the Horns Tavern. Soon after nine o'clock Godfrey emerged, and Gals followed him to the Skeltons' house on the outskirts. Gals waited. When the ostler appeared, Gals intercepted him. He was carrying a chicken under his coat for Godfrey's lunch. An hour later, the ostler came out on Godfrey's business again, going down to the quay at the west end of town to buy four small whiting intended for his supper.

Around five o'clock, 'a little after evening prayer', the watcher's patience was finally rewarded. Godfrey set about organising his escape. He came out of the Skeltons' and walked to the house of one of the Gravesend 'searchers', the customs and immigration officers of the day. Clearly he had been there before and knew his way around; the searcher's gate required a special knack but Godfrey let himself in with no difficulty. While he was there, the searcher gave him the information he needed and Godfrey then went to the King's Head tavern where he asked for a man named Thomas Low, master of the *Assistance*, a ship which had called at Gravesend, bound for Lisbon. Those watching Godfrey heard him ask Low if he knew him.

'No,' said Low.

'You shall know me better before we part,' said Godfrey and sat down with him. Godfrey now used the information that he had got from the searcher to bully Low, by pretending that he represented the owners of Low's ship. He threatened to arrest Low because he had not handed in proper accounts for his last voyage.

Poor Low went straight to his only ally, the bartender, who came from his part of the country, and asked him to find out if there was a writ against his ship. No writ existed, but by now Low was in such a state that he hid at the searcher's house for fear of arrest. Godfrey's work was done; Low was broken and pliable. Allowing Godfrey to sail on the *Assistance* would be a small price for Low to pay to escape arrest.

Meanwhile, Godfrey covered his tracks by telling the gathering in the King's Head that he had been on the road for two weeks, travelling around the coast, and that he had just come from the house of the Whig MP Sir Frances Rolle. He claimed he had missed a yacht that would have taken him around the coast to Deal and now he needed alternative transport.

By this time it was seven o'clock and Godfrey had drunk two bottles of claret. He was becoming increasingly talkative. It must have been Dutch courage that drove him back to the Horns Tavern, where he had first come across the suspicious port officials Skarr and Gals. They were there again. In a display of drunken confidence, Godfrey joined them. There was a heated discussion, fuelled by the wine, in which Godfrey was caught out while boasting of his knowledge of the geography of the Kent coast. Then he described a journey to Jerusalem, saying he had landed at Alexandria, near Aleppo. A man called Parker, who knew that area well, pointed out that Alexandria was nowhere near Aleppo, and he must mean Alexandretta. Godfrey tried to brush off the mistake but Parker was clearly annoyed by the man's bragging and led him into a trap. He asked him how many inns there were between Aleppo and Jerusalem. Godfrey produced name after name and Parker listened attentively to the growing list before pointing out that there was not a single one.

Godfrey then raised a toast to the Duke of Buckingham. Gals went next, drinking to the confusion of all those who had a hand in the Plot. At this, Godfrey 'was observed to hold the glass long in his hand until desired to drink, at which he put the glass to his mouth and drank a little, and flung the rest in the fire'. This was what they had been watching for – hard evidence that Godfrey's inclinations were not patriotic and Protestant but Catholic, conspiratorial and murderous. By now though they were drunk and it was the waste of wine that angered them. Godfrey answered their complaints by boasting of his skill as a wrestler, saying he was not afraid of anybody. Skarr challenged him to a fight. Godfrey accepted and told him to choose what form the bout should take. They settled on competing to see who could drink the most and parted, the best of friends, at about nine o'clock.

In the cold light of the next morning, Godfrey's refusal to drink the toast sounded a more insistent warning note, and the port officials went back to tracking his movements. He ate a lunch of roast mutton at the Skeltons' house and made a deal with them to feed his horse until he returned. He asked the ostler to buy a brush and comb to keep it well groomed; he told Skelton he intended to return within a week or so. At two o'clock he went back into town, the ostler coming along behind carrying his boots, saddle, holster and pistols. From the public stairs on the quay he got a waterman to transport him out to the *Assistance*, whose master he had bullied in the tavern, and he got on board.

The officials watching him saw no need to act; the boat could not sail without being cleared by the searchers. In London the previous day a £500 reward had been offered for Edmund Berry Godfrey's murderers. If that news had reached them in time, they might have taken more care. They did not know that Godfrey's friend, the corrupt searcher, had cleared the ship illicitly and privately. The *Assistance* unexpectedly up-anchored and sailed. Their bird had flown.

The account of Godfrey's escape landed on Samuel Pepys's desk in London five days later. The report came from the mayor of Gravesend rather than the river authorities, who were presumably loath to admit that one of their searchers had helped Godfrey slip away. Pepys immediately wrote letters by express to the commander-in-chief of the King's ships in the Downs, the sheltered anchorage off the Kent coast. He went personally to ask Secretary of State Henry Coventry to write to Plymouth and Falmouth, where his own authority did not run. Coventry sent instructions about 'a very suspicious person who goes under the name of Godfrey'. If the *Assistance* came near either port, they were to 'board her . . . cause the said Godfrey to be seized and brought on shore and kept in safe custody'.[5]

But Godfrey was too good at the game. He left the *Assistance* long before the navy could catch her, switched boats, then hired a horse to ride across country to Folkestone, arriving there at night on Wednesday, 23 October. The following day he went to the house of a reliable fisherman, James Sturgis, who had transported him across the Channel three months before, and asked to make the journey again, offering four guineas.[6] Sturgis landed his passenger at Boulogne that afternoon. Godfrey told him that if Sturgis ever needed him, he should go to the Duke of Buckingham's and ask for the Duke's friend John. Describing Godfrey, Sturgis mentioned the wig and the bushy brown eyebrows, denied he had a squint but said his sister had noticed the initials 'J S' marked on his handkerchief.

By now Pepys was hot on the scent. Trailing somewhat behind him was the Duke of York, who delivered the report from the Gravesend mayor to the House of Lords on Saturday, 26 October, whereupon Pepys was 'called in and desired to acquaint one of the secretaries [of state] with it', something Pepys, it seems, was too polite to tell them he had already done the previous day.[7] In the absence of any other information or clues about Godfrey, the Lords focused on the horse he had left behind at Skelton's. Poor Mr Skelton received an order from the Secretary of State to 'lay hold on whosoever shall enquire after the horse'.[8] It was a weighty task for a man whose heaviest duty in life was to convert his house into an inn at fair time. It must have been a relief that within four days the horse was taken from him and delivered to the Lady of the Manor as the abandoned possession of an absconded suspicious person.[9]

There were plenty of people more qualified to uncover Godfrey's mysteries than Samuel Pepys. The murder of Edmund Berry Godfrey was hardly a naval affair but Pepys had a duty to act because he was a Justice of the Peace for Kent. In September 1660, he had been sworn in so that he could wield legal powers in the royal dockyards there as well as in Middlesex, Essex and Southampton, although he admitted at the time that he was 'wholly ignorant in the duty of Justice of the Peace'.[10] He also had a personal motive. Godfrey had put one past him in slipping away from the coast despite the Admiralty Secretary's attempts to alert the ports. Now his investigations were helped by the Gravesend mayor. Hearing of Godfrey's new campaign coat, they traced the stall-holder who had sold it to him; when questioned, he did not just remember his customer, he knew where he lived. The stall-holder explained that he normally worked at a tavern in Cannon Street in the middle of London and he knew that Godfrey lodged across the road at the house of a 'haberdasher of hats'.[11] Four days after Godfrey reached Boulogne in Sturgis's little boat, Pepys questioned the landlord, who told him that his tenant Godfrey, now Pepys's quarry, was really called Colonel John Scott.[12]

In the last days of October, Pepys had Scott's lodgings in Cannon Street searched and a list was compiled of everything found there. The curious haul included a trunk full of mathematical instruments, ten guineas stored in his closet and a host of suspicious papers. These ranged from poetry to copies of political speeches. Among them was a copy of a document that Pepys recognised well, because he had written it for Parliament; it was a detailed analysis of the costs and strengths of England's army and navy. Scott's landlord was questioned by Pepys, the Lord Mayor of London, and Sir George Jeffreys, the Recorder, in effect London's senior judge. Behind the quiet questions of these three powerful men, all England clamoured to find the murderer.[13]

Nothing they learnt proved that Scott had killed Edmund Berry Godfrey. They heard which tavern he liked to drink in (the Bear, in Cornhill), that two of his closest friends were American sailors and that he had 'one or both crooked legs'. The landlord had heard that Scott was a Jesuit, but that was contradicted by the fact that Scott had claimed he was poisoned by Jesuits, and by his close association with several prominent politicians who abhorred Catholicism. Scott's credentials as a Catholic murderer were weak. Nonetheless, the circumstances of his disappearance and the papers found in his lodgings were suspicious enough for an arrest warrant to be issued, to come into force when Scott set foot back in England.

Scott learnt of the warrant while he was in France. He was furious. He had not been fleeing the murder and he had only intended to stay away a week. The task for which he had been sent over was completed, but he was unable to return to England. The decision to call himself Godfrey had been disastrous, drawing attention to him while he was on a mission of the highest secrecy and danger. Maybe he cursed himself; so many of the decisions he had made in his life had been self-destructive. Now he was stuck in France as the days rolled by and critical events unfolded without him. While he waited, anxious and angry, he learnt that the name of the man who had pursued him out of England was Samuel Pepys.

5
Saving Sam Atkins

Two days after John Scott's lodgings were searched, one of Pepys's clerks left his desk in the Admiralty's Derby House office and did not come back. He was twenty-one. He had a fondness for wine, women and staying out late. The seething city had fleshy, drunken delights to offer. Pepys had privately enjoyed these many times but, as a man of reputation, he ran a tight domestic ship and did not tolerate such behaviour in his employees. He had disciplined Atkins before, just as he had Will Hewer in the past. It was hard for a young man, living where he worked, under such a master. By nine o'clock the clerk had still not returned. Pepys told the Derby House porter to refuse to let him in, that night or ever again.[1]

The clerk, whose name was Sam Atkins, had left his desk because he had received a summons to go to a nearby inn. There a king's messenger, sitting with a glass of wine in his hand, told him that the Secretary of State wished to see him. When Sam asked him why, the messenger showed him a warrant for his arrest, asked for his sword and escorted him away. They paid a visit to Secretary Coventry's office. Then Sam was delivered to a house in Lincoln's Inn Fields. By this time, it was dark.

The house belonged to one of the members of the Secret Committee investigating the Plot. In the flickering candlelight, the Committee was in session. It was made up of a round half dozen powerful noblemen. To a man, they abhorred Catholics and were

35

leading the fight against the Catholicism lurking in the heart of the Crown. Their support of Titus Oates was complete. Oates's claims had exposed the Catholic violence they had all suspected. More importantly though, they knew that the trail of Oates's accusations might lead all the way up to the royal brother, the Duke of York. He, after all, would benefit from the King's murder. If the unfolding Plot required a helping hand from the Committee that was supposed to be investigating it, so be it; they would chase prosecutions and force confessions where necessary.

Among their number was the man John Scott had called his friend, the Duke of Buckingham. At their head sat Anthony Ashley Cooper, the sour and very clever Lord Shaftesbury. His portrait shows a man with a slender face and narrowed eyes above a hooked nose. His thin lips are clamped shut. He appears almost to be scowling. There is resentment in the look but also something calculating and coiled. He had to walk with sticks and was kept alive by a copper tube in his side that dripped poison from a wound that never healed.* These were the men that young Sam Atkins had to face – the men shaping Oates's Plot, giving form and meaning to England's mad prejudice, and putting real men on the scaffold so that London could see its enemy. The Committee intended to make a show trial of Sam.

Shaftesbury's Committee produced a seaman called Child. Sam and Child, both baffled, explained they had never seen each other before. Then Sam's main accuser, a namesake though no relation, swaggered in. Captain Charles Atkins told a story about Sam's attempt to recruit Child, on Pepys's behalf, to kill Sir Edmund Berry Godfrey because there had been a conflict between Godfrey and Pepys. Sam swung angrily on the captain.

'God, your conscience and I know 'tis notoriously untrue,' he said

---

* K. H. D. Haley, *The First Earl of Shaftesbury* (1968), p. 205 details the decision to operate on the cyst near Shaftesbury's liver and the subsequent decision, made after Shaftesbury had cross-examined the surgeons, to keep the tube open which 'led Tory pamphleteers to christen him "Tapski" as though he were a barrel of beer with a tap'.

and launched into a fluent, furious account of all their recent interactions, which largely involved Sam lending the captain money. He explained Captain Atkins's motive for telling this lie to the listening lords. The captain had held a grudge against Pepys for more than two years. In the summer of 1676, while in command of a small warship, the *Quaker* ketch, the young and inexperienced captain had ingloriously surrendered to a pair of Algerine galleys without firing a shot. Pepys, enraged, ordered him to return to face a court martial. Only a severe case of venereal disease contracted in the fleshpots of Tangier had saved the captain, for by the time he had recovered and returned to England, the crew of the *Quaker*, the vital witnesses, had sailed for the Americas. Nonetheless, he was thrown into prison and his father, the governor of Barbados, disowned him.

As a result, he was in a state of penury. He had been living on the charity of Sam Atkins and other generous types for some time. In Sam's view, the captain had now come to 'the last degree of necessity', and when the £500 reward for information leading to the capture of Godfrey's murderer was offered, he reached for the bait by putting his young friend – his enemy's employee – in the dock.

But Sam's protestations of innocence had no impact on the Secret Committee. They were not the least interested in the captain's quality as a witness – they wanted a prosecution. They questioned Sam's commitment to the Protestant religion and eventually, when the brave clerk refused to buckle or confess, they turned nasty.

'Mr Atkins,' Shaftesbury told him, 'we are to be plain with you. Here's a positive oath against you. We cannot answer to Parliament the doing less than committing you to Newgate.'

Even at the mention of the foulest prison in London, Sam refused to be intimidated.

'What your lordships please,' he said. 'If you send me to be hanged, I could say no more, or otherwise.'

The Secret Committee was prepared for this response. The Keeper of Newgate was waiting in the hall. Sam, whose day had begun quite normally, was carried off to a cell.

The young Protestant clerk could not understand why the Secret Committee would think he had murdered Godfrey, which – everyone knew – had been a Catholic crime. Thinking that there must have been some error on the Committee's part, he asked to be brought before them again. On 6 November a Newgate warder escorted him back to the lords. He had considered Captain Atkins's story, he told them, and he hoped to refute it.

'Why,' jeered Shaftesbury, 'Charles Atkins has said he will overturn you by other circumstances and show you the worst man living.'

Nonetheless, Sam had the captain sent for. When he arrived, Sam asked that the captain's story be read over. Shaftesbury refused this and told him to repair to his memory for the details, so Sam repeated the charges faultlessly then denied them categorically. Pepys and Godfrey had only met once, to Sam's knowledge, and they had seemed 'as good friends as could be'. There was no 'difference' between them, as the captain had pretended.

The Committee responded with angry incredulity, rejecting Sam's carefully considered defence. Frustrated, he tried a new tack. What if he confirmed the captain's story, he asked them? What if he told them that he had indeed said the things the captain pretended? It would be a lie, 'and if I invented a lie,' he cried, 'I must suffer for doing it.'

'Nay, nay,' said Shaftesbury, swift to reassure him, 'leave us to make the use of it. Do you but confess it. You shall be safe and we will apply it.'

If the lords were hopeful that Sam had finally understood what was wanted from him and would now comply to incriminate Pepys, they were to be disappointed. The clerk was braver than that.

'I cannot do it!' he declared. 'I hope I never shall tell a lie to any man's prejudice, though I meet with never so great a danger.'

Though they pressed and threatened him, he would not budge. Shaftesbury told him he would be made to seem Pepys's great favourite, privy to all his letters and fond of reading to him at night. He also claimed he could prove Sam was a Catholic.

'Do that,' said Sam, 'and I'll plead no more.' He had read Pepys books: the Bible, history books, and books on divinity.

'Never any popish books?'

'Never in my life, I assure your lordship, never any.'

Stubborn Sam was sent back to Newgate. Two days later, on 8 November, Captain Atkins visited him in his cell. Sam begged the gaoler not to leave him alone with his accuser (who knows what the captain might pretend was said?) but it was the Committee's command. The captain brought news of the arrival from Bristol of a new authority on the devilish Plot. William Bedloe was an old acquaintance of Titus Oates whose interest was sparked by the £500 reward for information.

Bedloe's story changed completely within his first twenty-four hours in London. When he arrived, Sam Atkins was in Newgate and Bedloe had never heard of him. That very afternoon, Bedloe had appeared before the King and the two Secretaries of State and told them that two Jesuits had offered him £4,000 to help murder Godfrey. Naturally, he had refused. Godfrey, he claimed to have learnt, had been smothered with a pillow in Somerset House. He listed the murderers. Sam Atkins was not on the list.

The following morning Bedloe gave his information again, this time at the bar of the House of Lords. He had revised it. He had learnt that Oates had claimed Godfrey was strangled; he corrected his story so that Godfrey was first smothered and then strangled. Overnight, he had also worked young Sam Atkins into his account, claiming that on 14 October, the Monday following Godfrey's disappearance, he had been taken to Somerset House, where in a dimly lit room a theatrical tableau had confronted him. Godfrey's corpse lay there, revealed by the opening of a dark lantern, with his assassins standing round. One of those, a young gentleman, told Bedloe he was 'Mr Atkins, Pepys's clerk'. King Charles was astonished at his changed story. 'Surely this man has received a new lesson during the last twenty-four hours,' he remarked.[2] Someone had indeed been bringing Bedloe up to speed, for he was to be the vital second witness Oates needed.

Captain Atkins came to Sam's cell with news of Bedloe's accusation and pressed him to confess the crime, for he would have a great reward for turning King's evidence.

'Being young men,' the captain said, 'we ought to lay hold on this fair occasion of making our fortunes.' But again Sam refused to comply. That afternoon, the Secret Committee summoned him to hear Bedloe's charges. Bedloe, however, was new to the game of the professional informer. He lacked Oates's brazen confidence, and feared that he would be discovered as a perjurer, so refused to be positive that the real Sam Atkins was the man who had introduced himself as 'Pepys's clerk' beside Godfrey's body. Bedloe said he had been in the lantern-lit room in Somerset House between nine and ten o'clock at night. Under pressure before the Committee, Sam was unable to remember where he had been on that particular evening but again protested his innocence at length. Shaftesbury had had enough of the troublesome young man and turned on him, saying that only a papist uprising would save him – otherwise he would be hanged. When Sam was sent back to Newgate this time, the irons were left on as punishment.

Bedloe's and the captain's versions of the murder were entirely different. Bedloe had named Robert Green, Lawrence Hill and Henry Berry (who all worked in the Queen's lodgings of Somerset House) as the murderers, whereas the captain had named Child. The Secret Committee was not in the least bothered. Nor did the fact that Captain Atkins was an ever more unconvincing witness worry them. He lacked that essential quality of an efficient liar, a good memory. At one point, he forgot what the seaman Child was supposed to have said to him and tried to get out of it by suggesting the Committee ask someone else to whom he had told the story. Sam Atkins described the captain looking 'very pensive, walking up and down the room, under an uncertainty whether Child had really said such things to him or whether he dreamt he had'. Sam surmised that the captain was starting to worry about the penalties for perjury. None of these inconsistencies mattered in the slightest to the Secret Committee. They were holding out a huge reward and would ignore the captain's blunders so long as he had his story straight by the time he got into the courtroom. Meanwhile, he flailed around, his eyes all the time on the £500.

The following day, Sam Atkins remembered where he had been on the night of 14 October. He could answer this new charge of Bedloe's. He managed to get a pen and paper, and scribbled an account of his movements. He had alibis. No sooner had he finished writing than the Keeper of Newgate seized the papers and took them to the Secret Committee. The Committee realised that the story they had given Bedloe would never stand up in court. He could not have seen Sam beside Godfrey's body in the dimly lit room, and Sam could prove it.

Meanwhile, Samuel Pepys made enquiries after his vanished clerk and learnt about his imprisonment in Newgate. Sam Atkins's youth and naivety meant that he never fully understood the reason why he was being charged; he always believed that one of the murderers had assumed his name. Pepys, however, was more sophisticated. He understood that the movement against Sam was really a movement against him. Indeed, had he not had the perfect alibi for the weekend of Godfrey's murder (he had been called to Newmarket by the King), it might have been him beside Godfrey's body, rather than his clerk. If Sam could be bullied into saying that Pepys had ordered Godfrey's murder, Pepys would fall.

Pepys's fall would have delighted Shaftesbury. The two men were old enemies. In 1674, Pepys had been elected to the village of Castle Rising, near the muddy waters of the Wash, but his opponent was a bad loser and labelled him a closet Catholic. The Commons were told that a great man, Lord Shaftesbury himself, had seen 'an altar and a crucifix upon it' in Pepys's old house.[3] When Pepys confronted him, Shaftesbury backtracked, saying it was all too long ago to be sure, that he had never seen an altar and had only a vague memory of a carving or a painting of the crucifixion. Eventually, Pepys was allowed to keep his new seat but not before he had written Shaftesbury a ferocious letter complaining about 'the injurious consequences' of Shaftesbury's 'ambiguity', pointing out that Shaftesbury's convenient vagueness was very damaging to him and brusquely asking him to 'perfect [his] recollections'.[4] Shaftesbury, the vindicated Pepys informed the Commons, had made no reply.

Pepys's fall, however, would have been merely a side-show for Shaftesbury. The security of Protestant England hung in the balance, threatened by the impending accession of a Catholic king. The issue of Pepys's master, James, Duke of York, was so fundamentally divisive that, behind the gentlemanly lunge and parry of Westminster politics, something much more serious was now at work. Sam Atkins was not the true target, nor was Pepys: the Secret Committee was aiming for the Duke himself. Godfrey's murder had been a part of the Plot and if the heir to the throne could be implicated in that murder, he would fall. As contemporary commentator Roger North put it,

through Mr Pepys, by like process of threats and promises (for he was an elderly gentleman who had known softness and the pleasures of life), they might have that murder charged on the Duke of York. For Mr Pepys, in desperate circumstances, might be as likely to accuse the Duke as his man Atkins was to accuse him.[5]

But the Secret Committee's plan underestimated both Atkins and Pepys.

As soon as he discovered what was in play, Pepys set about constructing Sam Atkins's defence. Within two weeks of Atkins's arrest, Pepys had put together a document establishing Atkins's family history, Protestantism and good behaviour. It read,

During which whole time of his service under Mr Hewer and Mr Pepys, there has not happened any blame chargeable on him either of debauchery, corruption, lying out at nights or other crime discovered by Mr Pepys more than an inclination sometimes of taking the advantage of his master's absence to spend his time out of doors.

For that fault, it said, Pepys sacked Sam in 1677 but was persuaded to have him back after Sam wrote a penitential letter. Pepys kept this letter 'as a constant witness against him'.

Ironically, when he began investigating his clerk's movements over the weekend of Godfrey's murder, he discovered that Sam only had an alibi because of debauchery and 'lying out at nights'. On the crucial evening of 14 October, between nine and ten o'clock, when he was supposedly seen in Somerset House, Sam Atkins had been out drinking with the sisters Sarah and Anne Williams and Captain Richard Vittles on the royal yacht *Katherine*. At half past ten that night, Vittles had put Sam and the girls in a boat at Greenwich and sailors had rowed them against the tide up to London Bridge, where the water was sluicing through the arches. There they offloaded the very drunk clerk and his two girls into a hackney cab. Pepys assembled a precise document, listing who could prove Sam's whereabouts at any given point over that weekend. Vittles, Anne Williams and Sarah Williams could 'prove how he spent Monday in the afternoon from 2 a clock to 12 at night'. The witnesses able to prove that young Sam, who was normally forced to live a monastic existence, had spent the whole of the rest of that night at home included Sarah Williams though not, prudes may be pleased to hear, Anne as well.

Pepys sought alibis. He wrote to a sea-captain with whom Sam had spent other parts of the weekend, asking him to recollect, write down and swear to an exact account of their time together. Pepys asked only for the truth. If the prosecution were to find one mistake, he pointed out, it would 'justly call in question the whole of what you shall say is true'. Pepys also sent for Captain Vittles, the little river-party's host, to pay him a visit at Derby House.

Over three months after his arrest, on 11 February 1679, Sam Atkins was brought to the bar of the court of King's Bench to be tried as an accessory in the murder of Sir Edmund Berry Godfrey.[6] The court was told that the three murderers, Green, Berry and Hill, had wrapped a sixpenny linen handkerchief around Godfrey's neck, choking and strangling him. These entirely innocent men had been found guilty the previous day, to the public's delight. Young Sam Atkins, the jury heard, had organised the murderers and cared for them afterwards. The momentum of their convictions seemed set to take him down with them. He pleaded not guilty.

The prosecution made their case. Captain Atkins was the first witness. One afternoon at the beginning of October 1678, the captain told the court, he had sought out Sam in Derby House to borrow some money and found him upstairs, writing all alone in his study. Young Sam got up to greet him and they stood under the great window in the large room talking about Titus Oates's recent revelations of a Popish Plot.

'Sir Edmund Berry Godfrey has very much injured my master,' Sam allegedly confided. 'If he lives, he will ruin him.'

'Is Godfrey a member of the House of Commons?' asked Captain Atkins, who knew that Pepys had, in the past, been questioned there about his religion. The clerk led the captain away from the window.

'No,' he said. 'Please be secret.' Then he asked the captain if he knew a Mr Child.

'Which Mr Child?' asked the captain. 'He that I used to meet at the Three Tobacco Pipes?'

'Yes. Is he a man that is stout, or to be trusted with a secret?' asked Sam.

'As to his valour,' replied the captain, 'I know nothing, but he has a very good character.'

'When you see him,' said Pepys's young clerk, 'send him to my master.'

Captain Atkins told the court he had duly arranged the meeting between Child and Pepys. Some time later, as he was out walking near Holborn Fields, he happened to meet Child, who said he had something private to say. They went to a shed at the back of the Three Tobacco Pipes and, after the landlord had brought them a pot of ale, Child offered Captain Atkins a job that would relieve his financial strain. It was a murder. The captain refused.

'I was to have one hundred pounds for my secrecy,' he told the listening court, 'but if I did reveal it, I should not outlive it.'

The broad-faced Lord Chief Justice William Scroggs broke in to confirm that Sam Atkins's master was 'Mr Pepys of the navy'.

'Yes, my lord.'

'Did Sam Atkins fear Sir Edmund Berry Godfrey would ruin his master, by discovering something about the Plot?' asked Scroggs.

'I understood so,' said Captain Atkins.

The prosecution turned to their next witness, a last-minute surprise for Sam.

'Now, my lord,' said the Attorney General to Scroggs, 'because it seems a strange thing that Mr Atkins, who says he is a Protestant, should be engaged in this business, we have a witness here to prove that he has been seen often at Somerset House at Mass.' Shaftesbury had kept his promise to prove Sam a Catholic.

They brought in a boy who declared himself to be 'about seventeen'. By his clothing he appeared to be one of the 'black guard', the lads who scraped a living by running errands and doing odd jobs about the Horse Guards' barracks near Whitehall. The judges were immediately uncomfortable at the sight of a witness who could so easily be bribed.

'Do you know what, if you swear false, will become of you?' asked one.

'I shall be damned,' the boy replied.

Sharp Sam Atkins, standing anonymously amid his throng of witnesses, called to him.

'What religion are you of, boy?'

'A Protestant.'

'Do you know me?'

'No.'

The court reprimanded Sam for being 'too bold with the witnesses' but his quickness had saved him. The Attorney General was flustered and stammered that the witness was not known to him and was not in his brief. He clucked angrily as the boy was ushered out of the courtroom.

'My lord,' said the Recorder moving things smartly along, 'I perceive it was a mistake; it was somebody else. We will proceed to other evidence.'

The next witness was William Bedloe. Asked whether the

defendant was the young gentleman he had seen beside Godfrey's body, Bedloe procrastinated.

'There was very little light,' he explained. 'It is hard for me to swear that this is he. I do not remember that he was such a person as the prisoner is; as far as I can remember he had a more manly face than he has, and a beard.'

The Lord Chief Justice tried to pin him down, but Bedloe refused to be categorical.

'I cannot say it was he,' he protested.

Sam Atkins never had any reason to doubt Bedloe's account. 'If Mr Bedloe ever meets with that manly face and beard again,' Sam wrote afterwards, the impostor who had taken his name could be hanged. Sam had no way of knowing that Bedloe had been coached against him or that the Plot was anything other than real.

By the time the prosecution had finished, they had made only a slim case against Sam. Captain Atkins's testimony contained only conversations; there was no crime there. William Bedloe refused to say that Sam was the man he had seen by the body, so there was no crime there either.

Until this point, Scroggs had been unrelenting towards Catholic Plot defendants. When he summed up a case, the jury followed his direction slavishly, meaning that he effectively dictated the verdict. The Plot was so secret, he believed, and its effects would be so devastating to the country and the Protestant religion that it was better to be overly warm in the courtroom than to be burnt alive by Catholic tyrants at Smithfield.[7] When Sam began his defence, however, Scroggs was positively helpful. Sam, intending to expose Captain Atkins's lies, launched into a tedious, meticulous speech but Scroggs cut him off.

'Hold!' he said, genially. 'You mistake, Mr Atkins, he does you no mischief at all. His account of his discourse with you is nothing to the purpose.'

Sam mistakenly thought the Lord Chief Justice was condemning him and began protesting his innocence.

'But what say you to Mr Bedloe's testimony?' interrupted Justice Dolben. 'Did you see the body of Sir Edmund Godfrey at Somerset House?'

'No, my lord. I am so far from that, that in all my life I was never in the house.'

The hesitant case against Sam Atkins was on the verge of collapsing.

'Then call a couple of witnesses,' said Scroggs, 'to prove where you were that Monday night, the 14th of October, and you need not trouble yourself any further.'

Sam summoned bluff Captain Vittles, who laid out his movements that weekend in laborious detail.

'How come you remember the days so exactly?' asked Justice Jones.

'Mariners are very exact and punctual,' offered Scroggs, pleased to endorse the witnesses for Sam, who he was now convinced was innocent. 'They keep accounts of every day, and have journals of all passages.'

Vittles was frank about the state Sam had been in that evening. By 'about eight or nine o'clock we had drunk till we were a little warm,' he told the court, 'and the wine drinking pretty fresh, and being with our friends, we did drink freely till it was indeed unseasonable. I must beg your lordship's pardon, but so it was.' His boatswain confirmed his account. It was quite clear that the sober man William Bedloe said he had seen in Somerset House could not have been Sam Atkins.

'My lord,' said the Attorney General, throwing in the towel, 'it is in vain to contend in a fact that is plain.' But, he was anxious to point out, the Plot witnesses' honesty was not in question. Bedloe had never sworn positively against the defendant, and Captain Atkins's claims had not been contradicted.

'I desire,' said the Attorney General, 'the company may not go away with a mistake, as if the King's evidence were disproved.' Scroggs waved the idea away.

'Not a tittle,' he said. Bedloe's reputation as an honest man was intact, and he could continue to testify against the Plot conspirators. The jury returned a 'not guilty' verdict and Sam, as was required, fell to his knees and cried, 'God bless the King and this honourable court.'

Scroggs's court had a perfect record of prosecuting those accused of complicity in the Plot; eight innocent men had been sentenced to death because of Titus Oates's story. Young Sam was the first of the accused to prove his innocence; the rest had been sunk in a hail of accusations which drowned out their denials, or been bullied by Shaftesbury into saving their own lives by condemning others.

'Mr Atkins,' said Scroggs, 'I should have been very glad that the rest, who have been condemned, had been as innocent as you are, and I do assure you I wish all mankind had been as innocent. For if any Protestant had been guilty of such a thing as this, it would have grieved me to the very heart.'

Good, straightforward Captain Vittles failed to grasp that further defence was unnecessary, and offered to produce a witness who could attest to Sam's Protestantism and give an account of 'what a good conditioned young man he was'.

'Well, well, captain,' smiled Scroggs, 'go and drink a bottle with him.'

The Plot could roll on, the witnesses could continue to send their victims to the gallows, but the first movement of the plot against Pepys had broken on the rock of his brave, forthright, stubborn young clerk.

6

The Temper of the House

It is thought . . . that they will hang Pepys.
A— B— TO THE DUKE OF ORMONDE, 13 MAY 1679

As Samuel Pepys proved himself and his household innocent of
Edmund Berry Godfrey's murder, Protestant England held its breath.
The Plot, it seemed, was real – the killers had run a sword through
the sad, brave Justice of the Peace because he had evidence against
them. The assassination of the King would surely follow soon then
many more Catholic swords would pierce many brave Protestants,
and England as it was would be destroyed. The country had to be
defended and into the breach stepped the elected representatives of
the people – the House of Commons.

The Commons were terrified about the threat to the country but
were also facing institutional death. Their debates would cease and
their laws would become irrelevant the moment the future Catholic
king abolished Parliament and gathered his taxes by force of arms. An
England ruled like that would be 'enslaved forever', cried one MP.[1]
'Should his Majesty fall by any unhappy stroke,' declared another, 'it
would not be in our power to defend the Protestant religion long.'[2]
Compelled to confront the terrible possibility of a Catholic successor,
the MPs became brave and warlike.

Loose opposition to the Crown had existed in the Commons for
some years. Now the opposition's ranks swelled, their alliances
became more consistent and crystallised around hostility to the Duke
of York. Their enemies called them Whigs, a contraction of a Scottish
word for raiders. They adopted the name in proud defiance. Those

49

MPs who supported the Crown also found themselves re-named. Titus Oates (who believed that Irish assassins were on their way to kill him) had begun to use the Irish word *tóraidhe* as a label for all his enemies – it meant robbers or wreckers, and was pronounced 'tory'. The Court party found themselves stuck with it. On this battle ground, the two-party system was born and christened.

Only a negligible minority questioned the King's right to rule. Everyone accepted that the operational decisions of government happened at a royal, not a parliamentary level – that is, in Whitehall Palace, not in the Commons. Everyone, Tory and Whig, believed Parliament should exist. Their differences stemmed from what they considered Parliament to be. Parliament began as a tax-gathering body, then asserted its right to a governing voice by withholding money if the monarch did something it did not like. Those with Tory inclinations saw their parliamentary role as being to vote funding for the King's policies. Whigs saw their role as defending Parliament's right to a voice, even at the expense of the King. The King, they thought, had a duty to rule in the interests of his subjects, and they would pull tight the purse strings if he failed in this. At this moment of acute crisis, the Whigs were willing to tread on royal toes if necessary. With the King apparently asleep to the threat England faced and his life about to be cut short, they stepped in as defenders of the Protestant faith. The many active and able Whig MPs became restless in their efforts to strengthen the Commons, shore up its rights and bring down their enemies.

The Whigs' first action was to get rid of the King's treasonous first minister. Now that the Earl of Danby's furtive plot with France to abolish Parliament had been exposed, the Whigs closed on him. When King Charles came, cap in hand, for money to pay off an army he no longer needed and could no longer afford, the Whigs granted it on two conditions: Danby must be dismissed and Parliament dissolved.

Dissolution meant a general election, which was bound to strengthen the Whigs since the country was up in arms about the

Plot and Danby's behaviour, but Charles had no choice. On 24 January 1679 he gave in and dissolved Parliament. He would not give up Danby so easily. On 1 March he declared that 'for diverse good causes and considerations' he had 'out of our special favour, certain knowledge and mere motion of our own' pardoned Danby of any treason or wrong-doing.

Charles II was capable of displaying great political skill, but this was a disastrous decision and it backfired. Pardoning a man who had been impeached by the Commons suggested that Charles had no regard for parliamentary authority – perhaps even that, at heart, he was an absolutist like his brother. The Commons were furious. 'An impeachment is to no purpose when a pardon shall stop our mouths,' said one MP.[3] Whig sentiment hardened and on 16 March Charles was forced to dismiss Danby, who was imprisoned in the Tower. In the past, Charles had been able to get his servants out. The previous November, the Commons had sent Secretary of State Joseph Williamson to the Tower; the King had released him within hours. Williamson's fellow Secretary of State Henry Coventry wrote to him at the time, 'I congratulate you on your release though by the temper of the House I know not who will succeed you.'[4] Now the Commons were angrier still and there would be no release for their next victim unless they allowed it. The Crown's servants could no longer hide behind royal coat-tails; if they were thrown into the Tower, they would have to get out by themselves.

The first elections in eighteen years followed the January dissolution and they were a disaster for Charles. Everywhere men voted to punish Danby and the Crown for their communication with France. Nevertheless, Pepys and Sir Anthony Deane, both Tories, won the two seats for Harwich, which had done well out of Admiralty shipbuilding contracts yet, even there, Pepys had to write to the mayor reassuring him that Deane had 'too much wit to be an atheist' and that he himself was no Catholic; the proof of his Protestancy was there to be examined in the parliamentary records.[5] Their election was a small victory in a sea of defeat. The Tories won just thirty seats, the Whigs a hundred and fifty.[6] When Pepys sat down in the Commons at the beginning of March, he was in a room full of men whose common characteristic was their hostility to Catholicism and his patron James, Duke of York.

None of Charles's prior experience as king had prepared him for the crisis he now faced. Whig strength had soared. The final touches were added to the Whig victory. On 26 February Charles had told the Duke of York that he must go into exile for the time being. He was 'truly sorry' for it, he said, but James should leave as soon as he conveniently could.[7] James left the country on 3 March.[8] Realising he had no viable alternative, Charles admitted the Whigs to the heart of power. On 21 April the Privy Council was reconstituted to take in prominent and vocal Whig leaders such as William Harbord.[9] At its head, Charles was forced to put the man whose efforts had united the Whig movement, and who had already proved more than a match for the Earl of Danby. From the court's point of view he was the prince of darkness, a canny politician who knew England better than most and who was capable of coordinating popular and theatrical politics on a grand scale, even in opposition to the ancient institution of the Crown. He was Sam Atkins's inquisitor and Pepys's old opponent, the Earl of Shaftesbury.

At this moment of great strength, the Whigs were mindful of their weakness – the possibility of Parliament's abolition at the moment of the King's death. They put forward a series of radical modernising proposals. One bill would have ensured that Parliament met regularly and not merely at the King's whim or because his pockets were empty. Another sought to limit the lifetime of any given Parliament to a maximum of two years.[10] But apart from the crucial exception of the Habeas Corpus Amendment Act, which was to serve the world well, the Commons' proposals ultimately came to nothing. The Whigs had no faith in legislation because they knew that an absolute monarch would abolish both Parliament and the laws it had passed. Driven to rage by their impotence, the Whigs turned their attention to dealing with that problem at its source. In a move that demonstrated the width of the gulf between Crown and Parliament, they tried to deny the Duke of York the kingdom by excluding him from the succession.

It was a massive step and the Whigs had to work up their nerve by advancing in small stages. On 27 April, William Harbord moved a bill to banish all Catholics from London. The Duke's banishment would not alter the fact of his succession, pointed out an MP. Lord Russell was the first to say what was in all their minds. 'I think we are but trifling hitherto,' he said. 'If we do not something relating to the succession, we must resolve, when we have a prince of the popish religion, to be papists or burn.' The time for talk, the Whigs threatened, was coming to an end.[11] Throughout, the King's loyal Secretary of State Henry Coventry 'spoke freely his mind' against exclusion and as a result was 'fallen upon with fury' by the MPs.[12]

Coventry's defence of the succession restrained the Commons but he had few allies. The House did not resolve to exclude the Duke of York that day, though MPs had grown bolder in their claims of his treachery. He had transacted with the Pope said one, and was now residing in Brussels among 'the thickest' Jesuits.[13] From Pepys's point of view however, a dangerous trend was emerging in the debate; the Duke's servants had come under scrutiny. These were men, the Commons complained, whom the Duke had put into 'offices of the highest trust', who paid him more reverence 'than to the King himself' and willingly carried out his treasonous commands.[14] The Commons might have fallen short of excluding the Duke but they had described a treacherous network of men who operated around him. The groundwork was done. The next day, they fell upon Pepys.

On 28 April, at the bar of the Commons, the rail which separated the ordinary people from the MPs, a captain complained that Pepys had sacked him 'for calling his lieutenant papist'. In the opinion of Robert Southwell, an intelligent observer and a friend of Pepys, this charge, with its implication that Pepys favoured papists, 'was very poorly proved'.[15] This, however, was just the first shot; a barrage of angry Whig complaints came in about problems in the fleet. As a result the House appointed a Committee of Enquiry into the Miscarriages of the Navy to examine the charges, and the fiercest Whigs were appointed as its members.[16] Chairing it was the MP for Thetford, William Harbord, 'the last man in England' Pepys wished any involvement with.[17] The new target of the House's temper had become clear. 'Mr Pepys,' wrote Southwell the following day, 'however prepared, must certainly be destroyed.'[18]

On that same day, 28 April, a small boat ferried a man into Folkestone from a French vessel out to sea.[19] He had come from Paris via Rouen and he gave his name as John Johnson. The apparently innocuous name was the same alias that Guido Fawkes had used during the Gunpowder Treason in 1605. The man had used aliases before; when he had left Gravesend six months earlier he had called himself Godfrey. His real name was Colonel John Scott.

He had been away for much longer than the week he had intended. As a result of Samuel Pepys's investigations and information from France, Secretary Coventry had issued an arrest warrant instructing the officers at Dover Castle 'at their peril' to secure Scott's person on his return and seize his 'papers and writings'.[20] Faced with certain imprisonment if he came back to England, Scott had stayed away. The warrant for his arrest was still in place but now he landed at Folkestone relaxed and full of confidence.[21] To Scott, the political air in England smelt better than it had in years. He had been pursued for most of his adult life and he believed that the Duke of York was the root of all his problems. The truth was that the Duke probably did not even remember Scott's name but Scott saw their relationship as a bitter rivalry. Now the Duke was hated and exiled, and Scott felt his star was in the ascendant. England was in the hands of the Duke's enemies; his moment had come.

The Duke's servant, Samuel Pepys, had been the man whose work had kept Scott out of England. It was no hard task for Scott to transfer a dislike born of years of resentment from the master to the servant, despite the fact that at this point he and Pepys had never even met.

An official from Dover who happened to be in Folkestone begged the Folkestone mayor to hold this 'John Johnson' and he was seized at the Prince of Orange inn trying to get himself a horse for London.[22] He confessed his real name to the Folkestone court. To explain his pseudonym he said, with a smile, that 'his father's name was John, and he was John's son'.[23] He was carried to Dover where he was interrogated before the deputy mayor and a local official. In his examination, Scott gave an inoffensive account of his trip from Gravesend the previous year: he had been summoned to France by the Prince of Condé, a veteran French nobleman and general, to survey several parcels of land and woods in Picardy and Burgundy. He came back now to 'see his native country'. He gave his profession as soldier. He offered to take the oaths that proved his allegiance to the Protestant Crown. He had come into Folkestone rather than Dover, the proper port of entry, to see James Sturgis, the fisherman who had carried him over the previous year 'who he had heard was in great trouble for doing so'.[24] But despite his charm, Coventry's warrant held. The deputy mayor imprisoned Scott while he awaited further orders.

On the day that Scott landed at Folkestone, a man rode in on horseback and went straight to a house where Scott often lodged. Scott was not there. Eventually finding Scott in custody, the rider 'seemed to be uneasy', the officials noticed. He and Scott saw each other but talked little, inhibited, the officials thought, by their presence. Questioned, the rider gave his name as Cavendish, an inhabitant of Spitalfields and a glover by trade. He was well known in Dover, he said, because he had hired a boat there to take him to Calais five days before. That was all the information the suspicious officials could get out of him before he abruptly rode off.[25]

Cavendish's short visit is telling and he gave away more than he might have liked. It was no coincidence that Cavendish was in Calais five days before Scott (who was in France, waiting to return) travelled to England; Cavendish had summoned Scott. It was also no coincidence that Cavendish's journey to Calais came two days after the Whigs were brought into the heart of government; the Whigs had sent him. That is, the Whigs summoned Scott.

At Westminster, the temperature continued to rise. The King tried to regain control, giving a speech to the Lords and Commons together on 30 April to reassure them that 'in all things that concern the public security, I shall not follow your zeal, but lead it.' He promised them that under a Catholic successor, Protestants would fill all important offices and their appointment would have to be approved by Parliament. If a Catholic king appointed Catholic ministers, Parliament could refuse to fund him; the King could think of no greater restraint on a popish successor than that.[26] The Commons was unimpressed. 'The speech is merely to delude the people with security, when there is none,' said one MP.[27] It was not the reality of Charles in all their minds, but the spectre of James abolishing Parliament and building a permanent army. However reasonable the present king might sound, nothing he could say would bind his heir.

On 1 May, with the Commons threatening action, Secretary of State Henry Coventry received news of Scott's arrest. He sent a trusted messenger to Dover to bring Scott under guard to London, 'and his papers if he has any'.[28]

Then Coventry wrote a letter intended for his nephew Henry Savile at the Paris embassy, informing him that 'Colonel Scott is taken'. From snippets of information his network of foreign spies had sent him, Coventry suspected Scott was up to no good. Eager to prosecute his captive, he asked Savile to find witnesses in France who knew Scott from his six months there, to 'come over to testify against him'.[29] It is indicative of the strain Coventry was under from sickness and the sustained Whig barrage in Parliament that he accidentally addressed Savile's letter to his number two at the embassy, John Brisbane.

Both men responded as best they could. Savile had heard on the grapevine that Scott 'has as bad a character here as he can possibly have in England'. Word had reached them that Scott was the Duke of Buckingham's agent, so Savile tipped off his uncle that Scott had powerful friends at court.[30] Since Buckingham and the Whigs were in the ascendant, Coventry had to be careful. His letter and part of Savile's reply were in cipher in case of interception. The embassy men began their investigation against Scott.

Their efforts were for nothing. In his Dover Castle cell, Scott calmly wrote a letter to the Earl of Shaftesbury, the thin-lipped Whig president of the King's reformed Council. For once in his life, Scott could be confident of his position. The letter was not a plea for release. It did not need to be; Shaftesbury knew he was coming, and why. Scott simply stated the circumstances of his detention. The letter was dispatched to London by a local ally, Mr Nephew. That night Scott was 'very merry and sat up drinking all night in Nephew's company, and they lay in a room together'.[31] He expected to be released and he was right; four days later, he was taken to London and set free. Then he disappeared.

When Scott had been chased out of England in October, Samuel Pepys had been in charge of the Admiralty. At Scott's return, the boot was on the other foot. After their victory in the general election, the Whigs had taken control of the Admiralty Commission, putting them in charge of Pepys and making his life difficult. Now his life was impossible, because he was also under investigation by MP William Harbord's Whig Parliamentary Committee. On 1 May he was hauled in front of the Committee. On 3 May, one observer wrote that the new head of the Admiralty 'desires to have Will Harbord for Secretary, so that Mr Pepys is to be pulled in pieces with complaints poured in'.[32]

By 5 May, Pepys was suffering under the strain the Committee was putting on him. He wrote to Sir John Werden, the Duke of York's secretary, who had reluctantly accompanied the Duke into exile in Brussels, to say how bad his position had become: 'As unpleasant as you seem to hold the place you are now in, I think the not offering you mine in exchange is one of the best instances I can at this time give you of the sincerity of respect borne you.'[33] Everything that Pepys hated had come to torment him. The new Admiralty Commission was unprofessional, inefficient and blind to the navy's needs because the Whig commissioners had no idea what they were doing. The King seemed to derive some enjoyment from their ignorance, and complimented Pepys that he alone was keeping the commissioners 'right' and the navy functioning.[34] On 6 May, unable to bear it any longer, Pepys wrote an impassioned and bitter letter to the exiled Duke.

He wanted to be appointed to the Commission – to be set on a level with the Whig eagles who had taken over the roost of his professional life. He was asking the Duke of York to bend his brother's ear. He said he had hardly been able to bear the 'fatigue' of the office of secretary in the days when the commissioners were knowledgeable. Now he had to inform 'those who should inform and are to command me'. His dignity was ruffled. Pepys, with the bantam-cock pride of the small of stature, was often on his dignity, but in this case his position was intolerable. For many years he had lived 'in a constant state of war' with these men of the Opposition, 'they censuring, and I defending, the management of the navy' and now he would get no respect from them 'upon terms so unequal, as my being brought down to be a servant to them, when the dignity of the trust I have so long had the honour of serving His Majesty in, might, I hope, be thought to have set me upon a level with them'. The Secretaryship had become 'odious'. He chose to resign from the position that had marked the high point of his career. The Whig commissioners who wanted his job had finally levered him out of it.

The cost of the resignation worried him. The Diary demonstrates his constant obsession with his financial state and the passage of time had not changed this. Now he told the Duke he would be in a 'very ill condition' if he was not rewarded by a pension or the Commissioner's position he wanted.[35]

As Pepys looked for a way out, the Commons pushed the King further into a corner. On 9 May, still furious that Charles's pardon of Danby had made a mockery of their authority, the Commons resolved that even to express the opinion that Danby's pardon was legally valid was a criminal offence.[36] Two days later, agreeing with one MP's view that 'as long as the duke is heir to the Crown, the kingdom is unsafe', the Commons boiled over. Whig after Whig leapt to their feet. 'If the Pope gets his great toe into England, all his body will follow,' said one MP. Sir Thomas Player stepped up to propose what had become inevitable but which was still taboo – 'a Bill for excluding the Duke of York by name, and all papists whatsoever from the Crown of England'. Brave Henry Coventry intervened, despite being very ill from gout and having been fallen on before.

'Acts of Parliament, we know,' he said, 'have not kept succession out of the right line [of inheritance], but brought in blood and sword.' If the Duke of York was excluded he would resort to 'desperate and irrecoverable counsels . . . Pray run not upon these extremities,' Coventry begged, 'before you have well considered of it.'[37] Coventry argued with the Whigs for a solid thirteen hours that day.[38] His appeals foundered on the perennial problem, trenchantly expressed by a Whig MP: to bind James with laws was like 'binding Sampson with withies [willow wands]; he will break them when he is awake'.[39]

When it came to a vote, those who wanted to exclude the Duke from the line of succession were counted in the traditional way, by leaving their seats. As the vast majority filed out, the remainder conceded defeat rather than have their pathetic number known.[40] Thus the House resolved to bring in a bill to exclude the Duke. Coventry's one-man battle for restraint had been lost, and by the 14th he had 'gone sick into the country'.[41] The Exclusion Bill was read for the first time in the Commons on 15 May.[42] It began with a weak attempt to absolve the Duke of direct blame for his religion; the papists with their wicked designs had 'traitorously seduced' James to Catholicism. Such language did little to disguise the violence of the bill, however. It was to be as if the Duke were dead. The next good Protestant in line would inherit the throne, and James would be guilty of high treason if he tried to behave as sovereign. If he entered the kingdom anyone seeing him was required by law 'to seize upon and imprison him'. If he resisted, they had an obligation to subdue him by force of arms.[43]

Nothing could have touched Charles's raw nerves more certainly than an attack on the direction of the Crown's descent and his rejection of the principle was total. This after all was the man whose own inheritance of the throne had been interrupted by Cromwell's republican government, whose father had died at the executioner's hand and who had been forced into exile on the Continent by civil war. But it was now clear to everyone that Charles's authority to rule was no longer 'by the grace of God', but by the grace of the people, who had invited him back as king. Government by consent had begun at the moment of Charles's Restoration. The intransigent approach that had been his father's style was no longer acceptable. Charles had to honour that consent but the implications of it horrified him, for what the people had given, the people could also take away. What was the Crown if the people could decide who wore it?

On 12 May, before the Exclusion Bill had been read, James wrote to Charles on Pepys's behalf, asking for him to be made an Admiralty Commissioner. Pepys was 'an old servant . . . that has long and faithfully served you' and 'is likely to suffer without your Majesty's favour'. The new Commissioners were still 'very raw', and the navy would deteriorate should Pepys be 'laid aside'. Charles was 'bound to do something' for Pepys given his long service and experience.[44] The request was admirably faithful but hopeless. It was politically impossible for Charles to show favour to those the Commons detested.

The wheels were in motion, and political observers could see what was coming. A well-informed parliamentary commentator wrote that 'It is thought . . . that they will hang Pepys.'[45]

There was another sign of the changed times. After a long absence, John Scott's patron the Duke of Buckingham reappeared in public, confident the Whig cause was in the ascendancy and speaking in the House of Lords 'scores of times, but, 'twas said, more pleasantly than learnedly'.[46] Information now arrived from France that would have been useful in prosecuting charges against John Scott, but Shaftesbury had already released Scott and he had disappeared. In a ciphered letter, Henry Savile at the Paris embassy told Secretary of State Henry

Coventry that Scott had given one of Louis XIV's senior ministers 'a map of all the ports and creeks in England'. Suspecting treason, Coventry hurried to show the letter to the King.[47] He was too late.

By 20 May, nine days after the Bill's reading, the politics of fear had flooded out of the Commons chamber and were running through the streets. A vast array of men and women stood against the Duke of York. Collectively these Whigs opposed the pro-French line of the government, displayed a virulent hatred of Catholic absolutism, and lived in fear of Charles's assassination by papists and his replacement by an absolute monarch in the form of James. Some were earls, some dukes, but the vast majority were merchants, brewers, landlords, shopkeepers, joiners, tradesmen, goldsmiths, adventurers, builders or hackney-cab drivers. Their antipathy to James united them across class borders. Their convictions were fired by pamphlets, newsletters, satires, broadsides, almanacs, plays and political tracts. They were not wits in Whitehall or courtiers with houses in the fashionable growing squares of the West End. They sang raucous ballads together. They met in smoky taverns and coffee shops, or on the streets where they lit bonfires and held processions. They had not one but many headquarters in clubs across London. Infamous among these was the Green Ribbon Club in the King's Head at the corner of Fleet Street and Chancery Lane. Among their wide and varied ranks were men of scrupulous political conscience, and others who came from the underbelly of the city, attracted to the celebrity that Oates and his cronies had brought to the role of the professional informer. On 20 May, Colonel John Scott stepped forward from their ranks to the bar of the House of Commons and accused Pepys of being a traitor.

7
Through Pellissary's Window

Tuesday 20 May 1679 was the fifth consecutive day of hot weather.[1] A guard standing outside Somerset House recognised Colonel John Scott going past clutching a bundle of papers, and greeted him. Scott, evidently distracted, said he was to 'impeach Mr Pepys' in Parliament and hurried off. The guard's companion reprimanded him for speaking to a villain like Scott.[2]

A little upriver, the whitewashed chamber of the House of Commons was packed with the Earl of Shaftesbury's Whig supporters. Samuel Pepys and Sir Anthony Deane, his fellow MP for Harwich, were sitting on benches cushioned by hay and green baize. The findings of the Committee of Enquiry into the Miscarriages of the Navy were due to be announced. Waiting among the last rearguard of the routed Tories, Pepys could have expected complaints about administrative fees and the usual insubstantial claims that the navy favoured Catholic officers. He had been answering the same complaints with great eloquence and indignation for years. Besides, since he had resigned, he no longer had to protect his job.

Outside the chamber, in the busy Commons' lobby, a skilled craftsman called Captain John Browne was waiting for a friend. Browne, a maker and engraver of fine cutlery, had just been to the House of Lords to see the King's cousin about a plate he was to engrave for the chapel at Windsor Castle. He was hailed, but not by the man he was expecting.

'Welcome friend,' said Colonel Scott. Browne had known Scott in France four years earlier. Scott was very glad he had bumped into Browne because Browne, he said, could do the King a great service.

'Do you not know Sir Anthony Deane?' asked Scott.

'No,' replied Browne.

'You know that you were with me at Monsieur Pellissary's house at Paris, that time when the two yachts were brought over from England,' persisted Scott. 'You and I saw Sir Anthony Deane through the sash-windows talking very earnestly alone with Monsieur Pellissary, and though you did not understand French, I heard and understood what he said.'

Browne remembered no such thing. Scott became impatient with him.

'Sir,' he said, 'you must now remember it for you are to be a witness for the King. I am this day to accuse Sir Anthony Deane and Mr Pepys to the House of Commons and you shall go into the House with me to testify it.'

'Press me no more in this,' said Browne; he would not do anything so unjust, even if it was for his own father. Angry, Scott demanded that he repair his memory by the next morning, 'for it was the King's business'. Besides, he added with an oath before stalking off, it was 'as true as the light shined'.[3]

In the chamber, William Harbord, the Whig chairman of the Committee, stood up to outline its findings before making way for his first witness. Colonel John Scott was almost completely a stranger to Harbord. They had met a day or two before, when Harbord's Committee had gathered its main informants privately at the Mitre tavern, Fenchurch Street, to prepare them for the attack on Pepys in the Commons. Scott's information, Harbord knew, would hang Pepys and Deane – if Scott could prove what he claimed.[4] But he had heard 'bad report' of this man, in his velvet coat and embroidered jacket, and was uncertain what to make of him.[5]

Scott came in from the lobby and stood at the bar of the House. Pepys had never seen him before but as he stared at him and turned the name over in his mind, memories began to stir – of murder, a chase and a flight from Gravesend.

In 'about August' 1675, Scott began, he had been invited to the Paris house of the treasurer of the French navy – the house with black and white marble floors, and myrtle and orange trees in the gardens. His name was Georges Pellissary, he was a Protestant, and he had shown Scott documents that had come from England.[6]

These papers, Scott told the listening MPs, included fourteen sheets written in English in a 'close' hand. They laid bare the workings of the English navy. They listed the quantity, age and condition of the ships in the fleet. They gave the names of the harbours the ships lay in, those harbours' strengths and weaknesses and the numbers of guns. The fleet's 'fighting instructions' since 1652 were provided, as were details of how sailors were organised in sea fights. The papers were annotated with helpful marginal notes comparing English and French strength. 'Our guns want a fourth part of the number of yours,' read one note. Another mentioned that English sailors' 'dissatisfaction . . . for want of their pay' could tempt them into French service. In short, the papers paved the way for a French invasion of England.

In addition, Scott said he saw 'five large maps or charts'. One showed Gravesend and the shores of Essex and Kent. The second showed the Medway from Rochester Bridge to where it emptied into the Thames. The rest were of Portsmouth, the Isle of Wight and Plymouth. They showed the sands, soundings and recently built fortifications. There were plans of Sheerness and Tilbury. Accompanying the papers and maps, said Scott, was a letter stating that Captain Deane would explain and interpret them. The English letter writer had clearly taken advantage of a providential situation to send these papers, maps and charts to France; 'The occasion . . . that brings these yachts is very lucky,' the letter read. Scott knew the handwriting, he claimed, because he had seen it since then. The letter was signed 'Samuel Pepys'.

Pepys must have been listening in horror. He recognised the event being described, of course. It was Deane's trip to France with the yachts for Louis's Versailles canal – the journey on which Deane had struggled with one hundred and sixteen horses and a broken trolley to haul the yachts from the Seine; on which Deane had been feted and dined by the French navy ministers. Now Scott was talking about exactly that. He told the Commons that Deane, walking in the garden of navy treasurer Pellissary's house, had stopped under an open window. Unaware of Scott's presence just inside, Deane had told a companion that he had carried papers and maps 'from Mr Pepys' to France. The papers had gone first to the Marquis de Seignelay, the French navy minister. De Seignelay's name must have provoked another rush of recognition for the listening Pepys; Deane and Will Hewer had feasted at his house. The papers were of such importance, Deane allegedly said, that Pepys would not have parted with them for £40,000, 'had it not been for the greater end'. The phrase resounded like a warning bell in the furious, Plot-fearing House of Commons.

Shortly after, Scott continued, Pellissary suggested to Deane that he come in and meet Scott. Deane, who had not known there was another Englishman in the house and did not want to be seen by him, had recoiled, begged to be kept away from Scott and demanded to know whether Pellissary had told Scott anything about the treasonous papers. Embarrassed, Pellissary lied and said he had not, then hurried into the house to tell Scott to stay out of sight. Scott was made to 'dine privately' elsewhere in the house that night. The listening Pepys may have remembered other details Deane had written to him about that meal: how Deane's son had translated between French and English, and how the party had danced as Pellissary's wife played the harpsichord.

After Pellissary saw the papers, they were sent to a third Frenchman, Scott told the Commons – one Monsieur Piogerie, 'a person of great knowledge in sea affairs'.* Scott had seen them at

---

* Monsieur Piogerie was rightly Louis Heroüard, sieur de La Piogerie.

Piogerie's lodgings. In disgust, he had said to Piogerie that he 'hoped that these great rogues that would betray their own country are not of our religion' and Piogerie, who was also a Protestant, replied, 'They are of the Devil's religion, let us drink off our wine.' 'There is a mystery in this business,' the Frenchman had added, 'more than I dare speak of.'

These conversations had happened four years before. Scott should rightfully have told the Commons straight away about Pepys's treason. To explain the long delay, he said that Pellissary and Piogerie had sworn him to secrecy. By their deaths, he told the House, he was now 'discharged from obligation of privacy'.

Scott had finished. He left the chamber. Pepys's mind must have been whirling. In April 1675, four months before Scott said he had seen them in France, Pepys had prepared exactly those papers and given them to Parliament.[7] The information they contained had been so detailed and sensitive that the worried Secretary Coventry had moved the House that the papers should 'not be exposed to public view' but instead kept safely by a committee. The House had refused and the papers were made available for any MP to see. Some had made copies of them.[8] When Scott disappeared from Gravesend six months before, his lodgings and possessions were searched. Among the odd assortment of mathematical instruments, political speeches and poetry were copies of exactly these papers. Pepys knew this.

As Scott left the Commons, Harbord brought in his second witness, Captain Moone, who charged Pepys and Deane with piracy. With a bit of theft out of the stores and by abusing Pepys's professional position, he said, they had acquired a privateer called *Hunter* to prey on Dutch ships during the last war. When England made peace with the Dutch, Pepys and Deane sent their privateer to France to prey on Dutch and (Moone had discovered to his astonishment) even English shipping. When Moone reported the abuse, Deane had him thrown in gaol and maliciously clapped on an iron shackle that made his leg swell and forced him to walk on crutches. Moone stayed in gaol, he told the Commons, for three years. Meanwhile, Pepys's brother-in-law, Balthasar St Michel, sailed to France to make sure that the English ship the *Hunter* had captured – the *Catherine* – was declared a legitimate prize.[9]

After Captain Moone, the Committee's third witness was a dapper and healthy-looking young man who Pepys knew well. His name was John James. He had been Pepys's butler.[10]

Pepys kept a Portuguese man in his house, said James, but the relationship between them was not like a master and servant. The Portuguese would go to his devotion at 3 or 4 a.m. when the house was asleep, and then he was allowed to sleep late. If he was in bed, Pepys would not disturb him. They dined together and Pepys let the Portuguese have as much as he wanted of any wine he chose. When they were at their devotions together on a Sunday, Pepys told the porters no one should interrupt them, 'though it were from the King himself'. When Pepys's brother died, the Portuguese had composed several psalms or masses which they sang mournfully and privately together for a fortnight. The man's name, said James, was Morelli. He was a Catholic priest. The implication was clear to all: Pepys was Catholic. The kept priest was a senior figure in a Catholic household. In Protestant England, however, he had to be disguised as something lesser to escape detection. John James told the Commons that he had heard descriptions of how priests lived openly in Italy and Spain. In every particular, he said, these descriptions were identical to how Morelli was treated behind Pepys's closed doors.

James's story was a long way from the truth. Cesare Morelli was not Portuguese; he had been born in Flanders.[11] Pepys had never been shy about his patronage of Morelli nor had he concealed Morelli's Catholicism. In the lonely years after his wife Elizabeth's death, Pepys had sought a companion with whom he could play music, his 'utmost luxury'. Thomas Hill, a music-loving merchant in Lisbon, found the young man for him in 1674. Morelli spoke Latin, Italian, French and Spanish, sang with an admirable voice and played the theorbo (a kind of lute). He had been living under the ungenerous patronage of a marquis in Lisbon, but had so little ambition that he was content with the pittance.[12] In his heart, though, Morelli longed to come to England. The marquis was loath to part with him, but after seven months of effort Hill was finally able to write to Pepys that 'as all things contribute, not only to your honour and advantage but to your gusto also, this Marquis is lately dead'.[13] Pepys had never hoped to find a servant who so completely fulfilled his requirements as Morelli did and, in gratitude, he sent Hill a portrait of himself. Hill's letter of thanks has the excited quality of a dog that knows it has performed an excellent trick.[14]

Warned by Pepys against sordidness and pomp (which he might have laughed at had he been able to read Pepys's Diary), Morelli joined Pepys's household for £30 per year. Pepys promised he would 'cherish him with a great deal of pleasure'.[15] When the story of a Popish Plot first appeared in autumn 1678, Pepys asked his great friend, the merchant James Houblon, to try to convert Morelli to Protestantism but Morelli was 'resolved in his religion' and politely refused to shift.[16]

The account of Morelli that John James now gave the Commons was altogether shadier than the reality. He claimed Morelli possessed all the materials needed for Catholic worship. Morelli had a private closet, the door of which could only be opened by a hidden mechanism. Here he kept his daggers, crucifixes, pictures of saints in gold and silver, a great number of writings and a trunk large enough to hold his and Pepys's habits 'and other things that they used in their service'. Such a collection, a kind of Catholic fancy-dress box, hidden in the labyrinthine houses of wealthy Catholics, was a standard feature. The men chasing the fleeing Gunpowder Plotters of 1605 had searched a series of concealed and ingenious hiding places, many of which contained just such collections of popish paraphernalia.[17]

Morelli, said James, carried three types of dagger: one to throw, another to poison and the third 'for a plain stab'. He had walked several times in St James's Park (where Charles II walked daily) with a dagger and pistol in his pocket.

To be converted to Catholicism, to attend mass or to possess

Catholic apparatus was illegal. Catholic priests were forbidden entry into England; any found within England could be executed. When, shortly after Edmund Berry Godfrey's murder, a proclamation commanded Catholics to leave London, Pepys had ignored it and kept Morelli in his house, said James. He had sent him away only later – secretively, in a rowing boat. Sheltering a priest was a capital offence.

With his final words, John James made it quite clear to the Commons that Pepys, though a high-ranking bureaucrat in the King's service, was first and foremost a willing henchman of the Duke of York. If sea officers came asking for jobs, James said, Pepys told them their cause was futile unless they could get on the Duke's list. When a 'person of great quality' requested Pepys discharge a man who had been press-ganged into the navy, Pepys said that even if the King himself was asking, he would not do it unless the order came through the Duke. When another man came with an order for employment from the King, Pepys 'puffed at him' and said Charles did not know what he was doing. Every detail James gave of Pepys's private life suggested that Pepys was loyal to the Catholic monarch-to-be, not Charles; to Catholicism rather than the throne.

James stepped away from the bar and the Commons exploded in agreement.[18] One MP told the House that he had spoken with Titus Oates in the lobby, who said that Morelli had begged to be put in charge of the plan to kill Charles. Another said that Pepys's crimes were 'one of the branches of the Plot'; the Catholic uprising in England was the 'Land-Plot' and Pepys's sale of naval secrets was a 'Sea-Plot'. The Commons' seventy-eight-year-old sergeant-at-law demanded that the papers detailing the charges should be put into the Speaker's custody and thus made inaccessible. It was a desperate moment. Without these, Pepys and Deane would have to rely on memory to prepare a defence. Clearly alarmed, Secretary of State Henry Coventry argued it was only reasonable that the accused should have the charges in writing.

The sergeant-at-law disagreed. It would be highly unusual for Pepys and Deane to be given written copies of Scott, Moone and

James's charges; he wondered whether defendants had ever been given such papers, in any court. They might possibly be given bare summaries of the charges, if and when the Commons thought fit.

'Then,' he added acidly, 'you may see what defence can be made for giving the French King such information as you have heard.'

Whether Pepys was invited to make a defence, or the sergeant-at-law's last comment compelled him to get to his feet, parliamentary privilege gave him the right to reply and the Speaker let him talk for some minutes. Two transcriptions of the speech were made. Anchitel Grey, the MP for Derby, took notes of debates in shorthand for his own convenience. His copy is concise with frequent editorial contractions.[19] Someone else also felt moved to pick up his pen and write. The second copy is among Pepys's own papers, now in the Bodleian. Its authorship is ascribed to 'Sir –', and while its accuracy is qualified by a remark in Pepys's own hand that 'it was taken very imperfectly', it contains more detail than Grey's professional, un-engaged version.[20]

From the moment he began to speak, Pepys had to walk the line between his anger and the respect that the House demanded. It was essential not to provoke its hostility, given his new status as a Catholic conspirator. It was a great misfortune, he began, to have so many things cast upon him, all at once and all by surprise. But, he added, he did not speak to complain. If he had failed in his duty to king and country, he ought to be thought the greatest criminal in the world. He could not ignore the secret nature of the proceedings against him and no sooner had he acknowledged the severity of the charges than his indignation burst out, 'But Sir!' He had never failed to obey the summons of Harbord's Committee from the hour of its first constitution and yet he had never heard one syllable of these accusations, which were 'totally foreign to every thought of my life'. He turned briefly to the case of the *Hunter*, declaring that he only knew about the ship through 'common fame' and had no personal involvement with her. Then he addressed 'Mr Scott's' charges, a crime of such weight 'at a time so dangerous' that Pepys said he would help in his own prosecution to have this dark matter 'changed to light'. He was quite sure he did not know Scott, nor did he know 'where his abode is'. He resented being forced to defend himself unprepared. The House had made a committee not a secret committee. Why had the Committee not asked him, instead of springing this on him?

By now his memory had made the link to the Gravesend incident and, realising this must surely be the same man, he told the House the bare bones of the story of the suspicious stranger's flight. He said he had advised the Commons and, as directed, taken action to try to stop the man. The House had commanded Pepys to 'be as inquisitive as [he] could'. Pepys passed on details to the Lord Mayor and the Recorder, who searched the man's London lodgings and found papers 'of very ill import'. If the gentleman who had stood so confidently at the bar was the same as had been pursued through Kent, said Pepys, then it looked 'like a pretty odd piece of skill', for the papers Scott had accused Pepys of sending over to the French were exactly the papers that had been found in Scott's house.

The point made, Pepys's indignation spilled over. He said he did not know if Scott was making this up to get even with him. However, he did know that communicating weighty secrets to the French was 'out of my province . . . entirely out of my watch'.

'He tells you that the papers in France . . . were signed by me,' thundered Pepys. ' 'Tis Scott's "Yea, by report"; 'tis my "No, before God Almighty".'

Perhaps one of the two MPs noting down Pepys's angry defence was sitting too far from him to hear clearly, or perhaps one man's shorthand was unable to keep up. The unnamed writer thought Pepys said he was unwilling to 'admit of any smile of any French ambassador'. Anchitel Grey thought Pepys had 'industriously' avoided coming within the French ambassador's smell.

Turning to the butler, John James, Pepys again questioned the Committee's methods. This was the information of a servant against his master, a member of the House of Commons entitled to certain privileges, and yet the master had not been told the charges were coming.

'It is a little hard,' Pepys told them.

It had been his misfortune to find that James was bad and had fallen into an amour with Pepys's housekeeper. It was Morelli's misfortune to hear the two lovers passing his chamber door late one night (here Pepys emphasised that Morelli, far from being a priest, was James's 'fellow servant'). Pepys and Morelli caught James and the housekeeper together at the 'unseasonable' hour of 3 a.m. It was a Sunday, Pepys told the House, briefly showing signs of enjoying himself; 'I thought the better day, the better deed.' Both the offending servants were turned out the same day and James had not been back except, Pepys suspected, to rob him.

Morelli was a tricky issue but Pepys thought it best to tell the truth. Morelli had sung psalms and he was a Catholic. Pepys confessed that he had sought a good scholar, a good linguist and a good musician, as a 'servant for my entertainment'. His business did not allow him the diversions that men of more leisure were entitled to. In Morelli he had found a harmless, perfectly qualified and inoffensive young man.

Before he sat down, indignant and spent, he moved to categorical denial. The psalms were anthems, it was no crime to sing them and they would offend no one who loved music as much as him. When the proclamation was issued banning Catholics from the city, Morelli did not remain secretively but left the city publicly into the country where he now lived. As for Morelli being a Jesuit, he was thought so moderate a Catholic in Lisbon that he was suspected of being a Protestant.

Pepys failed to rebut the charge that Morelli kept concealed weapons and priestly possessions. For all that, it had been an impressive impromptu performance.

Sir Anthony Deane, a more hesitant public speaker, stood up in the silence that followed Pepys's tirade.[21] He freely admitted he was part of the consortium that bought the *Hunter* in the Dutch war of 1673. His one-eighth share cost him £400. He had paid for the ship to be fitted out and if anyone had stolen stores out of the dockyard, that should be taken up with the man responsible. As for Captain Moone's honesty, he had captured a prize but made off with the proceeds and that was why Deane had him sent to gaol. On the question of the *Catherine*'s capture, he said she was in fact manned by the Dutch and so sailing under false colours, making her a legitimate prize.

Then Deane turned to Scott's accusations. Yes, he said, he had been ordered to build two boats for Louis XIV but these were not significant vessels. The canal at Versailles was 'the depth of my stick, about three foot and a half'. The French ambassador paid for them but 'I built them in obedience to the King's command, little thinking I should be questioned here for it.' He spelt out his reward: 'The King of France presented me with 600 pistoles, for my charges, and his picture set with diamonds, worth £200 and he gave my son a medal of £100.' He also explained that while he was there, he studied the organisation of their navy and gave his findings to English officials.

Protesting his complete innocence in the presence of God, he went rather to pieces at the end of his reply.

'I have twelve children to take care of,' he said. 'I have bewailed and lamented our station . . . I hope you will take it from a gentleman. If it should be the last word I should ever speak, I never carried script nor scroll from Mr Pepys to Monsieur Pellissary.'

Then he too turned it back on Scott. By chance an MP he had met two days earlier 'named this Colonel Scott to have given intelligence to the French Court'. The rumours of Scott's time in France were spreading.

Pepys and Deane could not now walk free. Those few friends they had did their best to soften the blow. Sir Joseph Williamson confirmed that Deane had indeed investigated French naval affairs and once, when de Seignelay came to England, had obstructed the French navy minister's secret plan to inspect the naval town of Portsmouth.

Some sort of trial was inevitable. The MP William Garroway warned against letting the House of Lords anywhere near the case. The upper house was seen as a bastion of popishness and royal support. Whether the Commons impeached them or let the Attorney General prosecute them in the cruel law courts, Garroway told the other MPs, 'you cannot leave it.'

Pepys and Deane's long speeches might have made them seem innocent, said William Harbord, but he would prove the allegations. As for John James, the Committee had £500 security from him for his honesty. The Duke of York might no longer be Admiral but these men were clearly still operating under the Duke's instructions to put the navy into papist hands. 'Pepys is an ill man,' said Harbord, 'and I will prove him so.'

William Sacheverell pressed for swift examination before the Commons. He suggested that it would be 'just' for Pepys and Deane to prepare themselves for an examination the following day. This utterly ignored the impossibility of Pepys and Deane assembling a defence relating to events four years earlier in another country. Sacheverell had dined with Shaftesbury and had actively prosecuted the Plot since its discovery; justice for Pepys was not a prime concern of his.[22] The House supported his motion that the accused be taken into the custody of the sergeant-at-arms.

Harbord, who had begun the report, hammered home the severity of the case. There should be no repeat of a recent occasion when one prisoner committed to the sergeant had been found drinking in the Devil Tavern. Harbord said if the House was in earnest 'I would have them committed to the Tower. Let them withdraw.'

The two men stood and, stepping along the line of benches, made their way out.

8

Fat Harry and the Scotsman

Samuel Pepys and Sir Anthony Deane spent the remainder of 20 and 21 May in the custody of the sergeant-at-arms. We do not know where he kept them but their movements were almost certainly restricted; they were the Commons' enemies, and William Harbord's warning that they were not to be seen in the Devil Tavern was deadly serious. On 22 May, the day the weather broke, they were taken back into the Commons, where Harbord went through the charges again. The MPs had to choose what to do next. Initially, the Whigs wanted to hear the case and find the traitors guilty themselves, and a parliamentary impeachment was 'very much talked of'.[1] But wiser heads prevailed and the Commons eventually directed the Attorney General to prosecute them in the regular law courts, where Henry Coventry's eloquence could not defend them and where Lord Chief Justice William Scroggs had a near-perfect record of steering Plot juries towards guilty verdicts. The decision made, Pepys and Deane were led out of St Stephen's Chapel into the thunderstorm and transported, under guard, past the blackened bones of old St Paul's cathedral and into the Tower of London.

As with all dramatic political events, the charges against Pepys provoked a flurry of written information. The Duke of Ormonde, away in Ireland, had a string of correspondents keeping him up to date with affairs. On the day of Scott's accusations, one of these wrote to tell him that 'the Commons chiefly spent their day on Mr Pepys and Sir Anthony Deane'.[2] He wrote again to say he thought the *Hunter* charges were not as substantial as the prosecution would have them appear, but had been 'aggravated to the height'.[3] The belief that the charges lacked substance ran through other letters written in those two days. 'No less than matters of treason and felony are laid at their charge,' wrote an MP who confessed he was not fond of either man, 'but by what I have heard I am apt to believe neither will be well made out against them.' He predicted that Pepys and Deane's defence would benefit from the 'warmth of the prosecution', and thought 'that their offences are magnified beyond due proportion'.[4] Sir Robert Southwell, also writing to Ormonde, agreed that the prosecution's evidence would probably 'shrink' at trial.[5]

Southwell, a friend of Pepys, was canny enough to see that the political climate would make the consequences of the charges severe. Pepys and Deane, he wrote, had both 'been sharers of the Duke's favour, and how slender soever the proofs be, they must taste the bitter cup'. And below the level of elegant correspondence, in the streets, the talk was violent. On 21 May, the Commons passed the bill to exclude the Duke of York from the throne for a second time, and the news spread like a fire among delighted Londoners. In a marketplace, the mother of John James the butler told a Mrs Harris that she feared for her son's safety as a witness against Mr Pepys. Mrs Harris cheerily replied that she need not worry, for Mr Pepys would soon be hanged.[6]

Pepys sat alone in the Tower, full of questions, trying to regain some control and composure after events had so fiercely and publicly felled him. His enemies' grand intentions must have been blindingly clear to him. He stood with the Duke of York, on the wrong side of the yawning divide that had opened in England. As for the individuals who had given evidence against him, he understood why John James had lied about his religion; the sacked butler resented him, and his testimony had been bought. Captain Moone's charges about the *Hunter* touched Sir Anthony Deane rather than Pepys, and he felt no need to answer them. The missing piece of the puzzle, the gigantic hole in Pepys's understanding, was Colonel John Scott. Pepys was at a loss as to what Scott's 'inducements' might be.[7] All he had to go on was the tantalising keyhole picture he had of Scott from exploring his Cannon Street lodgings six months before – a man who wrote poetry, and collected political speeches and mathematical instruments.

Among Scott's possessions, most bizarrely, had been the naval papers Pepys himself had drawn up. Why did Scott have them? Was it to prepare the attack on Pepys – so that he would be able to describe them in the House? Had Pepys's enemies really been planning this attack for six months? That was, after all, when Shaftesbury had charged his clerk with murder. If so, the presence of the papers indicated an unnerving degree of preparation. There was every chance that an MP on the other side of the parliamentary divide had given them to Scott. But the Plot had been very young then. Had they really decided to involve him in it that early? Was there a chance that Scott had genuinely seen the papers in France, and taken a copy to keep?

In captivity, Pepys tried to get to grips with all these questions. We do not know exactly where in the Tower he was imprisoned, nor do we know his degree of discomfort. 'People of quality', in the terminology of the time, were kept in rooms in some of the twelve towers which punctuated the walls of the inner ward. In some cases they would be allocated a room in the lodgings of one of the Tower officials, living the life of a 'paying guest' and enjoying some freedom to wander around the inner areas of the old fortress. At the other extreme, they would be kept in strictly guarded solitary confinement. The stone walls of some of the prison towers such as the Beauchamp Tower are decorated by the intricate carvings made by long-term prisoners from the ages before Pepys, who could import some of the comforts of home in the form of furniture, servants and wall-hangings. Old engravings of the interior of the Beauchamp Tower show it much as it is today, thick stone walls broken by windows set in deep gothic arches, a high ceiling carried by heavy beams and a wide stone fireplace. A prisoner could look out across the open ground in the middle to the massive central keep, the White Tower.[8]

It seems that Pepys was kept apart from Sir Anthony Deane.* However, he was allowed some contact with the world outside; as he pondered on the accusations against him, papers and people began to arrive at his cell. He must have been astonished at his good fortune. When his clerk had been in Newgate, Pepys had been barred from visiting him. The most useful thing to appear – probably on the third or fourth day of Pepys's imprisonment – was a nugget or two of information from Secretary of State Henry Coventry.

Henry Coventry was sixty years old and in constant agony from the gout that inflamed his joints. He had been a royalist in the Civil War and was a forthright supporter of the Crown now, so much so that he felt bound to justify royal policy even when the King was patently in error. The commentator Bishop Burnet called him 'a man of wit and heat, of spirit and candour', qualities he had shown in the Commons during the bitter struggles over the Duke of York. That might have been cause enough for him to funnel useful information into Pepys's cell, but Coventry had a further motive – guilt.

Coventry, it will be remembered, had helped Pepys chase John Scott as he fled Gravesend, and when Scott was seized in Folkestone on his return, it had been on Coventry's warrant. He had been anxious to prosecute the captive Scott, and had written to his contacts at the Paris embassy to gather witnesses against him. The embassy men had hunted for information and had quickly discovered that Scott had a bad name in France and friends in King Charles's court. But by the time they communicated this to Coventry, his interest in prosecuting Scott had entirely disappeared. In fact, Coventry had suddenly found an interest in using Scott himself, for quite a different purpose. Scott had come back to England claiming he had heard the deathbed confession of the Catholic Earl of Berkshire, who had been living in France. Scott alleged that the Earl had confided in him that there was 'a foolish and an ill design carried on in England', blaming it on 'the giddy madness'

---

* There is no indication in the letters Pepys sent from the Tower that he was communicating with Deane.

of some Catholics there and naming Lord Arundel (who had told Berkshire that 'the business could not miscarry'), Lord Bellasis ('an ill man . . . accustomed to speak ill of the king'), Lord Stafford ('all along a moving agent' in the business) and Lord Powis.[9] These were four of five Catholic lords accused by Oates of intending to take over the government after the King's murder, and imprisoned in the Tower alongside Pepys. This evidence had been Scott's passport back into England and Coventry – anxious to prosecute the Plotters – had believed that Scott might be telling the truth.

As a result, Coventry had delayed prosecuting Scott and even, perhaps, ordered his release once he arrived in London. Scott then disappeared and Coventry had trouble getting him to write down Berkshire's confession, since he could only contact him through a linen draper in Cornhill. Coventry wrote to this linen draper begging him to 'speak to Col. Scott to send me that in writing which he promised'.[10] Scott eventually obliged but then his reputation caught up with him. News reached Coventry from the Paris embassy that Scott had given the French a map of all the ports and creeks in England, and he hurried to tell the King.[11] So it was that Coventry knew that Scott, who he had released, was a traitor. Then, out of the blue, Scott accused Pepys. Coventry, suddenly understanding Scott's real motives for returning, and horrified by the consequences, had leapt to his feet to defend Pepys.

After the sergeant-at-arms took Pepys and Deane out of the Commons, Coventry had led an attack on Harbord's Committee and in doing so, did Pepys a huge service. He helped secure the prisoners' access to servants and papers – a snatched victory of crucial importance.[12] The incarceration, Pepys's friends had insisted, was to give him an opportunity to answer the charges; it was not yet a punishment. This also, undoubtedly, provided Coventry with the conduit by which he could pass on information to the imprisoned Pepys and make amends for having trusted Scott. He would certainly not have visited Pepys himself, for if he were seen to do so, there might be another royal servant in the Tower.

The information Pepys received was that Scott had tried to sell maps of England to the French. This information had already begun to seep into common knowledge; when Scott was arrested at Folkestone some people had mistakenly believed that this was the reason for his arrest, and Sir Anthony Deane had mentioned the rumour when he defended himself in the Commons. However, only Henry Coventry knew that his nephew at the Paris embassy, Henry Savile – 'Fat Harry' – could prove the rumour. Savile had written to Coventry ten days before Pepys was charged, saying that 'for certain' Scott had given the French 'a map of all the ports and creeks in England'. Coventry passed Savile's name on to Pepys.

Meanwhile, Pepys came to the conclusion that the main threat to his life was Scott's charge, and he set to work to overcome it with the busy efficiency that had shaped his career; by 26 May he was complaining of the shortage of time at his disposal, a remarkable position for an imprisoned man.[13] Scott had claimed that Pepys had sent the naval papers to the Marquis de Seignelay, then on to Pellissary and Piogerie. The last two were dead. De Seignelay, however, was alive and well and Pepys decided that, if he could get the Frenchman's word that he had never received the papers, the prosecution's case would collapse. This has to be seen as an illogical decision on his part. No English court was likely to put any credence in the word of a French minister alleged to be a co-conspirator. It shows an odd trust by Pepys in some inherent credibility conferred by aristocratic rank.

Pepys was feeling bullish. Armed with Henry Coventry's information, he decided to launch an immediate counter-attack on Scott, to prove that Scott had sold maps to the French, and so been guilty of exactly the crime he charged Pepys with.

When his clerk Sam Atkins was charged, Pepys never attempted to bring any counter-charges against Sam's accusers, although there would have been a strong case for doing so. He simply constructed a concrete defence for Sam. He decided to attack Scott because Scott had affronted him personally, but also because he was less certain of his defence than he had been of Sam Atkins's concrete alibi. What alibi could Pepys find for the broad charges against him? How could he disprove that he had put papers into Deane's hands at some unspecified point? And what if Scott really had seen the papers?

To try to get evidence against Scott and to secure de Seignelay's co-operation, Pepys turned to the two Paris embassy men, 'Fat Harry' Savile and his number two, the Scotsman John Brisbane.

Savile was not the most reliable of men in a crisis. His debauched behaviour had often stretched even the tolerant limits of Charles's court. He had served the Duke of York on land and sea, but then tested that relationship by getting himself emotionally entangled with the Duke's first wife, Ann Hyde. He disgraced himself again by trying his luck with the Earl of Northumberland's widow Elizabeth, entering her bedroom one night while staying at the Northampton-shire stately home of Althorp. She screamed for help and he had to run from the house. He was the younger son of a noble family, with the irresponsibility provided by an allowance of £1,000 a year, and was a bachelor because no respectable woman would consider marrying him. Nevertheless, he had a sharp brain and a deep know-ledge of France, which had been his habitual refuge on the frequent occasions when he had to flee England. Now he had an official post, not as ambassador (Charles knew him too well to take that risk) but as Envoy Extraordinary, the next best thing.[14] Life had recently caught up with him and he was in bad health: 'The return of my venereal pains,' he wrote, 'have thrown me back to dry mutton and diet drink . . . I wonder at myself and that mass of mercury that has gone down my throat in the past seven months.'[15]

His number two, the Scotsman John Brisbane, was a different matter. In Brisbane, Pepys had recognised someone after his own heart when they first met at a wedding fourteen years earlier, just as the Plague had begun to bite in earnest. Pepys clearly enjoyed the traditions of the time: 'And so after prayers, soberly to bed;' he had written in the Diary, 'only, I got into the bridegroom's chamber while he undressed himself, and there was very merry – till he was called to the bride's chamber and into bed they went. I kissed the bride in bed, and so the curtains drawn with the greatest gravity that could be, and so goodnight.' He then shared his own bed with Brisbane, whom he instantly assessed as 'a good scholar and a sober man'. Brisbane described Rome to him, 'which is the most delightful talk a man can have of any traveller. And so to sleep.'[16]

After that they kept in touch, inspecting a new book on Turkish customs together and visiting the gambling den run by the groom porter at Whitehall Palace. Pepys was fascinated by the 'profane, mad entertainment' and was astonished to see 'people in ordinary clothes' wagering two or three hundred guineas and drunken groups pooling their stocks of gold without any idea how much each had put in.

Brisbane pressed me hard and tempted me with saying that no man was ever known to lose the first time, the devil being too cunning to discourage a gamester; and he offered me also to lend me ten pieces to venture, but I did refuse and so went away.[17]

On 26 May, his fourth day in the Tower, Pepys wrote to these two men – a short note to John Brisbane, written as to a friend, explaining that he had been made dependent on Brisbane's help. Scott's 'severity and villainy' had to be matched by 'honest industry and thought-fulness', he wrote. His more formal letter to Savile gave all the details. He enclosed it for Brisbane to read, seal and pass on to Savile. 'It is with as much unwillingness as surprise that I find myself driven to give you this trouble,' it began apologetically, before explaining that his enemies aimed 'at no lower mischief than what concerns my life'. Pepys asked Savile to investigate Scott's charges. The best defence, Pepys told Savile, would be 'your conferring with the Marquis de Seignelay . . . he being a person of too great honour (I hope) not to own the truth'. He intended, he informed them, to lay at Scott's door the very same crime Scott had 'so villainously' accused him of – having sold maps to the French king, and boasted of it. If they had any knowledge of this – which, he said, he had heard they did – he begged for the details.[18]

He wanted de Seignelay's response put into some form 'fit to be offered in evidence to the court'. Pepys could never expect the great marquis to travel to England to be his witness. His helpers, including the lawyer John Hayes, took high-powered legal advice on this question from 'stout, jovial Mr. Saunders, the great royalist barrister, the honestest and best-natured fellow in England'.[19] Edmund Saunders advised that an ambassador could examine an overseas witness and pass their testimony to King Charles, for endorsement with his signet. It would then be admissible in an English court. That is, de Seignelay's written testimony would be acceptable; he would not have to show up in person.

In the world outside the Tower, King Charles, whose patience with the rebellious Commons had been tried to the limit by their attempts to exclude his brother, suddenly struck back. On 27 May, the day after Pepys dispatched his letters to France, the King stopped the Commons reading the Exclusion Bill for a final time in the only way he could; he prorogued Parliament. The bonfires and ringing of bells stopped and, one observer reported, 'Men know not what to say or do, but expect great changes.' Royal authority had silenced Parliament. The Whigs were furious. In London, an uprising seemed likely. Shaftesbury swore he would have the heads of those who had advised Charles and told the King in disgust that there was no need to hold a candle to his face 'for his intent was visible by his actions'. Charles had preserved his brother's inheritance at the price of distancing himself from his people, who were 'mightily troubled'.[20]

A four-day hiatus followed Pepys's letters to Paris, giving him time to reflect on his situation. He was no stranger to the Tower, which had dominated his local skyline for fourteen years when he had lived and worked at the Navy Office in Seething Lane, only two or three minutes' walk from its crumbling walls. No longer used as a royal palace, it still housed the royal menagerie which made its outer buildings a popular destination for sightseers. Exotic animals had arrived over the centuries as gifts from foreign rulers. Elephants, rhinos, apes, leopards and bears had all lived out chilly lives within the Tower's stone walls. In the thirteenth century a resident polar bear drew crowds as he swam in the Thames to catch fish. In Pepys's time, the lions were the main attraction, kept in the semi-circular outer Barbican, the first of three towers set in the moat, guarding the entrance and accessible to the public. The armoury continued to have a garrison and it provided somewhat insecure storage for the Crown Jewels. Colonel Blood had tested that supposed security eight years earlier, coming within an ace of escaping with the royal regalia.

Pepys had been inside the Tower many times. He had hunted for treasure there in October 1662, seeking £50,000 supposedly buried in butter barrels in the arched cellar of one of the towers. The guards made him leave his sword at the Water Gate. Without his sword, fashion dictated he could not be seen out-of-doors without a top-coat, so he sat in a nearby alehouse while his boy ran home to fetch it. He and his friends had dug sporadically for many days, spurred on by thoughts of their share of the reward. In the end they gave up, sent out for food and 'upon the head of a barrel dined very merrily'.[21]

Four years later the Tower served as a high place to watch a fire growing in the City, and he had gone walking through the streets 'seeing people almost distracted and no manner of means used to quench the fire', which swallowed up the densely packed houses with their fuel of pitch and tar, and the warehouses of oil, wine and brandy and eventually London itself.[22]

Pepys's naval business had taken him in and out of the Tower as well, inspecting new storehouses and magazines or dining with the Lieutenant. From Norman times, it had been the place where the choicest enemies of kings and queens were incarcerated but it was increasingly being regarded as the prison proper to the House of Commons, and Pepys was just one of a number of Plot 'conspirators' locked inside.

In the spring of 1669, Pepys's great Navy Office ally Sir William Coventry (Henry's brother) had been sent to the Tower by the King. Sir William, with his frown and flat mouth, was a thorough bureaucrat, loyal to his friends but seen by others as sullen, ill-natured and proud.

The King found his staunch anti-French position troublesome.

Sir William had an enemy, the Duke of Buckingham (who, nine years later, John Scott was to call his friend). The two men could not have been more different. Buckingham was a theatrical bon-viveur, savage, witty, lecherous and unreliable. Broad-faced and double-chinned with wide-set, watery eyes, he was capable of plotting against King Charles's interests, while using his charm and long history at court to stay within Charles's closest circle. He fought violently and frequently. He killed one of his mistresses' husbands in a duel. In his first five months in this mistress's thrall he was involved in five public fights and sent to the Tower three times. Nonetheless, Buckingham could always charm himself back into the King's good books.

Buckingham had written a play, *The Country Gentlemen*, lampooning the serious Sir William as 'Sir Cautious Trouble-All', a conceited bureaucrat who sat in the middle of a ring-shaped desk with his papers arrayed around him, spinning himself around on a revolving chair. Sir William had such a desk – indeed, he had shown it to Pepys, who thought it 'very convenient'.[23] When Sir William complained to King Charles, Buckingham quickly sent Charles a copy of the play without the offending lines. Sir William humourlessly declared that any actor who took the part would have his nose slit, then challenged Buckingham to a duel. An ancient law made it a grave offence for one Privy Councillor to challenge another and Charles (pleased to have the excuse) sent Sir William to the Tower. Charles also imprisoned Sir William's nephew for delivering the challenge – that same Henry Savile to whom Pepys had now written in Paris. It was an early glimpse of the two camps of the plot against Pepys.

Pepys visited Sir William in the Tower, then spent the evening with the Duke of York, who was angry about the affair because Henry Savile had been committed not to the high-status Tower but to the Gatehouse prison among the rogues. Honour was put right before the end of that day; Savile was transferred. Because these were the carefree Diary days, Pepys devoted rather more inches of his entry that night to an after-dinner game, 'the Duke of York and Duchess, with all the great ladies, sitting upon a carpet on the ground, there being no chairs, playing at "I love my love with an A because he is so and so; and I hate him with an A because of this and that." ' Some of the suggestions, Pepys thought, were very witty.²⁴ The King soon released Sir William and Savile. The episode was a world away from Pepys's situation now. His was no quick imprisonment, ordered on a whim. A carefully orchestrated plot was in motion, and the crushing power of the Commons was against him.

Then, suddenly, there was a ray of light. In the four days that followed the dispatch of Pepys's letters to the Paris embassy, someone in his team, probably his lawyer John Hayes, realised that there was a way to get him released. France, Scott and defence testimonies were all entirely irrelevant. The Commons warrant for their imprisonment – signed by the Speaker – did not say why Pepys and Deane were being imprisoned. It simply ordered the Lieutenant of the Tower to take them into custody and 'detain and keep' them 'until they shall be discharged'.²⁵ It was invalid in law. The mechanism of habeas corpus should compel their gaolers to bring them before a court. There they could make the complaint, and the court would have to release them. Parliament had been prorogued and could not therefore imprison them again. Pepys's team requested a court appearance. It was granted. Unexpectedly, freedom beckoned.

The following day brought warm spring rain, and Pepys and Deane were taken the length of London to the court of King's Bench, a simply constructed series of wooden bars, benches and tables which occupied one half of the end wall of Westminster Hall. The hall was a noisy meeting place for all ranks of society and was full of people and their animals, escaping the showers. It was a popular place for cutpurses and the 'men of straw' who displayed a straw tucked into their shoes to show that their testimony was for sale. Along each of the two long walls there was a series of stalls, selling anything from books and prints to felt hats and reading spectacles. The floor was strewn with rushes to keep the dust down, and above was the vast hammerbeam roof, the timbers of which were supported by carved angels.

'Angels work wonders in Westminster Hall' ran a popular joke, referring to the gold coin bearing an image of St Michael the Archangel, the retainer paid for a barrister's services. When state ceremonies demanded it, the woodwork of the courts and stalls could be dismantled and the thieves, straw and animals removed.

Pepys and Deane stood with their backs to the busy hall, at the bar of the court, facing a formidable line of judges perched on a raised oak bench. A hefty table covered in green baize lay in between. The Chief Clerk and some twenty-five officers and clerks sat around it, working at their rolls. On the back wall behind the judges, wall-hangings displayed the royal arms in silent endorsement of the court. A few feet to the left of the defendants was a high wooden tower, from which spectators could look down on proceedings. To their right, in the other corner of the hall, was the court of Chancery, an exact mirror image of King's Bench.

They said they wanted to be discharged because the warrant was invalid. The Attorney General, their prosecutor, was ill in bed. He sent his servant to tell the court that no evidence had yet been produced. Rightfully, his absence should have been entirely irrelevant but the judges hesitated. 'The court being at some stand', Justice Pemberton argued they should remain in prison. It was, he said, a commitment by Parliament 'for matters said to be of the most dangerous importance'. The Commons was a superior court to King's Bench. Because Pepys and Deane had been committed by a hostile Parliament, they were put outside the reach of the other courts. King's Bench was not of 'competent jurisdiction' to overturn the imprisonment, they were told. The judges decided that the Attorney General would be sent for and ordered to demand the missing evidence from Mr Harbord. The hopeful ray of light went out. The Lieutenant of the Tower was told to return with Pepys and Deane on Monday.[26]

Disappointed and back in the Tower, Pepys settled down to wait for replies from France. His next court appearance was two days away. Since the charge was treason, the court would consider him guilty unless he could prove himself innocent. Treason was so devastating, yet so secretively plotted, that the court heavily favoured the prosecution. No smoke without fire, the thinking ran. Normally, the defendant was not allowed the details of the charges before the trial – Pepys was extremely lucky to know what he was charged with but he had no useful evidence. Even if he could find witnesses, he could not force them to attend and could not have them sworn on the Bible. There was a heavy presumption in a God-fearing time that that if a man was prepared to swear his evidence on the Bible, what he swore was true. Once his trial began, Pepys would have no access to a lawyer and it would all be over in a day.[27] The prosecution, on the other hand, simply had to produce a coherent accusation supported by two witnesses, who were sworn and were therefore considered to be telling the truth. Without a second witness to his charges, Scott could not prosecute; with one, his prosecution would be almost irrefutable. To his alarm, news reached Pepys in his cell that it was 'whispered' one Sir Robert Welch was to be the second witness.[28]

Pepys's friends tried to reassure him. Morelli, banished into the country by anti-Catholic legislation, wrote with the music of one whose first language was not English: 'Your innocence speaks for you, and the storm with which you have been menaced, will be dispersed to their confusion, who only seek your destruction.' He listed the names of twelve men in Lisbon and London who knew him not to be a priest. 'Had I been such,' he pointed out, 'I should have been obliged, on pain of excommunication, to clothe myself as a priest in Portugal, instead of living at Lisbon four years in the same dress I wear here.'[29]

On 2 June, the last day of the legal term, Pepys was hauled back into court and arraigned. His three accusers told their stories again and Pepys's team scribbled the details. There was no sign of the whispered second witness, Welch, but that meant nothing – he would be most effective as a surprise at trial. The Attorney General, Sir William Jones, was present, now fully recovered. Pepys deeply disliked Jones, calling him 'that insolent, mutinous lawyer'.[30] Jones was a Whig partisan. Like Scott, he was a protégé of the Duke of

Buckingham's, and as an MP was openly in favour of excluding the Duke of York from the succession.[31]

At the bar, Pepys saw Scott for the second time in his life – indeed, was forced to stand just a few feet from him as Scott swore his evidence about the encounter in Pellissary's garden again. The air between them must have crackled with indignation. James and Moone's statements were also read, and they too swore them to be true. The case was now in the court's hands. Pepys and Deane pushed for bail but the Attorney General declared that while he had two witnesses for the piracy and felony charges against Deane and so was ready to prosecute, he had only one witness for the treason charge against them both. Jones said it would not be too hard on the men to go without bail, since the start of the next law term was less than three weeks away. He would 'endeavour to get other evidence in order that it could be tried in the next term,' he said. Pepys and his lawyer both noted the exact words. Pepys's timetable was laid out; he had less than three weeks to prepare a full defence.

The clock was ticking and Pepys was acutely anxious. When he got back to his cell he sent off duplicates of the letters to Paris in case the first had not arrived. He added a note to Brisbane saying he now knew that Scott had given maps to another senior Frenchman, the Prince of Condé. Perhaps Brisbane would be able to prove that? If Brisbane could find one of the maps Scott had made and sold, he should send it immediately as it would be 'beyond all other evidences in my vindication'. He urged Brisbane to hurry because Attorney General Jones was trying to 'improve the villainous information against Sir Anthony Deane and me in this matter to the most dangerous degree'.[32]

What seemed crucial to Pepys was de Seignelay's denial of Scott's story. After three days, letters finally came back from 'Fat Harry' and the Scotsman Brisbane. They contained very bad news. 'Fat Harry' gave no concrete information, reporting only that Scott was 'of so despicable a vile reputation in all places where he has lived that a real criminal would be very unfortunate to suffer by his means'. Brisbane was darkly realistic and suggested that de Seignelay might not think it was in the interests of France to help him. 'The ruining such a one as I take you to be,' he wrote, 'would possibly appear to him to have some merit in it.' What was much worse, neither man had spoken to de Seignelay. In fact, de Seignelay was not within 'any possible distance' of them finding him, for he had 'gone to visit his sea-ports'. Pepys now had fifteen days before his next court appearance and de Seignelay was not expected back in Paris 'at least this fortnight'.[33]

9

Jobs for the Scotsman

John Brisbane was hard up. As Pepys entered his second day in the Tower, the Scotsman, marooned in the extravagance of Parisian diplomatic circles, declared he was in 'the greatest distress' that he had ever experienced. He had been very poor in his life but never as poor as this, and he had fallen into debt for the first time. 'At least,' he wrote to Henry Thynne in Secretary of State Henry Coventry's office, 'I never owed as I do now more than I am master of to pay.' He asked Thynne to help him procure 'Mr Secretary's protection', so that he might be relieved.[1] A very promising letter from Coventry arrived with remarkable speed. It had been sent for entirely different reasons and the two letters crossed in the post. It told Brisbane to make ready for a summons to 'an employment at home' that was, wrote Coventry, 'not yet so certain as I can aver it but I pray be upon the wing. You may be suddenly called for if all things go right.' He did not say what the new job was, though Brisbane thought he could guess. 'We are not yet got out of the clouds,' Coventry added without being explicit about the complication. 'I hope by God's blessing we may but at present it is very dark.'[2]

When the sympathetic John Evelyn came to dine with Pepys in the Tower on 4 June, Pepys was still hoping for a useful testimony from de Seignelay, the French navy minister.[3] The next day, with the arrival of Brisbane and Henry Savile's letters from Paris, he was forced to consider that more closely. The letters told him that not only was de Seignelay away from Paris and out of contact, he had recently fallen into 'excessive devotions (accompanied with vapours)', hysterical displays of Catholic dedication which had become fashionable in the French court.[4] Brisbane was pessimistic about Pepys's chances of getting a useful testimony from de Seignelay because, he thought, the zealous marquis was likely to take huge pleasure in ruining a Protestant – as Brisbane said he took Pepys to be. This was not at all the type of behaviour Pepys had been led to expect from de Seignelay, who he had heard was honourable.

The second weakness was one that Brisbane had warned Pepys to consider carefully. He had identified the central flaw in Pepys's strategy. By Scott's account, de Seignelay and Pepys were partners in crime. If de Seignelay claimed Pepys had never given him the papers, the prosecution would argue that he was covering for Pepys. So even if he agreed to give evidence, it would not benefit Pepys's defence. Furthermore, the help of a French Catholic might well confirm rather than diminish the prejudice against him. However, Brisbane wrote deferentially, 'If you persist in the thought of having him spoke to', he and Savile would 'do it with great zeal and sincerity'. Pepys wrote back immediately, thanking them for their letters in flowery terms. In the absence of choice, he would take the risk; they should still try to speak to de Seignelay.[5] Then he considered what to do next.

Unlike his wayward clerk Sam Atkins, saved by a hard night's wenching on a royal yacht, Pepys had no alibis. Scott had not pinned his crime to any one place or time that Pepys might contradict. By Scott's story, Pepys had put the treasonous letter and papers into Deane's hands at some unspecified point before Deane sailed to France on 9 August 1675. Scott's account of hearing Deane's conversation through the open window in Pellissary's house that summer's day, and of being furtively hidden away by Pellissary to dine alone in a back room might be impossible to disprove. Pellissary was dead. So was Piogerie. Now the only living Frenchman Scott had said received the papers, de Seignelay, might do more harm than good to

Pepys's case if he came forward to deny the claim. Scott's charges had been perfectly engineered. His story would become irrefutable if a second witness came to his support. That left only one possible flaw in Pepys's enemies' plan: Scott himself. Within six days of Pepys's arrest, he had discovered that Scott's 'virtues' (as he sarcastically called them) were 'so well-known' that there was little fear that Scott's credit would be greater than his.[6] If he could not prove his innocence he would attack his prosecutor. It was imperfect, but it was all he had. He went after Scott.

By 9 June, when hot winds warmed the cold Tower stone, Pepys had new information that suggested Scott had travelled widely, spending time in the West Indies and the Netherlands, where he had apparently been notorious.[7] Pepys had a tip-off that details of his crimes might be available in the Dutch official records. Scott had been a military man, a major before he attained his current rank of colonel but, Pepys heard, he had stolen Dutch government money and deserted the services. Pepys had been given the names of two men who might know something. The names probably came out of brave Henry Coventry's office. The Secretary had defied the Commons when Parliament was sitting and he continued to do so now the House was prorogued. The Whigs would destroy Coventry at the next Parliament if he was found helping Pepys, so the information he passed on left only the faintest paper trail. It shows up in a letter Pepys wrote that day, remarking that a Mr Puckle might be useful to his investigations but had unfortunately left London for Flanders a few days before.[8] James Puckle was one of the government's agents there and he reported to the Secretary of State's office. His movements were Coventry's business. Puckle had run into Scott before, taking many 'false' papers from him and sending them to Coventry at Whitehall.[9] Coventry knew he could be useful to Pepys.

Pepys had no direct way of contacting Puckle. He needed someone he could trust in Europe with resources and time on their hands. In a bizarre reversal of circumstances it became clear that the man who could help him was the man whose patronage had landed him in trouble in the first place; he needed the exiled Duke of York, currently in Brussels. The Duke was already hated by the Whigs – he could not do himself any further damage by helping Pepys.

To avoid burdening the royal brother with excessive information, Pepys put the details in a letter to his secretary, a discreet and able man called Sir John Werden, who bore but privately detested the bitter exile on the Continent. In early May, he and Pepys had confided in one another on the shortcomings of being close to the hated Duke. From the Tower, Pepys now wrote to Werden – referring to his past letter from the letter-book in front of him – that 'the place I am now in is yet worse than either of the two you and I last complained of'. He listed Scott's charges, asked Werden to follow the tip-off on Puckle and to pass it all on to the Duke.[10] In a letter to the Duke the same day, Pepys was entirely frank. His service to the Duke had precipitated the charges, despite his adversaries' pretence that his crime was 'Popery and other like chimeras'. But his loyalty to the Duke and his belief in eventual vindication were unshaken. He did not know,

which of the two enjoys the greater pleasure; whether Mr Harbord in public, from the contemplation of the conquest his malice has obtained over me, or I in private, from what my innocence tells me I shall some time or other (if any justice may be hoped for) obtain against him.

He referred the Duke to Werden for the details, 'wherein your present aid and direction may be of instant benefit to me under my present misfortune'.[11] It was all clear-sightedness and deference, the calm tone of the dependable servant, but Pepys's last thought to Werden showed his anxiety; any help that came would need to come fast, for by the time the letters reached Brussels, the court term would be less than ten days away. He suggested as politely as he could that they should find Puckle quickly.

Pepys sent one more letter in pursuit of Scott's reputation that day. This went to an 'honoured friend' of his, a man who had sat in parliaments with him since 1673 and with whom he had exchanged many letters of gentle banter about such matters as his 'many holidays'.[12] This friend was an MP, an acute parliamentary observer who could smell political trouble coming. His name was Sir Robert Southwell. He had bleakly predicted before the charges that Mr Pepys 'however prepared' would be destroyed, but he nonetheless now felt compelled by long affection to do what he could. He had learnt some scraps of information about Scott and, without hesitating to wait for Pepys's permission, had passed them on to a contact in Rotterdam. Good men draw other good men to them, and his contact was to prove a diligent and energetic investigator. Pepys seized on Southwell's efforts, passing him what he knew about Scott in the Netherlands and begging him to 'make use of this night's post' to encourage the contact to 'let no time be lost in his enquiries'.[13] Southwell was clerk to the King's Privy Council and it is possible that behind his helping hand lay the private support of King Charles.

The next day Pepys was attended in the morning and again after lunch by, as he put it, 'a man I love mightily'.[14] The phrase comes from his Diary thirteen years before, but time had done nothing to diminish his affection for the visitor. This was James Houblon, one of the five industrious merchant sons of a great merchant father. Pepys had been enamoured with the brothers, and he had them all to supper one winter's night in 1666. They had stayed until eleven o'clock – a 'great pleasure,' Pepys noted, 'and a fine sight it is to see these five brothers thus loving one to another.'[15] But James Houblon was the dearest to him, and at an early stage of their relationship Pepys had resolved never to lose contact with him. Houblon's visit on 10 June was the only time he could get to Pepys in the Tower but Pepys was thankful for this 'visit to the lions', and not merely for the pleasure of his company. Houblon's commercial activities meant he had a wide network of trusted and well-informed business associates in continental Europe and he agreed to put some of them at Pepys's disposal. Pepys promptly wrote out a list of questions for Houblon to investigate about Scott's activities on the Continent.[16] After Houblon had left, Pepys – his brain racing with the pursuit – sent a note with further thoughts and questions. Houblon forwarded all these to his contacts abroad.

It was too early to expect news about de Seignelay from the cash-strapped Brisbane at the Paris embassy. The London–Paris post took three to four days if the winds allowed the packet boat to sail on time, so Pepys's last letter would only have arrived there on the 8th or 9th. Nevertheless, unknown to Pepys, another letter from Brisbane was on its way to him.

From the beginning, Brisbane's letters did not come straight to Pepys. Despite their friendship, Brisbane was loath to begin a direct correspondence with an accused traitor. So he put his letters to Pepys in with those he was sending to Secretary Henry Coventry, for him to 'peruse', a precaution that Brisbane thought 'not unfit while he [Pepys] lies under a public accusation'.[17] The system spread the load of guilt on Coventry's broad shoulders. Coventry in turn passed them on to Pepys in the Tower.

Brisbane's boss at the embassy, 'Fat Harry' Savile, was close to Coventry by the tie of family. Even at this time of illness and political stress, affection shows in their correspondence. 'I wish you more health than your uncle and more content than most of your friends have here,' Coventry signed off one of his letters.[18] Now, with the promises of a new employment, the benevolent family arm was being put around Brisbane too, but it was hard to know how to refer to the unnamed job and Brisbane (though he wanted the job badly) had to put his words delicately. His tone with Coventry was all allusion and flirtation.[19] Coventry, in return, made it clear he wanted Brisbane to help Pepys. 'I would be glad you could do him any service,' he wrote on 4 June, 'for on my conscience his accuser has done him a great wrong.'[20]

Brisbane leapt to his new patron's suggestion. He immediately wrote a fresh letter to Pepys. Again he sent it to Coventry to look over before forwarding it to the Tower. Brisbane said that he thought this necessary because of Pepys's 'calamity'.[21] However, it suited him that Coventry would read it and see how willing a servant he was.

While the ink of his signature was still wet he flung golden sand on the page – a French speciality that stuck and sparkled in the light like flecks of gold leaf.[22] It impressed English recipients.[23]

The letter was an attempt to help Pepys. Brisbane reiterated his near-total ignorance of Scott, who was so much a 'stranger' that he did not even know 'any one man that has ever conversed with him'. He had a dim memory that Scott had tried to sell maps of English ports to the French, but he could not remember who had told him that. He used the most curious language however, becoming oddly specific when he described Scott's maps. He pretended that the descriptions were imagined, drawn from the little he knew of Scott as a man. 'According to my character of the personage,' he said, he thought the maps would be 'finely painted upon vellum . . . but in effect either not true taken, by hazard without art, or the necessary observations and expense; or barely copied from our own, and the Dutch prints, which are to be bought very cheap.' They would be 'maps of large scale, variety of colours, and with the ornaments of designing'. Brisbane, for all his ignorance of Scott, clearly knew more about Scott's maps than he pretended.

To date, Brisbane was Pepys's only agent actively searching for evidence that would build a material defence, and this deeply ambiguous response rather stumped Pepys. In fact, Brisbane knew about Scott's maps because of what had happened immediately after Scott's calm reappearance in England. At that point, a little over a month ago now, Brisbane had received the note from the exhausted Coventry mistakenly sent to him instead of Savile. It had read, 'Colonel Scott is taken.'[24] Because Coventry seemed desperate to prosecute Scott and asked for 'whatsoever evidence you can send against him', they had made all the enquiries they could. Though Brisbane did not see Scott's maps, he heard about them from the many that had. Their investigations took a week, and then Savile sent Coventry the ciphered note that Scott had 'for certain' given maps of England to French officials. So it was that Brisbane could paint such a picture of Scott's work for Pepys.

Brisbane wrote to Pepys in such strange conjectural terms because he was protecting himself. Although Henry Coventry appeared to be becoming a powerful patron, Brisbane did not like to be reliant on his fellow man. He had already been too close for comfort to the destruction of the King's first minister, the Earl of Danby, for it had been his former boss, the ambassador to France Ralph Montagu, who brought Danby down. At that time, Brisbane had guessed what was about to happen and gone behind his boss's back to warn Danby.[25] But Danby had been felled with an efficiency that amazed Brisbane. The news of his impeachment had reached Paris two days before Brisbane or anyone he knew 'had any letter about it' and he concluded that 'it was either sent hither quickly, or foreseen'. It gave him a sense of the ruthless power of the Whigs in the Commons and made him acutely aware that he had endangered himself by having tried to help the disgraced minister. Brisbane had heard the warnings on the street that 'it was the right work of a Parliament to hang great officers of State', and knew that Henry Coventry, who had made enemies of the Whigs again and again, might end up on the gallows.[26] However attractive it was to climb in under Coventry's wing, he would be a fool to trust the bold, hated Secretary of State's power to protect him for ever. He also knew that John Scott had powerful friends.[27] So, while he bowed to his new patron's requests to help Pepys against Scott, he chose words that would not incriminate Scott too directly, in case he himself should be left exposed. In addition, he knew his mysterious job might mean he would soon be working for a commission made up of those very Whigs.

By 12 June it was being whispered at Whitehall that Brisbane was to be summoned back to London for some other employment.[28] The news was controversial; Whigs and Tories were now at war over the position in question but the King, though conceding temporary ministerial posts to the Whigs, was anxious to keep his bureaucracy in the hands of loyal Tories.

On that day, Pepys hit upon a different strategy. He realised that if he could simply prove that Scott had not been in Paris in August

1675, he could destroy the prosecution. The rumours of Scott's criminality reaching him in his cell had refocused him; if Scott was capable of even half of what was said of him, he was certainly capable of lying about his presence in Paris. With the court term only eight days away, Pepys wrote to Brisbane again (though he had not yet received a response to his last letter) asking for more details. For the first time, his customary authority was replaced by humility. He offered his 'thorough submission' to Brisbane's advice but added, apologetically, 'I cannot but resort to you once more in a particular or two wherein a little information (if it might be had) might be of no small benefit to us', namely whether Scott had indeed been in Paris. It was 'not impossible' that Scott's landlord at that time could tell. It might not 'be very hard to recover' the landlord's name from the English in Paris.[29] Pepys had no idea who Scott's landlord was. This was not 'a little information'; Pepys needed a city-wide investigation. He promised to bear the costs of an investigator if Brisbane could find one for him.

Brisbane, though, was preoccupied with other matters. Coventry had not named the employment that he intended for Brisbane but the London rumours had reached Paris. Coventry's enigmatic phrase – 'we are not yet got out of the clouds' – had referred (though Brisbane did not know it) to his attempts to stop the job going to that 'bustling fellow about the town' who had harried Pepys and showed Scott the way to the bar of the Commons, William Harbord.[30] On the verge of success, Coventry sent Brisbane the official summons to return on 16 June.[31] Savile, on hearing the news, wrote a shining endorsement of his number two:

I find his Majesty has been pleased to recall Brisbane. I hope it is with some prospect of providing otherwise for him . . . for he has no fortune but knowledge and merit, in which he will be found to have a great estate wherever that coin is current.[32]

It looked very likely that Brisbane would indeed be provided for. The King, Coventry indicated, 'has something in his breast for you', for Coventry had been careful to tell him about Brisbane's financial condition. Brisbane was now confident that his first suspicion was correct. From the rumours, 'and from Mr Pepys's condition, it has not been hard,' he wrote to Coventry, 'for me to guess that you mean his employment.'[33] He was earmarked for Pepys's old job. It was a clear conflict of interest. If Brisbane succeeded in his task of helping Pepys, Pepys would be reinstated and Brisbane deprived of the prize: the prestigious position of Secretary to the Admiralty.

If Brisbane took the job and left Paris, Pepys would not have a committed agent there. Without an agent, he would be unable to assemble a material defence. It was about to be made brutally clear what the result of that would be.

10

The Light and Darkness

Richard Langhorn was a fifty-five-year-old barrister. He had a nice house on a lane which ran north out of Holborn into the fields of Middlesex, an office in the Inner Temple, a wife, and children whose misadventures on the Continent he occasionally had to fund. He was generous and sufficiently wealthy to ask for friends' fees to be paid in 'love and affection'.[1] As a Catholic and as the solicitor for the Jesuits, he was vulnerable. After seeing the stones of St Paul's cathedral split by the Great Fire, he had been accused before a parliamentary committee of starting it, on the strength of a casual overheard comment he had made about London's destruction.[2] In reality, Langhorn was no traitor and hoped that the Crown (although it would lose out 'infinitely' on taxes) would ultimately be strengthened by the disaster. Sounding more puritan than Catholic, he had asked at the time, 'Who can say that in this God has not been just? This City was too rich, too proud, too wanton.'[3] Such quasi-Protestant beliefs and his loyalty to the Crown were not enough to save him.

Langhorn first learnt of a Catholic plot to kill the King on 29 September 1678, when he heard that priests had been arrested on the information of Titus Oates.[4] The name rang a bell. As an errant Jesuit trainee, Oates had once brought Langhorn a letter from his youngest son (a fellow trainee) in Spain. That had been their only meeting. Over the next week, Langhorn paid as much attention to developments as anybody. He was finishing work late the following

Monday, and rain was beating down, when a sodden messenger from
the king's council arrived at the door of his chambers in the Temple
with a warrant made out for the arrest of John Langhorn. Langhorn
pointed out his name was Richard, but the messenger thought that a
minor detail. To correct the error, Langhorn went with him to
Newgate prison where he told the chief gaoler that he could not
justifiably be detained on a warrant in the wrong name. The gaoler
was indifferent. He threw Langhorn into close confinement, to be
kept to his cell.

Langhorn sat quietly in his cell for nearly two and a half months.
His assumption that the wrong would be undone gradually turned to
anxiety. On 10 December, he petitioned the King, protesting his innocence and asking for details of the charges against him. He wanted
to speak freely with his friends and send 'for such witnesses as I
should have occasion to use for my defence'. He put the petition into
the hands of the gaoler, there being no other hands to put it into.[5]

He never got an answer. Six days later, he was taken from his cell
to the chief gaoler's house where he found the Earl of Shaftesbury
and two other lords. They told him he was charged with high treason
and the evidence would take away his life. They believed him guilty,
but they had heard of his good character. Claiming to be moved by
'charity and compassion', they advised him to save his life by making
a full confession of the Plot. Langhorn was amazed; his conscience
was clear. Shaftesbury, feigning concern, said he thought Langhorn's
close imprisonment was illegal. Langhorn should be free to move
around the gaol, and his friends allowed to visit him.

Nothing changed. Three more months passed, then the other two
lords reappeared in Newgate. Shaftesbury had sent them to offer a
full pardon. They had the paper in their hands but Langhorn's
conscience prevented him from accepting a pardon for a crime he had
not committed and he rejected their offer. Like Pepys's clerk before
him, he would not be bullied into turning King's evidence and
incriminating others. His wife was the only visitor he was allowed,
and only then with the gaoler in the room. He told her he did not

know what he was being charged with and was afraid he would be surprised at trial, so she brought him a shortened narrative of the Plot trials since his arrest. The gaoler seized it and barred her from further visits. A friend was then given licence to visit. He told Langhorn of a changed outside world. Evidence had been brought against him by witnesses who had already been believed by other juries. The fact was of sufficient force to have driven Langhorn mad 'had not God been merciful'. The witnesses' testimonies, said his friend, had created 'such a strange abhorrence' of Langhorn's religion that anything said against him would be believed by any jury.

Just before Whitsunday, restrictions on his friends' visits were lifted and they came to him. They brought what information they could, mostly narratives of Plot trials printed with the permission of Lord Chief Justice Scroggs at the sign of the Bible on Chancery Lane. As he read them, his lawyer's mind detected the inconsistencies. The witnesses against him – Titus Oates and William Bedloe – seemed unable to keep to their own stories. They had constructed an account that would not bear its own weight. Too many people had been implicated. The 'Plot' was riddled with holes. Here was something. Langhorn could not defend himself against specific charges that were still unknown, but he could discredit the prosecution witnesses' evidence and force the court to set them aside. He began assembling the contradictions. Oates had 'affirmed several things which could not subsist to be all true'. Bedloe had sworn himself flatly perjured, claiming at one trial that the defendant was a stranger to him, and at a later trial the opposite. Even the court had admitted they were 'ill witnesses' and Bedloe readily admitted the worst things that could be said of him, but having the King's pardon thought himself safe. Both were guilty of the same treason they accused others of, having been complicit in the Plot.

Langhorn had one big advantage over previous defendants. Oates and Bedloe had not faced a lawyer at trial because treason defendants were not allowed one. This time, because Langhorn was himself a lawyer, they had no choice. He therefore met his trial with optimism when it came on 14 June, a windy and wet Saturday in Whitsun week. He had managed to summon some witnesses. He knew the law and thought his information would be enough to destroy the prosecution's credibility. In tempered times it might have been.

On the way from Newgate to the Old Bailey he learnt just how England had changed in the nine months of his imprisonment as he ran the gauntlet of a hostile and vociferous crowd who had taken to pelting Plot victims with whatever came to hand. At the Old Bailey, he finally understood the scale of the barrage of charges against him. He had planned to stir up sedition, depose Charles II, slaughter his subjects, subvert the country's government, alter the Protestant religion and levy civil war. The prosecution made Langhorn the administrative hub of the Plot. He pleaded not guilty.[6]

The court quickly realised that Langhorn's strategy was to attack Oates and Bedloe's inconsistencies. 'Does your defence consist wholly of this sort of matter,' Scroggs asked him disparagingly, 'objecting the incompetence of the witnesses?' Could Langhorn make no answer to the fact? It is hard not to feel for him. He replied that he had no choice but to 'disable the witnesses', for his imprisonment and ignorance of the charges had prevented him from preparing any other defence. He would try to lessen their credit with the court. Scroggs softened a little.

'Do lessen it, if you can,' he said. 'If you have any witnesses to take off their credit, or contradict them, call them.' The Lord Chief Justice's heart did not warm often, and the court's sympathy was not easily won. They were unwilling to admit to inconsistencies in evidence that had already sent men to the gallows.

Again and again, the court denied Langhorn the opportunity to trip Oates and Bedloe up. Oates's story involved a seditious Jesuit consult, or meeting, on 24 April 1678, at which it was resolved to kill King Charles. After the consult, Oates told the court, he had been commanded to report to Langhorn that assassins had been chosen. Hearing this, Oates said, Langhorn had lifted 'up his hands and his eyes, and prayed to God to give it good success'.

'When was this?' Langhorn interjected. Oates replied vaguely that it was a day or two after they signed the consult document, at the end of April or beginning of May. Langhorn jumped in.

'Dr Oates,' he said, 'do you know the day of the month? You have asserted the day of the month formerly, please do it now.' Justice Pemberton intervened to save Oates from embarrassment and barred that line of questioning.

Oates spun stories about seeing commissions from Rome on Langhorn's desk which promoted the five Catholic lords (now, like Pepys, imprisoned in the Tower) to ministerial roles after Charles's assassination. Langhorn listened silently as Oates painted a picture of in-fighting between him and the Queen's physician. The physician, Oates said, had demanded £10,000 to poison the King, which Langhorn thought was excessive since 'it was in the public good'. Then the lawyer saw another opening and tried to catch Oates out on his movements. Oates claimed to have first visited Langhorn in November 1677. When, asked Langhorn, had he departed back to his Jesuit college in France? At the end of that month, Oates replied. When did he arrive there?

'I think it was 10 December,' said Oates, 'I will not be positive.'

Scroggs leapt to Oates's aid, saying of the plotters in general, 'All their defence lies in catches upon a point of time, in which no man living is able to be positive.' Oates was allowed to be vague; Langhorn's precision was made to seem a Catholic trick.

Denied the opportunity to expose the prosecution's inconsistencies, Langhorn questioned whether they were believable witnesses. They had been complicit in the Plot, pardoned and were being rewarded for their testimonies. At the mention of reward, Oates protested that, quite to the contrary, he was £700 out of pocket.

'Mr Langhorn does suppose that the witnesses are corrupted and bribed,' said Pemberton, choosing to ignore the legal point in favour of a good blast of outrage. 'Do you think, Mr Langhorn, that the King will bribe his witnesses?'

Langhorn pointed out it had only been a question and Scroggs stuffily told him to answer that question himself. Justice North turned up the heat; if Langhorn was saying that Oates and Bedloe had been bribed to commit perjury, he had to prove it. Langhorn would not relent. He had been told in prison that Bedloe had received £500, but the court had grown tired of the argument and told him it would get him nowhere.

Tenacity and desperation forced Langhorn on. He pressed the point. There had been a proclamation which invited people to make discoveries about the Plot for reward. It was fair, Langhorn argued, for a reward to be offered for the capture of a defendant who fled, but it was an entirely different matter to encourage witnesses that way. That was an invitation to commit perjury. Until now he had avoided seeming to doubt the Plot's existence, but this exploration of the true motives of the prosecution witnesses was tantamount to denying the Plot. Nonetheless, he pushed further. Oates claimed he was £700 out of pocket because of his work on the Plot; Langhorn said he could prove that Oates had been penniless before the Plot was heard of.

'What is that to the present purpose?' asked Scroggs. 'It goes to no part of the evidence.'

Langhorn's answer hit the nail smack on the head and drove it into the heart of the Plot. If Oates had indeed been poor, it was impossible that he should have £700 to spend 'without a purse being made for him'. If he had been given such a sum, the only possible reason would be 'to give this evidence'. Oates was being employed to lie. Scroggs's response was unmoving, cold, hopeless.

'If you have any more witnesses,' he said, 'call them and make an end of them; if not, then you may observe what you will to the court and jury, after the King's counsel has done.'

Richard Langhorn made two crucial mistakes. He had no chance to prepare irrefutable evidence. Instead he had to rely on his wits and it is a tribute to these that, despite the court's hostility, he came close to destroying Oates's credibility. Early on, he skewered Oates with a question about his companions at the Jesuit consult in April. Oates had said there were nine or ten of them. Scroggs told him to name them.

Oates named Father Williams, Father March, Sir John Warner and 'the rector of Liège'.

'What was the rector of Liège's name?' demanded Langhorn.

'Warren, I think,' replied Oates, 'I cannot tell names so exactly.'

'Go on, sir, pray.'

But Oates confessed he could not name any more. Langhorn leapt on the admission, pointing out that he had named them before, as was shown in the records of the House of Lords. Langhorn listed other names from that record and Oates agreed they had been there. Langhorn pointed out that if he could remember them, Oates should certainly be able to, but someone had briefed Oates on the workings of the law and he taunted Langhorn with it.

'If you can show a record of what I said there, do,' he said.

Scroggs supported him. If Langhorn could produce, 'as you may if you have been diligent', a copy of the record in the House of Lords, verified as an accurate copy, it would be acceptable evidence. 'But,' said Scroggs, 'to put Oates to remember a record without book, must not be, it would be hard for him to undertake that.'

Without the evidence, Langhorn had to move on, leaving Oates's error unproven. Again the opportunity to discredit the Plot's main witness had been taken from him.

Langhorn's lack of opportunity for preparation caused him recurrent problems. He was fluent in Oates's claims, as a result of the long hours spent studying them in Newgate, but he had no evidence about them. He sought to prove – with a witness – that Oates had not travelled to the April consult with Sir Robert Brett. Oates had sworn he had done so and that statement was on record in the House of Lords' Register.[7] Scroggs told Langhorn to produce the paper for the court. He did not have it. He instead asked permission to examine Oates about it now and compare his answers with the Lords' Register later. Scroggs was implacable; if Langhorn wished to refute Oates's claim, he first had to produce that paper in court. Scroggs knew perfectly well that the Lords' Register proved Langhorn's claim. He could have a low opinion of the official record when it suited him and he growled that, in any case, the evidence Langhorn wanted was 'but a memorial taken by a clerk', prompting Langhorn to cry, 'It is the journal of the Lords' House my lord!'

Having inadequate evidence at his disposal was Langhorn's first mistake. His second was greater. He had prepared his witnesses. It is extraordinary that a man thought to have achieved 'great eminency' in law could have done this, or have allowed it to be done (assuming that Langhorn's friends deferred to his legal experience before taking such a step). Moreover, it is extraordinary that it was done so badly. This colossal misjudgement tells us, more than anything he left in writing, about the agony of the long months inside Newgate.

Sir John Warner's gardener was the first to display signs of the problem. He was there to disprove Oates's claim that Sir John had been among his companions on the journey to the Jesuit consult in April. The gardener testified that Sir John had not stirred from his home in Watton all April and May. Justice Pemberton asked him whether Sir John was also there in June and the gardener replied, disastrously, 'My lord, I cannot tell that, I only speak to April and May.' The court sat up to that. Why could he not remember June? It was more recent, after all.

'I took not so much notice of him in those times,' the gardener answered.

Scroggs asked him why. The gardener broke.

'Because the question, my lord, that I came for, did not fall upon that time.'

Scroggs's delight at pinning down the squirming gardener was evident in the way he spelt out the situation to the jury. The witness could only answer with relation to the months he had been prepared for. He turned to Langhorn. 'This, I am afraid, will go through all your St Omers men.'

He was right. The next witness claimed Mr Poole, his music master at St Omers and another of Oates's alleged travelling companions on 24 April, did not in fact travel to England until 'June, or May'.

'Or April?' mocked Scroggs.

'No, it was the month of June.'

Asked whether he mistook the month he replied, 'Yes, yes.' The listening courtroom laughed. 'No, no,' he corrected.

The rot had set in. Another witness claimed Oates had not left St Omers until the latter end of June.

'Yesterday you said the latter end of July,' replied the unrelenting North. 'Call another witness.'

A grim humour crept into the proceedings. 'He speaks much more to the purpose today, Mr Langhorn, than he did yesterday,' remarked Jeffreys of a further witness.

'And much louder,' agreed North.

Mrs Grove, with whom Oates claimed he had lodged when he came over, asserted that she could name all her lodgers for April and May and that Oates was not among them. She remembered exactly who was in the room he claimed to have stayed in at that time, and was quite sure it was not him. Who lodged with her in June? She looked blank and admitted she could not answer since she 'was not to be examined further than the two months' of April and May.

The disaster was completed when Langhorn summoned another landlady, the owner of the White Horse tavern, where Oates claimed the April consult had taken place. Oates began to speak.

'Is this Mr Oates my lord?' she interrupted. 'I never saw him before in my life.' It was unlikely that she could have forgotten him. Oates had a face that made passers-by turn to stare.

Scroggs met this with incredulity. 'Was there nobody never in your tavern, but who you knew? What! Can you tell all the people that were ever in your tavern?'

Langhorn had Oates reaffirm that there were fifty or so at the consult. The woman was then asked about the size of her house. When she asserted that it was 'a small inconsiderable house' with no room that would hold more than a dozen, she was immediately contradicted by several bystanders who all asserted that it had rooms that could hold twenty, thirty or even fifty people, and had done so.

Langhorn hoped neither the jury nor the court would reflect upon him for this. Scroggs retorted that it reflected badly on all his evidence. Langhorn, utterly dejected, replied, 'I have been a prisoner for so long, and I know nothing but what friends and relations inform me.'

Having lost the support of the court, Langhorn's case was slipping away from him and he began to flail around. Again he asked to use the Lords' journal and again he was denied. He tried to have other witnesses brought in, but by law the court could not summon witnesses for a treason defendant. He asked to use evidence from earlier trials, in which Oates and Bedloe had referred to him; again the court refused him.

'Then you take off the defence that I have, and make it as if I had never any,' cried the lawyer.

As if on dramatic cue, a man approached the court. His entrance must have created something of a flurry in the crowded room since Scroggs asked of him, 'What do you come for sir? What is your name?'

'My name is Castlemaine,' replied the man.

He was the Earl of Castlemaine, a brave man who was both a loyalist and an eloquent defender of Catholic rights. In October, Oates had denounced him as a Jesuit and now Castlemaine, who had also seen the holes in the Plot, was compiling a condensed account of the Plot trials in an attempt to awaken England to the miscarriages of justice Oates was presiding over.[8]

Castlemaine had come to inform the court that some of the waiting defence witnesses were 'so beaten and abused without, that they dare not come to give their evidence, for fear of being killed'. One, he added, was so injured that 'we cannot tell but it may cost him his life'.

The court declared its horror and promised punishment if the perpetrators were found. A more compassionate court might have considered Langhorn's shaken witnesses in a new light at this information, but the court failed to connect what was going on outside to what was going on inside. Langhorn felt no benefit from Castlemaine's bold intervention and very shortly the Earl had a new case to write up.

The prosecution made their case swiftly and Scroggs's summing-up was merciless. The jury were equally swift at returning a guilty verdict. The Recorder, George Jeffreys, said the verdict agreed with the prosecution's evidence and a great shout of agreement went up in the hall. Others convicted of involvement in the Plot the day before were brought in to receive sentence. Jeffreys said that among the men at the bar he was very sorry to see one that 'has understanding of law, and who has arrived at so great an eminency in that profession,' but Langhorn had forgotten 'that it is not only against the rules of all Christianity, but even against the rules of his profession, to attempt any injury to the king'.

Then he read the awful sentence:

That you be conveyed from hence to the place from whence you came, and from thence you be drawn to the place of execution, upon hurdles; That you be there severally hanged by the neck; that you be cut down alive; that your privy members be cut off; that your bowels be taken out and burnt in your view; that your heads be severed from your bodies; that your bodies be divided into four quarters, and your quarters be at the king's dispose. And the God of infinite mercy be merciful to your souls.

The court filled with the sound of the crowd's acclamation.

That was not quite all. Langhorn's execution was delayed, giving time in which his Protestant wife pressed him to confess anything he could. The thin-lipped president of the Privy Council, the Earl of Shaftesbury, came on his sticks to the lawyer's cell and persuaded him to reveal all he knew about where his clients, the English Jesuits, kept their wealth.[9]

There was nothing heroic about Langhorn's subsequent revelations. Telling himself it was his duty to the King, he listed all he could remember of the Jesuits' secret funds and earned a further reprieve while someone looked over the papers in his chambers to expand his statement. The results of his diligence stood to make an impressive contribution to the Crown's wealth, as he revealed riches totalling between £20,000 and £30,000.[10] It was a great breach of faith but he and his friends believed this would lead to a full pardon and he attached a petition, in which he declared his innocence.

His hope was cruelly dashed. It was made clear that giving up impersonal finances was all very well, but only naming names of further plotters was likely to save him. Part way through the reading of a final desperate petition to the Privy Council on 10 July, the reader was ordered to stop.[11] Shaftesbury's Council was no place for a Catholic to find sympathy.

By 14 July Langhorn's affairs were complete and his speech for the scaffold was prepared. In thirteen numbered points he condemned acts of treason, declared his loyalty to the King and that he died a member 'though an unworthy one' of the Catholic Church.[12] Like all the men executed for complicity in the Popish Plot, he confessed no guilt. He had none to confess. He had wondered in his prison cell whether there could ever be unity between the Catholic and Protestant religions, but had been told by the Newgate prison chaplain that there was no hope of fellowship between 'the light and darkness'. Langhorn had politely declined the chaplain's offer of a second visit.[13]

When he came to be put on a hurdle, a piece of fencing used as a sledge to be dragged through the streets, the sheriff took his speech from him, for he was to be allowed no papers on the scaffold. Langhorn was forced to give it from memory as best he could above the great noise of the people. 'I believe it is impossible to be heard,' he said. Before a crowd that could see nothing between 'light and darkness' he forgave Oates, Bedloe and the nation and asked that the blame for his death not be put on any individual. After a prayer he asked the executioner whether the rope was right.

'Yes,' said the executioner, 'do you forgive me?'

'I freely do,' was the response. He crossed himself, privately recommended his soul to God, and asked for it to be taken 'this instant into paradise'. To the executioner he said, 'I am ready, and you need stay no longer for me.'[14]

The details of Richard Langhorn's legal ordeal were circulated about town by Plot-watchers, and must have reached Pepys in the Tower. Langhorn's long isolation in Newgate trapped him into mistakes that Pepys now had to avoid. His first advantage over Langhorn was that, while he did not have them in writing, he had at least heard the charges. His second advantage was that his Commons allies had ensured that his imprisonment should not prevent him constructing his defence, and got him access to his papers and his friends. Langhorn's case showed that any copies made of paper evidence had to be witnessed as accurate. Paper evidence had to be to hand in the courtroom. So did witnesses, and it could be fatal to coach them. But above all, it showed that it was a most dangerous policy to attack the character of the prosecution witnesses. With the Marquis de Seignelay out of reach, this was what Pepys had decided to do just five days before Langhorn was tried.

11

Catastrophes

All that separated Samuel Pepys from a defeat like Richard Langhorn's was the evidence in France. His investigator there, John Brisbane, had been summoned home. Things were going catastrophically wrong.

It seems likely that Pepys learnt of Brisbane's new job from Secretary of State Henry Coventry; his office prepared a regular news sheet, and Brisbane's employment was due to be announced on 19 June. It was a courteous gesture on Coventry's part to tell Pepys before telling the public. Pepys must have been surprised, but rather than let anxiety overcome him, he set to work and found himself a replacement agent to go to Paris.

He sent Balthasar St Michel, the brother of his dead wife Elizabeth. Pepys called him Balty. Early on, the poverty-stricken Balty had proved an unwelcome addition to the family by quietly trying to borrow Pepys's money from Elizabeth. He had pestered Pepys for naval employment through the early 1660s, but Pepys resisted, 'for fear I shall not be able to wipe my hands of him again when I once concern myself for him.'[1] Balty harassed Elizabeth; she tearfully petitioned Pepys, and in 1665 Pepys buckled and found Balty work in the Guards, then at sea. Surprisingly, Balty did rather well and Pepys confided in his Diary that he had become 'a good serious man'.[2] Several well-paid naval employments followed, and in 1668 Pepys confidently presented him to the Duke of York. He had rescued Balty from professional disaster. When Pepys was charged, Balty was the navy's mustermaster at Deal, allocating crews to the ships and managing the books. He had been due to be posted to Tangier, but the King, at Pepys's request, held the position open while Balty repaid fourteen years of favours by coming to Pepys's aid.

In some ways he was perfect for the Paris job. He needed to be there anyway, to collect a defence against the charge that he had had a part in Anthony Deane's piracy. He had been raised in France, he was loyal, resourceful and energetic and, given his naval background, at home in the underbelly of Paris. He was wrong for it in almost as many ways. His judgement was often flawed, indignation flared easily in him and he was a painfully verbose correspondent. He was also a spendthrift – every new naval employment had been celebrated with expensive clothes. With help from the faithful merchant James Houblon, Pepys organised two Parisian merchants to supply Balty's French currency and keep an eye on his spending, and sent him off. A letter warning him to keep his head down and avoid mentioning his own name or Pepys's chased him out of London, overtook him on the road and was waiting for him in Paris, a stony welcome to remind him that he was not on holiday.

Pepys wrote telling John Brisbane that Balty was coming, to lessen the load and take instructions. 'I beg you therefore,' Pepys added humbly, 'to give him leave of waiting on you from time to time.'³ Balty would need Brisbane's help to get access to the Marquis de Seignelay; it would be disastrous to insult the prickly Brisbane by suggesting that Balty was replacing him. Pepys avoided mentioning that Balty had been charged too, saying only that he had 'business' of his own in France. He had no way of knowing that the mention of Balty's name would profoundly unsettle the nervy Scotsman.

That day, 19 June, a letter from Brisbane arrived at the Tower. Pepys was to appear in court the next day and hoped it would contain useful evidence, but he was disappointed. Brisbane had heard that Scott was not a traitor but an artist; he copied, enlarged and decorated maps he found in books. If true, this was a major blow to

Pepys. The man with this information had shown a 'backwardness' in wanting to discuss the matter; Brisbane had not pressed him, so still had nothing that Pepys could use in court. Almost as an afterthought, he added that he had finally spoken to the Marquis de Seignelay the previous day. This was what Pepys was waiting for but again, Brisbane let him down. 'I was forced to confine my discourse to the business I went for,' he wrote, 'wanting time to touch your matters.' The Scotsman was the most useless investigator. He said he would not raise the subject of Pepys and the treasonous papers with the Marquis, but would wait to see if the Marquis mentioned it first. This hesitant approach was bound to fail; absurdly, even Brisbane thought so.[4]

Responding, Pepys buried his frustration in polite formality. It was irrelevant that the maps were copies – what mattered was that Scott had tried to sell them. His subtext is clear; he had no defence and his trial might come as soon as tomorrow. He needed evidence. Did Brisbane not understand? As for de Seignelay, Pepys still thought he would tell the truth, if only Brisbane would ask him directly. One can almost see him throwing up his hands in exasperation as he told Brisbane to do as he thought fit.[5]

With only one night before his next court appearance, Pepys considered his position. Promising rumours had reached him. As a free man, Pepys had been a great theatre-lover, and he had begun to think of Scott's infamous, villainous life as a play with 'several scenes'. He had heard about a lawsuit in The Hague over some sort of forgery, and that Scott, as a colonel in the Dutch army, had run off after stealing Dutch money. There had also been a conflict with a solicitor in his regiment there. But Pepys could hardly go to trial armed with rumours. Henry Coventry's man James Puckle would be able to swear to some of Scott's crimes, but where was Puckle? Though it had been over a week now, Pepys had heard nothing to indicate that the exiled Duke of York might be looking for Puckle. Worried that the unreliable post might have failed him, Pepys had asked a sea-captain bound for Brussels to tell the Duke of his 'condition'.[6] But still there was nothing but silence. Tomorrow the gaoler would take him to King's Bench. He had gathered even less of a defence than Richard Langhorn. His only hope was that the court would allow him more time.

Suddenly, and quite unexpectedly, an opportunity presented itself. An acquaintance offered to talk on his behalf to a man who knew Scott well. This was a potential witness, in London, who could come to Pepys's defence in court. Pepys grabbed the lifeline. Declaring his 'utmost thankfulness', he wrote down all the rumours he had heard, for the witness to consider. In eleven 'queries' Pepys revealed the full extent and limits of his knowledge. He needed to know more about Scott's mapmaking and attempts to sell his maps; the history of Scott's life in various countries; his service to the French Crown; his relations with French navy ministers de Seignelay and Pellissary; his usual lodging in Paris, and whether he was really there in the summer of 1675; and what Scott's standing was now in France. The list exposed the state of his defence so completely that he was reluctant even to record it in the neat letter-book that contained copies of all his outgoing post; instead, he kept the copy on two smaller sheets of paper and only stuck it in later.[7]

The useful potential witness was called Sir Ellis Leighton. Pepys had met him briefly in the 1660s, noting after a dinner party that he was 'one of the best companions at a meal in the world'.[8] Leighton had a bawdy taste that may have appealed to Pepys's vulgar side.[9] A less admiring contemporary, however, described him as most immoral and vicious.[10]

It is worth taking a closer look at Leighton. He had become notorious in the early 1670s for misusing his position as secretary to an old and lazy ambassador in Paris to extort huge fees. In October 1676, Whitehall stepped in to examine claims that Leighton was demanding up to £500 to release English ships taken by French privateers.[11] Henry Coventry sent John Brisbane to investigate in Dieppe, where Brisbane was mobbed by furious merchants and captains issuing 'oaths and execrations' against Sir Ellis.[12] Leighton was sent to the Tower but he escaped on the way there.[13] A letter was issued to 'take good care to watch the ports'.[14] Sir Ellis fled to the Cornish port of Falmouth disguised in peasant clothing but wearing silk undergarments, as a maid who joined him in bed discovered. He evaded capture and sailed for Bordeaux, but in 1677 he gave himself up and was taken to the Tower.[15]

Even there, he kept a sense of humour and promptly asked to be released on the most spurious grounds. He wrote to Sir Henry Coventry:

If I should say I were sick for want of air I should lie, for I never knew any difference of air if the drink were good. If I should say I were sad I should lie for I spend all my time in showing Harry the Eighth's codpiece to all the women that come to see the rarities of the Tower.[16]

He was neither sick nor sad, he told the Secretary of State; he was broke and wanted to be set free. After his release he disappeared to France again. In July 1678, Coventry sent a ciphered letter to Brisbane in Paris, saying 'Sir Ellis Leighton is newly gone over without having given the Court any notice of it. I pray have a strict eye upon him and give me account how he comports himself there.'[17]

If Pepys had had time to consult Coventry about getting Leighton's help, Coventry would have advised against it – but Pepys, with only hours at his disposal, did not have time. Coventry had monitored Leighton on that trip to France because he had travelled with the Duke of Buckingham. The Duke's movements were being closely scrutinised because he appeared to be negotiating privately with King Louis of France. Buckingham had travelled with an entourage and among those men had been Colonel John Scott. Pepys had just put his whole defence into the hands of one of Scott's closest allies.

Sir Ellis would have been perfectly qualified to help design part of the plot against Pepys. He had been working on privateer cases in France when Anthony Deane's privateer *Hunter* had sailed into Dunkirk with the captured English merchant ship *Catherine*. He would have known the details and could, by talking with Captain Moone and bending the facts a little, have given the *Hunter* charge its final shape.[18] Pepys eventually realised how foolish it would be to summon Sir Ellis as a witness, but by that time Sir Ellis had the full details of his defence. Only then did Pepys get word that Sir Ellis had decided not to appear publicly against John Scott.[19] Too late, Pepys realised the scale of the catastrophe: Sir Ellis was, he wrote guardedly, 'a person of such a fame, that though his acquaintance with Scott could no doubt enable him to inform me much concerning him, I am not very desirous of meddling with him'.[20]

The following day, Friday 20 June, five more of Titus Oates's victims were executed. Thomas Whitbread, sixty years old, was the head of the English Jesuits. John Fenwick, William Harcourt, John Gavan and Anthony Turner were Jesuits known to Oates during his time in their faith. He had enmeshed them all in an intricate fantasy, involving repeated attempts to shoot Charles II with silver bullets which had been twisted to inflict a brutal wound. To explain why Charles was still alive, Oates told a tale of a series of providential loose pistol flints that stopped the guns going off. Gavan, the youngest, had tried every sort of defence in their trial a week earlier but he had failed, even being directed by the court to be more polite to Oates. The only mercy shown to them was that they were allowed to meet their death in the act of hanging. Their corpses were drawn and quartered.

On the same day, the first of the new term, Pepys and Deane were taken back to the court of King's Bench without a shred of useful evidence. Nonetheless, they were on the offensive and, for the second time, presented the argument for their release: the warrant for their commitment gave no reason for their imprisonment. The Attorney General confessed that he had not yet finished preparing their prosecution so there could be no trial that day. The court could not reasonably deny Pepys and Deane their rights a second time. It released them. They were free.

Their freedom lasted only a moment. The court had heard John

Scott, John James and Captain Moone's affidavits against them on 2 June. On the strength of these, it immediately placed Pepys and Deane under arrest.[21] Only the King and Parliament could put prisoners in the Tower; the court had its own prison of King's Bench, part of the notorious Marshalsea complex in Southwark. It was less comfortable than the Tower, and ridden with gaol fever. Pepys and Deane were to be imprisoned there.

Pepys made it very clear that this had been his intention. 'Sir Anthony Deane and I,' he wrote to the Duke of York's secretary, 'have (though otherwise to our inconvenience) got ourselves removed from the Tower of London to the King's Bench.'[22] The discomfort of the new prison was countered by the fact that they now had the full power of habeas corpus at their disposal. The court had discharged them from their parliamentary imprisonment, so would no longer feel obliged to keep them confined on Parliament's behalf. The English legal practice of habeas corpus dictated that, after a certain period without trial, the prisoner had to be discharged. It was a bullish tactic on Pepys's part. If his enemies failed to try him, he would go free. He refused to rot in a Whig prison.

They left the Tower with a bill for four weeks and six days' accommodation of £6 9s 6d.[23] Pepys tried to minimise their discomfort in King's Bench. The marshal of the prison was called Cooling; Pepys wondered if the man might be related to Richard Cooling, an old friend who in 1660 took Pepys for dinner to plan great money-making schemes.[24] He was in luck; they were cousins. There is evidence that the string-pulling worked. Pepys's loyal friend James Houblon made regular trips across the Thames to the 'Patten' in Southwark. The Golden Patten was an inn beside the King's Bench prison. Pepys, it seems, was allowed to meet visitors there.[25] From the tone of his letters, it is clear that he now had access to Anthony Deane as well.

The Attorney General's lack of preparation had bought Pepys an extra two-and-a-half weeks. Balty had just arrived in Paris and, if the Marquis de Seignelay was willing, might conceivably get his statement sworn and sent over in time. Pepys would not trust to de Seignelay, however. He had to prove that Scott was a bad witness. From his cell he could do very little but write letters. He had written to the Duke of York in search of James Puckle and had heard nothing. He needed help, but he was a Plot conspirator. His helpers would have to be brave and loyal. After three days in King's Bench prison, he realised that they were already at work.

Henry Coventry had taken matters into his own hands. Quite probably he wished to undo the damage the Whigs had done, now that Parliament's doors were closed and he no longer had to battle against their assault on the Duke of York. Again he demonstrated the heat and spirit for which he was known; throwing caution to the wind, he summoned James Puckle to England himself.

Puckle thought he was coming over to be a witness for Sir Anthony Deane, which baffled him since, he later wrote to Pepys, Deane was 'a man I never see, nor do I know him, nor have had any correspondence with him'.[26] But when he arrived in London and reported to the Secretary of State, Coventry told him to visit Pepys instead, explaining that Pepys's accuser was John Scott. Puckle understood immediately. His long experience of Scott was enough for him to declare, even without further investigation, that he believed Pepys to be innocent. He was certain that his testimony would 'clear' Pepys of this 'clamour about Admiralty papers', and he set off to find him. Coventry had made an inexplicable mistake (perhaps his gout had been particularly inflamed that day) by failing to tell Puckle that Pepys was in the Tower. Puckle went to the Admiralty Office at Derby House.

He tried several times to get in and see Pepys, and in the end the porter 'grew impertinent, looking on me as troubling him too much', and Puckle gave up and returned to the Secretary of State's office. When Coventry mentioned the Tower, Puckle's nerve failed. The information he carried would be highly beneficial to Pepys, but not if Pepys's enemies could argue that Pepys had told him to say it – which might happen, if he was seen visiting the prisoner. Puckle was a taciturn man, but a canny one too.

He returned to Brussels feeling rather put out by the whole frustrating experience. What with Coventry's misleading summons and failure to mention the Tower, the Derby House porter's rudeness and failure to correct the mistake, and the fact that Puckle had not in the end seen Pepys, it had been a rather pointless journey. What was more, he wrote to Pepys, 'the people do believe, you have not been my friend.' He explained what had unfolded in a letter, which he signed off 'without ceremony' and with a terse command for Pepys to 'excuse scribbling'.[27] In the Derby House porter's uncooperative behaviour, and the rumours on the street that Pepys was somehow Puckle's enemy, we catch the echo of a thousand whispers, and glimpse the breadth of the plot against Pepys.

Puckle had learnt to obey the Secretaries of State during his years as an English agent, and the Duke of York's ever-cool secretary was on hand in Brussels to smooth his ruffled feathers. From there, Puckle sent Pepys a paper detailing all he knew about Colonel Scott, by his own confession 'badly writ' but containing only 'so much as I am sure to prove'. In Puckle, Pepys realised as he read, he finally had a witness to prove that Scott had tried to sell English maps to the French. It also contained a surprise which turned all Pepys's preconceptions on their head. Scott's 'low virtues', his treachery and possession of naval papers, his copying of maps, and his crimes in Holland were only one side of an increasingly complex man. John Scott had worked for King Charles's government. He had been an English spy.[28]

Puckle's paper brought both hope and mystery into Pepys's cell. On the day of the charges William Harbord, trying to bolster Scott's legitimacy as a witness, had told the Commons that the former Secretary of State Sir Joseph Williamson 'thought Scott the ablest man in England for a West India voyage, and it was a pity to lose him'.[29] Williamson had been the government's spymaster. How much did Charles's court really know about Scott? Anxious to keep Puckle's sympathies, Pepys wrote to thank him for his 'justice and friendship', to apologise for his 'unsatisfactory usage' by the porter and to quash the suggestions that he himself had ever done Puckle any wrong.[30] Puckle's presence in court was going to be essential.

The following day, 24 June, a second paper brought another ray of light into Pepys's cell. It came from Robert Southwell. It will be remembered that Southwell, the Privy Council clerk with the sensitive political nose, had already taken it upon himself to pursue, on Pepys's behalf, rumours of Scott's crimes across the Channel. He had a contact there, one Nicholas Reeve, a cheerful and attentive man who liked a challenge. At Southwell's request, Reeve had ridden out from his home in Rotterdam to discover what he could in The Hague. The resentment he encountered there at the mention of Scott's name had stunned him. Everyone he spoke to described Scott in the most extreme terms: a godless, profane man; a false and traitorous suborner. After careful investigation, Reeve found evidence of a crime that 'may be of great moment for Mr Pepys', for it involved Scott falsely accusing a man – that same solicitor that Pepys had heard about – and having him imprisoned. Reeve could prove it, since there were written attestations in the official records. He intended to go back for them the following week.[31]

Pepys's Dutch investigations bore fruit through the rest of June. As his confidence rose, something of the old commanding tone returned, and when he secured himself an agent in the Netherlands, it was almost as though the man was still answering to the Secretary of the Admiralty. Captain Gunman, a 'sober, frugal, cheerful and temperate' seaman, as John Evelyn called him, and captain of a royal yacht, had carried many illustrious passengers on Pepys's orders in the past.[32] Pepys gave Gunman a long list of questions to ask a Mr Hutchinson, a contact of James Puckle's in Rotterdam.[33] Pepys wanted to know about Scott's being hanged in effigy or convicted of forgery; whether he had stolen Dutch government money; about his lawsuit against the solicitor; and Scott having been beaten by a well-known diplomat for having spoken 'ill words' against the King.[34] Sober Captain Gunman extended himself far beyond Pepys's requests and returned a document he earnestly titled, 'To prove Col. John Scott a scandalous person not to be believed'. He gave the names of twelve witnesses to prove that Scott had lied, stolen, cheated, associated with evil men and spoken violently against the English Crown.[35]

The charming Nicholas Reeve, meanwhile, was unstoppable. Reeve made at least four trips from Rotterdam to The Hague in June and Pepys praised his 'extraordinary diligence and dexterity'.[36] It was a huge relief to know that, outside the cell walls, Scott's story was being methodically harvested. On the second trip, Reeve stumbled across two men also following Scott's trail. They worked for the Duke of York; Pepys's anxious letters to his exiled master had paid off. Reeve was the most disciplined of the three men – one of the others languidly reported that it would 'take some time' to get proofs – and he immediately took control, dividing up the tasks.[37] One was to find out whether Scott had deserted the Dutch army; another was to try to prove a rumour that Scott had promised to launch a surprise military attack on England. Reeve himself focused on getting the testimonies proving Scott had lied under oath before.[38]

Reeve did better than his companions. It took him longer than he expected; the court delayed giving up the testimonies, but he remained cheery. 'I have, I think, so surely effected my desires that God willing hope next week to send what I promised,' he wrote on 27 June. 'If I miss my mark 'tis not for want of right aiming.'[39] By the beginning of July, he had copies of the testimonies in his hands. With every letter from Reeve, Scott's reputation crumbled further. Pepys began to imagine a devastating victory in the courtroom: Reeve displayed so much method, he wrote, that it 'might lead a stranger to think that instead of Scott's arraigning of me, I had in my care the management of a charge against him'. The extraordinary stories that were now funnelling back to Pepys gave him, he delightedly wrote to Southwell, 'little reason to suspect the world's thinking my accuser a saint'.[40] But as he prodded, the murky world of his accuser began to stir and Reeve wrote craving secrecy, for there was a Frenchman 'also very inquisitive into the legend of Scott's life here'.[41] Who he was or what he wanted, Reeve had no idea. But Sir Ellis Leighton, and probably Scott and the Duke of Buckingham, now knew exactly which parts of Scott's life Pepys was investigating. Any men or women who could testify against Scott were vulnerable to being bought or bullied. Pepys would do well to tell his investigators to pursue Scott quietly.

As Pepys's counter-attack on Scott gathered momentum, contributions began to come in unsolicited. A Mr Custis in Bruges sent two documents listing new crimes. Pepys had not asked Custis for information; Custis had seen a letter from a Mr Kennedy. Pepys was not even in contact with Kennedy, who had heard of Pepys's predicament from somewhere else. It gets better: Kennedy had never written to Custis, he had written to another man, who had gone off on an extended journey. Custis had seen the letter by chance, opened it on the absent recipient's behalf, and jumped in to help, 'out of delight in the defence of innocence', he said.[42] This kind of thing was happening all over Europe. Scott had spent a lifetime making enemies, who were now dry tinder for the spreading fire of Pepys's investigation. At the centre of it, in his cell, sat the little former secretary to the Admiralty who, with pen and paper, had lit the match.

On 26 June, King Charles made his position absolutely clear by sending Pepys a fat buck from the Royal Chase at Enfield.[43] It was all the embattled king could do. He had to tiptoe in his own realm. His brother, the Duke of York, could not even set foot in the country – but three days later, Pepys had a rare treat. The Duke's secretary had slipped back into England to visit the court, and he sent a kindly note to Pepys's cell. 'I am very unhappy,' Pepys wrote back longingly, 'that I cannot wait on you, the better to enquire after the state of our absent master.'[44] King Charles, in sudden defiance of the Whigs, sent a summons to the gaoler saying he 'would speak with Mr Pepys, now prisoner in your custody, at one this afternoon'.[45] Pepys was carried from prison gloom to spend snatched time with old friends in the splendour of Whitehall Palace. What was said remained secret, but Whig eyes saw Pepys there, and the Attorney General was told of the visit. He later tried to make trouble in court by claiming Pepys had been attempting escape.[46]

By 27 June, Balty had arrived in Paris. He had taken his son, Pepys's nephew, with him, and the boy sent Pepys a delighted letter describing Paris as the most beautiful town in Europe. He showed off by writing in French and Latin, and said that if he could only do a little dance in the letter, his uncle would see all his learning. He addressed it to Pepys as Admiralty Secretary at his old Derby House office.[47] Balty, with a father's gentleness, had kept quiet about Pepys's fall.

As he had been instructed, Balty headed to the embassy to consult John Brisbane.

Brisbane's poverty was eating at him. He had outstanding debts to pay before he could leave Paris. He had arranged to send his family and furniture home but, he warned Henry Coventry, 'Truly except you order me to run away I cannot go myself till I have paid all that I owe here.'[48] These concerns had driven any method or focus from his attempts to help Pepys. He had been reduced to mad dashes around Paris looking for answers. He had spent Monday afternoon and evening 'running about the town to find out somebody that could inform' him whether Scott had been there in August 1675.

The Scotsman had had one moment of bravery and success. Leaving a meeting with Louis XIV's foreign secretary, he had encountered a Monsieur de Gourville on the stairs. De Gourville served the Prince of Condé, a veteran military commander of renown to whom Scott had allegedly tried to sell his maps. Brisbane seized the opportunity and joked, as de Gourville passed him, that the foreign secretary had no time to see him. The French gentleman smiled and stopped. In that case, he said, he would speak to Brisbane instead; what news from England? Brisbane plucked up his courage. He had heard, he said, that de Gourville had bought maps of the English coast. The Frenchman's smile vanished.

'On my place in Paradise,' he said, 'there is nothing in that.' John Scott had offered them a hugely expensive chart but, he said, 'we are not stupid and if I wanted a map of England, I would send a 30 sol piece to London to buy it and have it enlarged in Paris for a lot less than that joker was demanding.'[49]

Brisbane had to confess he had underrated Scott's ability to sell his 'cockleshells for jewels'. 'I wish with all my heart,' he told Pepys, 'I could furnish you with better materials.' But he barely had time for his own affairs.

The news that Balty was due in Paris had come as a shock. Balty's name was familiar to Brisbane. While investigating Sir Ellis Leighton's extortionate charges, Brisbane had heard about the *Hunter* privateer's controversial capture of the English merchant ship *Catherine*. The *Hunter*'s owners, Anthony Deane included, had argued that the *Catherine* had been manned by Dutch (not English) sailors, so was a legitimate target for their English privateer. The debate wore on without resolution until Balty sailed over on behalf of himself and the other owners and persuaded the French to endorse the capture. Brisbane was quite sure the capture had been illegal. He was not alone. Henry Coventry also remembered when the case of the *Hunter* was heard by the council: 'it looked very black and I am afraid is hardly grown white with age.'[50] Brisbane considered Balty a criminal.[51]

When Brisbane got Pepys's letter saying that Balty was on his way out, he wrote one back explaining that he would have nothing to do with him. He thought Balty could prove 'a snare'. He posted the letter to Henry Coventry. The Secretary of State looked over all his letters before forwarding them to Pepys's cell, to ease Brisbane's anxiety about corresponding with an accused traitor. But Coventry chose not to forward this one to Pepys. Because it was a refusal to help, he thought Brisbane should explain himself to Pepys in person when he returned to London.[52]

So no one stopped Balty knocking on the embassy door.

He began to explain to Brisbane that he was in Paris on his own business, to answer the *Hunter* charges. Brisbane, prone to anxiety, and exhausted from overwork and the strain of debt, experienced a sudden lucidity. Everything became shiningly clear. It was a conspiracy. Pepys, he realised, had written letter after letter asking for help with a treason charge against him, yet Brisbane had not had it confirmed by anyone else that Pepys had in fact been charged. Evidently, Pepys had fabricated the whole affair, in order to man-oeuvre Balty into the embassy to get Brisbane's assistance and wriggle out of the *Hunter* crime. Brisbane would have no part in it. He threw Balty out of the embassy and wrote a furious note to Henry Coventry complaining of Balty's foul behaviour. He had trusted Coventry, he said, and had Coventry not pushed him, he would never have touched Pepys's case at all.[53]

With less than two weeks before his court appearance, Pepys's French network had just fallen completely to pieces.

12

The Signature

The news of Balty's disastrous meeting with John Brisbane took six days to reach Pepys's cell. It arrived on 3 July, completely unexpected. Pepys was concentrating on a letter pressing the reluctant Brisbane to talk to the Marquis de Seignelay. An anxiety had begun to infect him that de Seignelay might see merit in destroying him, and that his enemies would get to de Seignelay first and persuade him to confirm their lie about receiving Admiralty papers. After six weeks as a prisoner, Pepys's confidence was starting to slide.

When Will Hewer arrived with the post, Pepys put down his pen to read Balty's distressing account of being thrown out of the embassy. Pepys's fragile network had ruptured. He picked up his pen to stitch it back together. He reassured the affronted Scotsman that he need have no fear of getting mixed up in the *Catherine* affair; Pepys was not involved in it one bit. The task of answering the charge lay wholly with Sir Anthony Deane, who expected trial soon and seemed 'not only prepared for it but zealous in the hastening of it'. Pepys himself only needed help to answer John Scott's charge of correspondence with de Seignelay; he did not expect Brisbane to help Balty. He would order Balty to stay away from the embassy.

He signed off asking 'ten thousand pardons for the troubles this misfortune of mine has (to my great affliction) heaped upon you', then he immediately wrote a warning to Balty to keep clear of Brisbane. Balty could no longer be Brisbane's assistant, so Pepys created a new role for him, setting him to work on the other two characters in Scott's story: Georges Pellissary and Monsieur Piogerie. Loyal James Houblon's two merchant friends had already begun to investigate these men; Balty's new task was to join the merchants and discover everything he could. Were they dead, as Scott claimed? What had their religion been? Was Scott really at Pellissary's house the day Deane visited? Pellissary's servants might remember. Had Scott even known Pellissary? Pepys wished Balty health and, with blessings to his little nephew, sealed the letter and sent it off.[1]

Pepys found some comfort that day, in good food and friendship; a piece of venison from John Evelyn, and Evelyn himself to share it with at dinner.[2]

Oddly, John Brisbane had calmed himself down by yelling at Balty. He would have liked to have helped his old friend Pepys more, but self-protectiveness (or cowardice) had stopped him. Every coward fantasises about bravery. As his time in Paris drew to an end, the departing diplomat did his duty by visiting the court at St Germain to say a formal farewell to Louis's ministers. The occasion marked the end of his three years in Paris. Perhaps this gave him some perspective. The Marquis de Seignelay was there. In the lavish environment that had become so familiar, Brisbane suddenly felt unexpectedly brave. His former caution no longer seemed necessary. He walked over to the Marquis and said:

I must speak with you. I would not touch the business if I imagined it would cause you the least pain, but I am persuaded your answer will be easy for you to give, and satisfactory to me. An Englishman of consideration, Samuel Pepys, has been accused of a criminal correspondence with you, for sending you draughts of our ports and coasts.

De Seignelay looked at him thoughtfully.

'I was sent to England by my king,' he remembered, 'to regulate the common affairs of both fleets. Pepys did then communicate to me the number and strength of the English ships. But, upon my honour, I have never had any correspondence with Pepys, good or bad.'

In the mad final Paris moments, Brisbane found time to put this conversation in a letter to Pepys.[3]

Pepys had it by the 7th. It relieved his fear that the Marquis, thinking Pepys's permanent removal from the English government would benefit France, would join the ranks of his accusers. But de Seignelay was mistaken; Pepys had never met him. After a quick investigation by his friends, Pepys realised de Seignelay was referring to a time when the English and French were openly cooperating against the Dutch – back in 1671, before Pepys had even joined the Admiralty. De Seignelay had confused him with the Duke of York's secretary at the time. The misunderstanding had to be corrected. It would be disastrous for de Seignelay to begin telling people that Pepys had in fact given him naval information. Another task for Balty.

Balty, a free agent now, was throwing himself into his work. He had the help of the two French merchants who supplied his money, François Trenchepain and Antoine Pelletier. The loyal James Houblon had arranged these, but Pelletier was also an old acquaintance of Pepys and Balty's, known from the trip to Paris they made with Pepys's wife Elizabeth, just before her death in 1669. Balty and his men made a dogged and loyal little team, infinitely bolder and more capable than John Brisbane.

They were examining the servants of the dead navy treasurer Georges Pellissary, in whose house Scott said he had heard Anthony Deane through the open window. They had got off to a promising start. Pellissary's former secretary told them Pellissary had 'no acquaintance' with Scott, who could not, therefore, have been in the house.[4] The secretary had never seen any such papers from England. Pepys, however, was beginning to pre-empt what his prosecution might argue; if Pellissary had kept the papers secret, he told Balty, his secretary might not have known about them. It would be best if Balty questioned all Pellissary's servants. Hopefully they would be Protestants, like their dead master; it would do no good to have Catholic witnesses. The secretary had offered to show Balty the house; Pepys told him to accept, and talk to Pellissary's widow if possible. He should keep his eyes open for five large maps – a nonsensical request since, even by Scott's account, these had not remained with Pellissary. So far, Balty had been cagey about his motives and had not mentioned the treason charge to Pellissary's secretary, but Pepys now felt he should come clean with the household. After all, Scott's lies were almost as damaging to Pellissary's memory as they were to Pepys.

London was beginning to swelter. On Wednesday 9 July, the last day of the court term before the long summer break, fat, warm raindrops fell occasionally from a still and heavy sky. Pepys and Deane were again in Westminster Hall before the raised wooden benches of the court. In four or five days, Attorney General Jones said, he hoped to have further evidence against them; they ought not to be bailed. He produced three new affidavits to show that Pepys and Deane had tried to suppress evidence against them.

One was from Mary Harris, the wife of the messenger at Derby House. This was the second time that Pepys's old workplace had been mentioned. She said that the previous month, a man called at her house looking for her husband's friend John James, Pepys's ex-butler and now one of his accusers. The visitor pretended James was wanted for an important job. After several visits, he revealed his true colours as a friend of Pepys's, swearing violent oaths against James for disclosing his master's secret Catholicism.[5] The court asked whether the mysterious visitor could be produced; he could not. Pepys was nonplussed and said simply that he did not need to suppress anything James had said.

There was a new affidavit from Scott, and he swore to it solemnly at the bar. He had been in the Tower, he said, and had been shouted at by one of the Plot prisoners. The man had threatened him for accusing Pepys, warning him that the papists were 'not yet brought so low' that they could not retaliate. A short time after Scott had finished speaking, and by complete chance, this prisoner appeared in the Hall to push for bail. He was standing close to Pepys and Pepys, unwilling to be associated with another accused Plotter, muttered that he would rather the gentleman did not come to his aid. The man replied courteously, quietly saying that Scott's story was a lie.

The third affidavit was from an ironfounder who, in a rambling tale, claimed that two years earlier he had witnessed a notorious Jesuit come to Scott to offer him Pepys's favour. The implication was that Pepys had realised long before Scott charged him that Scott knew about his crime, and had tried to buy Scott's friendship. Pepys told the court that he had never spoken to the Jesuit. Scott piped up that some twenty people had asked him to be friends with Pepys.

'Who, then?' demanded Pepys. But Scott could only name one, a clerk of Pepys's who had sought him out in a coffee house; for the third time, the name of Derby House was heard. Pepys asked to see the ironfounder's affidavit. It bore that day's date – a last-minute bit of work by the prosecution. Pepys pointed the fact out to the court. Scott blustered, saying he had been unable to reveal it before because his French informants Pellissary and Piogerie had been alive, and him sworn to secrecy. This sounded pathetic and he conjured another reason. At the time, he said, the Duke of York, 'his greatest enemy', had been in power. Since Pepys had been the Duke's favourite and confidant, Scott could have expected no justice. This was a similarly ill-considered excuse; there had been nothing to stop Scott mentioning this incident in May, when he brought his other charges. But the Attorney General was leaping to Scott's support.

'And this my lord will be allowed (I doubt not) for a good reason,' he said. But the court was less than impressed by Scott's explanation, and there was a muttering of discontent on the judges' bench. Scroggs tried to move things along.

'We are here to discuss whether it is bail, or no bail,' he told them.

It was dawning on Pepys that there was an absurdity at the heart of the ironfounder's affidavit. If Scott had kept what he knew secret until he stood up in the Commons, how could Pepys have discovered that he needed to silence Scott back in 1677? He made a note of this contradiction and, aware now that his adversary was making mistakes of logic, went on listening carefully.

As the judges began to debate the possibility of bail, the Attorney General interrupted them.

'The matter whereof these men stand accused is of great moment,' he protested. 'Given these affidavits, bail ought not to be granted. And your eloquence and rhetoric will be more seasonable when you come to your trial,' he muttered to Pepys. To reiterate the seriousness of the charges, he asked Scott to lay them out again.

When Scott came to the part of his charge when he claimed to have recognised Pepys's signature, he was asked how he knew it was Pepys's.

'I know it to be his by the many things I have since seen signed by him,' he said.

Quite reasonably, Scroggs was unimpressed by this explanation and he made the point to the court; Scott had not known Pepys's signature before he saw the letter. Scott, taken aback by this unexpected hostility from the Lord Chief Justice, could think of nothing to say. He had suddenly realised how flimsy it sounded.

The court wondered whether Pepys's signature was sufficiently remarkable to remember. Scroggs asked Pepys to write it out for them. The judges agreed it was remarkable. Pepys informed the court that his signature had often been faked by others. His clerks could prove how easy it was to copy, but he kept the fact to himself. He might need it at trial.*

Scroggs had shown a rare display of support for Pepys and, well aware that he should capitalise on it, Pepys made the point to the court again: Scott had not known his signature before he saw it on the papers. How could he possibly have recognised it? Quite unexpectedly, and for himself disastrously, Scott snapped.

'The court is mistaken,' he said, 'in thinking I have said I have never seen his hand before I saw that letter. I never said any such thing.'

Uproar in the courtroom. Even the more partial judges disliked being told that they had not heard something when they had heard

---

* This might make collectors think twice about the high prices demanded by rare book dealers for Pepys's autograph on run-of-the-mill navy documents.

it, just minutes before. Scroggs and Judge Dolben insisted he had plainly said it. Pepys joined them indignantly – and then stopped. He realised he had his accuser pinned.

'Since you would now have it otherwise,' he said to Scott, 'declare where and on what occasion you have seen my hand.'

Scott, as was his way, sought refuge in the dead. Captain la Piogerie had shown it to him, he said. Piogerie had had twenty orders – all signed by Pepys – while he was major of the fleet in the Channel. Scott gave a date.

'That is impossible,' Pepys told the court. He had been paying close attention to the details of Scott's claims. He was putting into effect advice he gave Balty; the best way to trap a liar was to snare them with their own detail. Scott had already given the court an account of Piogerie's movements and – by that account – Piogerie could not have shown Scott those orders before he showed Scott the letter. The court was impressed.

Scott was thunderstruck, and he stood, stock still, unable to think of a response. Then he turned, walked away from the court, and disappeared into the crowd that was buying books and chattering in the Hall.

The Attorney General, in a state of some disorder, began scooping up his papers. This was not the first time this kind of thing had happened since the Plot was discovered, and he found it deeply embarrassing. The matter had been handed down to him by Parliament, he explained, flustered; he was only doing his job in objecting to bail. The court must do as it saw fit. As he too disappeared into the crowd, the Lord Chief Justice turned to his fellow judges.

'They seek to impose any stories on us and fox us with information,' he growled. 'For my part I am ashamed of it.'

It was the first time since the beginning of the Popish Plot that he had shown any real dislike for the prosecution's evidence. He turned to Pepys and Deane, suddenly friendly and energetic.

'You are Englishmen,' he declared, 'and God forbid you should not have the rights of Englishmen.' So much Englishmen, Pepys answered brightly, that they served in the Commons – a 'signal instance' of their Englishness! If the court would bail them, Pepys reasoned, they would stay as close to London as was necessary and give in whatever bail was demanded. They did not wish to spend the long hot vacation confined.

The judges voted unanimously for bail but they set it extremely high. Four of Pepys's friends, including James Houblon, had to put up £5,000 each. Pepys had to raise £10,000, twice as much (as Pepys told Balty in a different context) as a really great man could earn in a year.[6] The total bail of £30,000 each would be equivalent at the time of writing to £4.5 million.[7]

In earlier Plot trials, even when he had guided the jury not to shed innocent blood, Scroggs had put much trust in the prosecution's stories. Pepys left Scott so unmasked that Scroggs was forced – for the first time – to confront the fact that evidence against Plot 'perpetrators' might not be true. After this remarkable day in court, his behaviour changed. At the next Plot trial, Scroggs was markedly tougher on Titus Oates than ever before, picking him up on the detail of his evidence, and the defendant, George Wakeman, was acquitted.[8] Pepys's moment of cross-examination brilliance may have had effects far beyond his own case.

For Pepys himself, very little had changed, except that now he was tied to his friends by bail. The charges still hung over him. Ironically, he had fewer rights now than when cooped up in prison, because on bail he fell outside the mechanism of habeas corpus; his eventual trial or discharge was no longer guaranteed. The prosecution had the long summer break to prepare their case. Attorney General Jones was to be replaced, and his successor might be a man of even less generous inclinations.

For all Scott's disasters in court today, Pepys had seen a violence in him. Scott was not simply a witness with a testimony – he seemed to have a vendetta. At one point, Pepys had asserted he was a Protestant, and Scott had jumped down his throat with a whole new story about seeing a trunk full of crucifixes bound for Pepys's house.

In the previous week, though Pepys did not know it, Scott had approached an old associate from France and trailed a bribe in exchange for his testimony. Pepys and Deane had only been saved from trial because the man was decent, and refused.[9] If Scott came up with a second witness (perhaps one whose financial needs were a little more pressing), the jury would most likely find Pepys and Deane guilty as charged.

Pepys's need to construct a tight defence was more pressing than ever. But there was something Scott had said in court; the Duke of York was his 'greatest enemy'. Pepys must have wondered about this complaint. The Duke had never mentioned Scott.

13

Scott's Glory

He likewise (during his glory) summoned
the Dutch government to surrender . . .
EDWARD SACKVILLE TO PEPYS, 23 JULY 1679

For John Scott it began – like so many stories that end with disgrace
– with ambition.

He was born in Ashford in Kent, five miles from Scot's Hall, the
vast house that dominated the landscape of his early childhood. Scot's
Hall, of which no trace remains, was the seat of the great Scott
family, once immensely powerful throughout Kent.[1] John Scott had
no known link to them. He was the son of a bankrupt miller.[2]

Scott's father died while the boy was very young and his miserably
poor mother took her son by the hand and sailed to America to make
a new life. They had nothing, but the American colonies, clinging to
the edge of a vast and unconquered continent, were full of promise.
Hard-working settlers arriving on the shores of New England were
cutting back the trees, planting crops, building farms and carving
lives for themselves. Here, far from everything they knew, the widow
and her son might begin again.

She put the boy to work as apprentice to a farmer in Hempstead,
Long Island, and he drove the cows into the woods in the morning
and back again in the evening for milking. There was a tragic
accident in those early days; out hunting in the fields with a light
birding gun, Scott shot and killed a young girl. He was removed to
the eastern end of Long Island and employed to look after hogs in
the woods. As he grew older, he set up a little business with a
borrowed boat, trading goods between the Long Island natives and

the main Dutch settlement – New Amsterdam, on the island of Manhattan. He married Deborah Raynor, the only daughter of a prominent magistrate, and built a house in Southampton to be near the girl's father.[3] He had made a prosperous little life for himself. But this world was small, and his ambition made it a prison.

His eyes turned to the Atlantic. Beyond it were the grand stone buildings and opulent courts of the Old World. Most of the settlers had turned their backs on the Old World, longing to be free of its constraints – but not Scott. The subsistence of the pioneer did not excite him. He was drawn to the authority and wealth emanating from England. Though he could barely remember it, it was his home.

He could read and write a bit; he picked up languages easily, he had an excellent memory and quick wits – a 'nimble genius', as one person put it. He had no family pedigree or connections, no wealth and no education to speak of. But he had a growing sense of his own potential, the latent ability that separated him from other men. His self-belief bordered on arrogance, and the Long Islanders could see that he thought himself 'somewhat above the common man'.

He waited and traded, building up his reserves and keeping one eye on the ocean. In 1660, when word reached him that Charles Stuart had come out of exile and been triumphantly restored as King, Scott sensed that the moment had come. He bought himself passage and sailed to England.

At twenty-eight, he was one year older than Samuel Pepys who – just like him – had been born into neither power nor wealth.

The London he arrived in was that teeming timber London that was soon to burn. It seemed vast, stretching all the way from the medieval magnificence of Westminster to the imposing fortress of the Tower. After a short time in the throng, Scott realised that the busy new King and his preoccupied officials paid little attention to the distant New England colonies. He spent the last of his money on fine clothes and, 'giving himself out to be someone', walked into Charles's court disguised as a gentleman.

Whitehall Palace at the Restoration was a hotchpotch of timber-framed and stone buildings, tennis courts, a tiltyard and cock-pit, sandwiched between the Thames and St James's Park. The stone ceilings were covered in gold, the walls faced with wood panelling carved with 'a thousand beautiful figures'.[4] In 1660, the young Pepys, his mind full of the naval position he was about to begin, as Clerk of the Acts, had admired the antique marble busts on display.[5] In the Banqueting Hall the ceiling was by Rubens and in the Privy Gallery a painting twelve feet long showed Henry VIII sailing from Dover to France in a squadron of four-masted ships, as the cannon fired the royal salute and vast retinues of loyal noblemen and servants lined the shore.* On Christmas Day 1662, nearly a year after Scott secured access to the court, Pepys walked through 'a most brave cold and dry frosty morning' and, arriving too late for Communion at Whitehall, chose instead to admire this painting. His naval work had become his great joy and he was a diligent student; he noted that ships were built very differently in Henry's time.[6]

The same painting represented a world of wealth and status to Scott. Desperate to be accepted into it, but (beyond his new clothes) lacking the credentials, he pulled a noble background out of thin air by claiming kinship with the Scotts of the grand and ancient house of Scot's Hall. The house, according to John Evelyn, was 'a right noble seat handsomely built with a handsome gallery. It stands in a park well stored with land fat and good.'[7] Scott paid it a visit for reconnaissance, to the confusion of the family, who received him as a stranger and entertained him only for a brief time.[8]

It was an expensive façade to maintain. Scott needed money, but a man of noble descent could hardly be seen working. Then he met Major Daniel Gotherson and his wife Dorothea at court. Dorothea was a Quaker with a penchant for giving hellfire sermons. Like John Scott, she claimed descent from the Scot's Hall Scotts – but with more justification. Her great-great-grandfather, a Scott, was a man of

---

* The Banqueting Hall is the only part of the old Whitehall Palace that still survives. *The Embarkation of Henry VIII* now hangs in Hampton Court.

prodigious talent for siring bastard children and his liaison with a woman called Jeane was the origin of Dorothea's illegitimate line. In the King's presence, Scott told her that he too was related to the Scot's Hall Scotts, 'which I was ready to believe,' Dorothea said later, 'because some of our ancestors' pictures were very like him.'

Scott spun an elegant story to explain why the major and his wife had never heard of him. He had been banished to America for daring to cut the girths of the parliamentary horses during the Civil War, he said. He had lived among the natives in Long Island and bought a large tract of land from them. He showed Major Gotherson a document, apparently proving he had 'lawful Indian title' for the purchase. Then he struck. On 11 July 1662, Scott sold Gotherson 1,600 acres of Long Island that did not belong to him. Ambition had driven him to commit his first great crime.

The deal made Scott rich and ruined the Gothersons. Major Gotherson's 'intent was to go thither to dwell', but he was to die a few days before the Great Fire. They never saw any benefit from the land. He died in debt, with his English lands mortgaged so Dorothea and her six children received no rent. She petitioned the King, and sent letter after letter organising searches for their land in America, but to no avail. Scott's 'insinuating lies and large boasts' had earned him £2,000 and £200 in jewels, which he showed off in Old England and then New England, to which he returned in the late summer of 1662.

Scott had swindled the Gothersons with huge charm. Seven years later, Dorothea still blindly believed that he intended to do 'what lies in his power' for her.[9] Even sixteen years after the cheat she still did not accept that Scott had stolen from her, obstinately asserting that he was simply 'not in capacity of serving me right or himself either as to that particular concern of possessing the land'. Scott had been very clever indeed. He had seduced the Quaker woman; they had had an affair. Her wronged husband discovered this and brought in a 'wench' to live in the house as a chaperone to his wife, then – in a neat piece of marital justice – got the chaperone pregnant. After the major's death the two women found their common ground, and the 'wench' went to America for Dorothea in search of the land. Dorothea should have been furious with Scott, but she had fallen for him.

He came back into America flamboyant and changed, telling his old acquaintances he had received substantial favours from the King. It was an easy lie and it bought their admiration. It was also a fantasy that he wished was true. He seems to have genuinely felt that, in London, he had found a setting where his ambition could be fulfilled. He sensed his potential to become one of the great men of Charles's court. He became a zealous defender of the Crown in Long Island, and tried to bring a case of high treason against a man who made derogatory remarks about Charles.[10] For show, he employed an extravagant number of servants. He dressed his wife like 'a great Lady', to which the simple girl submitted, and he had her train carried like a countess's. The 'gentleman's garb' he had put on at court had convinced the English; now her clothing would persuade the colonists. But the real Deborah Scott was never the aristocrat he wanted her to be. Before long, his mind turned away from her, and he planned his return to England.

His flamboyance had persuaded the New Englanders that he carried real weight at court. Three groups rushed to ask for his help. New Haven colony asked him to deliver its complaints about the overbearing behaviour of its much larger neighbour Connecticut, which had all but swallowed it up. Two Long Island towns, Southton and Southold, asked him to win charters of independence for them; they paid him £500. The third request came from a group of influential men from Massachusetts and Connecticut; they were engaged in a land dispute and wanted Scott to persuade the government to rule in their favour.[11]

Crime paid, in cash. Cash bought respect. Scott was enjoying himself. He would build a mansion appropriate for the ambassador and politician he had become. There was a patch of land on Long Island that he particularly wanted. The problem was that the town of Setauket lay on it. Scott sat down and wrote a document granting him land on Long Island. With a pen or black lead he drew the

King's picture. At the bottom, he forged the signatures of King Charles and one of the Secretaries of State. Then he dropped a fat globule of hot yellow wax on to it and stamped it with an elaborate seal. He took it to Setauket, showed it to the townspeople and offered to swap their land for his, which was a greater quantity. For fear of the power he wielded, most of them agreed to sign the exchange. There were those that refused; Scott forged their signatures.

He sailed into London at the beginning of 1663 loaded with money and confidence. He took to calling himself captain, though he had never been a soldier. Empowered by the colonists, he could bring real influence to bear in England. He had spun concrete gains out of thin air and fantasy. On 2 March he negotiated a deal easing relations between New Haven and Connecticut. Then, with the help of a little bribery, he got a letter from the King in favour of his Massachusetts and Connecticut friends in the land dispute.[12] He never managed to get Southton and Southold's charters of independence, but he kept their money anyway. Then he happily sold the still-ignorant Major Gotherson another 115 acres of Long Island.

Scott became so engrossed in his London politicking that his affairs in America went to seed. His family had moved to the estate at Setauket, recently vacated by the former inhabitants, but his wife was having trouble putting corn on the table for their 'great family' of servants and there was a bill to be paid for 3,000 feet of planking for the new house.[13] Worse, the displaced townspeople of Setauket had started to realise their new land had not been Scott's to give. On 12 June, a faithful but harassed friend wrote asking Scott to return home with haste, for his credit with the Long Islanders was at stake.[14] But Scott's adventure in the Old World was too exciting to worry about such details.

He was befriending some of the most powerful men in England, key players around King Charles like Lord John Berkeley, Sir George Carteret and Joseph Williamson. To impress these, he spent his money as freely as he had got it easily. He felt a particularly close tie of friendship to Williamson, who accepted his advances courteously.[15]

Through Williamson, Scott was introduced right into the heart of government, to the Secretary of State. He presented the Secretary with expensive gifts.[16]

Scott had known for years that he was capable of greatness, and now the court could see it too. This was the moment to secure decisively his rightful place in Charles's administration. He realised he wanted to return to Long Island, but not as some bit-part player; he would be master over it. He would bring royal command to America. He would aim as high as he could. He sat down and wrote a petition asking Charles to make him governor of Long Island.

It is impossible not to admire the sheer gall of the bankrupt miller's son. His petition was bursting with brazen lies.* He claimed that his father had advanced £14,300 over the years to King Charles I and had died serving him. He repeated the lie he had told Dorothea, saying that 'as a small expression of his loyalty' he had as a boy cut the bridles and girths of some of the parliamentary horses during the Civil War. For that, Parliament sent him to New England where he was dealt with 'most perfidiously'. He had worked his way back to greatness, however, and now owned nearly one-third of Long Island.[17]

He got the petition to the Secretary of State and on 26 June 1663, King Charles declared that he was 'fully satisfied of Scott's particular abilities to serve him'.

There was, however, one hurdle to be overcome; Lord Stirling had recently sent in a petition claiming the governorship as well. Before the government could give it to Scott, they had to consider Stirling's petition.[18]

This was a disastrous discovery for Scott. He had to find a way to strengthen his petition and safeguard the employment he felt was rightfully his. He realised that he already knew how to. He had been given a letter. It was a royal command to the New England colonies. In it, Charles ordered the colonists to enforce certain laws restricting

---

* These have been happily endorsed by his biographer, Lilian T. Mowrer, who provides an account of Scott's early life based entirely on his petition.

trade between them and the Dutch in New Netherlands.[19] At the moment, the regulations were being ignored, which was costing the royal coffers thousands of pounds. The government thought Scott could be relied on to deliver the letter of command to the colonists on his next crossing. But its contents gave him an idea.

Ten days later, he appeared before the government committee that controlled the American colonies and which was deciding between his petition and Stirling's. He told them a story that made him seem a loyal subject and the obvious choice for a responsible colonial governor. Charles's colonies were in danger, he said. The Dutch were beginning to intrude on to the mainland of New England, and Manhattan and Long Island, but were failing to obey English laws there. It sounded like a creeping invasion. The committee heard him attentively, then asked him to write up a paper explaining this 'Dutch intrusion'. They wanted details of Dutch military strength there. They also wanted Scott's thoughts on how to make the Dutch 'submit to his Majesty's government' and, in case that should fail, how to drive them out of the New World altogether.[20] Scott, though he did not know it, had set something vast in motion.

He persevered with his noble façade, and even when it slipped he was not shaken. In the winter of 1663, one Mathias Nicolls met Scott dressed in mourning black. Mr Scott of Scot's Hall had died, Scott explained, and he had been left the estate in the will. News of the death of his 'relative' seemed to have reached him very late: Edward Scott had died in the spring. Edward had lived apart from his ill-matched wife for twelve years, so had greeted the birth of a son with understandable consternation.[21] He thought the child, Thomas, had been 'got by somebody else, at Oxford' and refused to acknowledge it as his heir. However, before his death, Edward owned the child and left him his estate. This family drama was widely discussed; Pepys even mentioned it in his Diary.[22] Nicolls therefore knew Scott's claim to be the heir was bunkum and said as much. Scott persisted, claiming that Thomas was indeed a bastard and he, John, was the dead man's nephew and the true heir. He would prove it in court. Of course, no such hearing ever happened.

Full of hope, Scott returned to America and was back by 9 December. His career was soaring, his fortunes high. Armed with the letter containing the King's command on the trade laws, and the fruits of his work in England on the colonists' behalf, he was at last a genuine full-blown royal servant. He also carried a medal showing the King's effigy (awarded to him, he gave out, for some signal service), and a blue garter which he said the queen had taken off her own leg and handed to him. He could not resist it; he claimed he had been made a Gentleman of the Queen's Bedchamber. He also had with him the Gothersons' young son, put into his hands by the besotted Dorothea. Scott had promised to give him a noble American education.

Scott delivered the King's command to the court at New Haven colony. The court jumped to attention and sent out a declaration 'to be published in all the plantations of this colony' that the command should be obeyed. Then they hurried to forward the letter to the other colonies.[23] Scott's standing soared again. He began making land purchases and sitting in the local courts.[24] It seemed, at this strange, euphoric moment, that he had arrived. He had become a respected man, of standing in the community and carrying with him all the tantalising power of the opulent court across the Atlantic. But it was a sham. He had built his reputation on lies. His success had come far too fast for him to learn discretion, judgement or integrity. He had only ever done what was best for him. In his apparent success, he could not see that his position was desperately fragile. In the middle of December it fell to pieces.

It began with Connecticut. The great English colony was anxious to expand. It had eyed nearby Long Island greedily. Long Island had Dutch and English villages on it; the Dutch were clustered at its western end, which they called Breukelen, and were overseen by the main Dutch town of New Amsterdam, which lay across the river on the island of Manhattan. The English villages were dotted around the rest of the island, independent from any colony. To the Connecticut

1 *Detail from* View from Lambeth Palace *by Wenceslaus Hollar. Pepys was accused in the House of Commons (no. 4 on the right of the picture) and appeared in court in Westminster Hall (no. 5). Westminster was alive with the same anti-Catholic fervour that had infected the streets and coffee houses of the City, a short distance downriver.*

2 *Sir Anthony Deane (shown here in a portrait by Sir Godfrey Kneller) was perhaps the most gifted shipwright of his generation. He was Pepys's fellow-accused, imprisoned with him for selling naval secrets to France. Deane bore the brunt of the piracy charges.*

3 *Charles II (studio of John Riley). By the last years of his life, experience had lent a sombre weight to the once rakish king. The Popish Plot forced him to walk a tightrope, balancing the rights of monarchy against the resurgent power of Parliament.*

4 James, Duke of York, as Lord High Admiral *by Henri Gascar. This was painted before anti-Catholic legislation forced him to resign his post. Samuel Pepys's close association with the future king helped make Pepys a target for the plotters.*

5 *Intolerant Lord Chief Justice William Scroggs presided over the trial and execution of many innocent men during the Popish Plot. Pepys's clever exposure of inconsistencies in John Scott's evidence may have helped win him round.*

6 *Richard Langhorn, lawyer to the Jesuits, was tried for complicity in the Popish Plot while Pepys was in the Tower. He defended himself as Pepys did, by attacking the witnesses against him. Though entirely innocent, he was found guilty and executed.*

7 *Godfrey's murder. Detail of engraving from broadside entitled 'England's Grand Memorial'. This shows Sir Edmund Berry Godfrey's corpse (top), and the men convicted of his murder being hanged and disembowelled – the standard punishment for treason.*

8 *The Earl of Shaftesbury (portrait by John Greenhill) led the Whig campaign to prevent the succession of a Catholic king. A clever man with a flair for inciting the English to fervent anti-Catholicism, he helped to establish modern party politics.*

9 *George Villiers, Duke of Buckingham, was John Scott's patron and one of the instigators of the plot against Pepys. He could be extremely violent – he killed Lord Shrewsbury in one of his many duels – but his great wit helped secure the king's forgiveness again and again.*

10 *Henry Coventry (portrait by Mary Beale). He combined the roles of home secretary, foreign secretary and spymaster in Charles II's government. His actions allowed John Scott to return from France to accuse Pepys, but he made up for it by supporting Pepys surreptitiously in every way he could.*

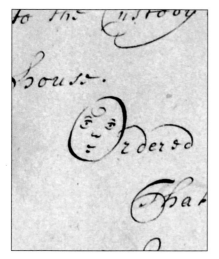

11 *The Mornamont volumes contain transcriptions of the sober documents Pepys collected about Scott's life. This pleasing addition appears on page 4, inside the capital 'O' of the Commons' order to investigate Pepys. It is a tiny smiling face.*

12 *The court of King's Bench (by Hollar), where Pepys faced the judges, took up part of the north end of Westminster Hall, next to the court of Chancery (right). It was a noisy meeting place for lawyers, traders and cutpurses, where 'men of straw' showed their testimony was for sale by sticking a straw in their shoe.*

MR SAMUEL PEPYS
Given to Sir Jas. Houblon 1681

13 *Samuel Pepys. This portrait (artist unknown) was a gift from a grateful Pepys to his friend James Houblon. Pepys joked about having bribed Houblon's children into reminding their father of his kindness. Fondness aside, the strain of the ordeal can be seen in Pepys's face.*

14 and 15 John Scott acquired a copy of this map of Britain by Carr and Tooker (right), replaced their names with his and published it as his own (see detail below). This was typical of his plagiarism but he committed more serious offences when he offered maps of England's coastline and coastal defences to the French.

EEN Perfecte aenwijsing om te reysen door Englandt by Post, seven Engelsche mijlen yeder uyre in de Somer, ende vijf in de winter, gelijck een order in alle Post-huysen daer van te vinden is.

Beschryvinge van alle de Post-wegen die in Engelandt zyn, van LONDEN tot EDENBURGH in Schotland, de Plaetsen alwaer men versche Paerden kan krijgen, de wijdte en distantien, met de namen en Post-wegen, die van de principale Steden en andere Steden, Casteelen ende Dorpen, uyt-spruyten in yder Provintien Welck bekent sijn by verscheyde Teykens of Caracters als hier boven is aenwijsende, seer noodigh voor alle reysende persoonen in 't voorseyde Koningrijck. In 't light gebracht en geteyckent door J. S.

quinque milliaria in hyeme unâ conficiuntur.
minorum viarum à præcipuis Civitatibus aliisque Urbibus excurrentium, per

JOHANNEM SCOT, Nobilem Anglum.

16 The Wreck of the Gloucester *by Johan Danckerts. The painting makes it look as if the ship has been gently beached. In reality, the wreck was a violent catastrophe that cost the lives of nearly half the 350 people on board.*

governor John Winthrop and his government, the powerful John Scott seemed the ideal person to persuade all the Long Island villages to enter into Connecticut's control. He approached Scott, and Scott accepted. Winthrop awarded him magistrate's powers to negotiate for Connecticut and, on 14 December, Scott swore an oath that he would carry out the charge faithfully.[25]

But when Scott approached the Long Island villages, he quickly realised that they had no desire to be ruled by Connecticut. Five of the villages had joined together to form a 'combination' and protect themselves from Connecticut's pressure. Their 'combination' needed a leader. Though Scott came representing Connecticut, they knew he had been a Long Island man from the start. They invited him to break his oath to Connecticut and become their president.[26]

It was the most critical decision of his life. Connecticut was one of the two most powerful colonies of the New World. If he rejected Connecticut's friendship, he would become leader of a weak alliance of Baptists, Mennonites and Quakers. He should have turned down the presidency out of hand. But Scott knew something that very few others in America did. His suggestion back in London that the Dutch should be pushed out of the New World had gathered pace, and before he left he had heard it whispered that the King's brother, the Duke of York, was to be the inheritor of the conquered lands. If Scott was in control of Long Island when the Duke arrived, then he would be the obvious choice for governor. Looking ahead to a royalist future, on 11 January 1664 he broke his promise to his allies in Connecticut and accepted the title of president of the Long Island villages, to remain so until the King or the Duke established a government there.[27]

Filled with visions of King Charles congratulating him and the court applauding, he set about taking Long Island for the English. He summoned 170 men, and demanded that the Dutch villages surrender. Peter Stuyvesant, the Dutch governor, called Scott's forces a 'ragged troop intent upon plunder', but Scott was serious.[28] Every-where he threatened fire and violence. At Breukelen, he whipped a little boy about the head and neck with his rattan stick because the boy would not take off his hat to the royal flag. The rest of the Dutch inhabitants proved equally unwilling to bow to President Scott and his English king. When New Utrecht failed to recognise King Charles's authority, Scott's forces captured the blockhouse and fired a royal salute. Stuyvesant sent three envoys to deal with him, but Scott was incandescent. 'I will stick my rapier in the guts of any man who says this is not the king's land,' he cried to them. In the heat of the moment, he yelled out that the Duke of York would take not just New Amsterdam but the whole of New Netherland.[29] The Dutch, who had no idea their colonies were in any such danger, heard this in horror. The English were planning to conquer them. Scott's revelation sent Stuyvesant hurrying to fortify his city and strengthen his military. Meanwhile, Scott's attack failed and fizzled out.

Stuyvesant wrote home asking for reinforcements of ships and men. In return, he was sent a motley crew of sixty soldiers and some helpful advice about building fortifications. The Dutch at home anxiously asked Charles II to confirm that the western end of Long Island was rightfully theirs. Charles did not bother to reply. He was bent on conquest. He had been told by two of Scott's friends at court, Berkeley and Carteret, that three ships and 300 men would be sufficient to conquer New Netherland. On 12 March, he gave his brother a patent for a great tract of land in the New World which took in Long Island and the Dutch lands. The Duke swung into action to claim it.

Meanwhile, Scott's small military adventure had proved a disaster. He had upset the Dutch, the Connecticut authorities and even the Long Island villagers, who were now swallowed up by Connecticut. Governor Winthrop was furious that Scott had broken his promise to act on Connecticut's behalf. On 10 March, the Hartford court drew up a proclamation for Scott's arrest listing ten charges from 'seditious practices and tumultuous carriages' to 'usurping authority, forgery and profanation of God's Holy Day'.[30]

They sent a marshal to make the arrest. He was John Gilbert, a literal man. Told to demand speedy answers from people who might know where Scott was, he charged the deputy governor of Massachusetts with abetting and concealing Scott before the poor man had a chance to open his mouth.[31] Despite this excessive zeal, it took nine days and the help of a company of armed men for Gilbert to find Scott – at home. They seized him, then – afraid Scott would be rescued – Gilbert hired natives to lead them to Hartford by back-woods trails. Scott was committed to gaol wearing long iron chains and foot-locks.

Those who believed Scott really was an agent of the Crown anxiously spoke out against his arrest. The governor of New Haven, where the people remembered the good services Scott had done them in London, wrote to Connecticut complaining of the 'surprisal of Capt. Scott', who was 'taken violently from off his own land'.[32] There was a popular groundswell of pro-Scott protest, supported by numerous petitions; one from Flushing said that if the people would not rise for Scott 'the very stones' might justly do so. His wife, 'big with child' and generally pitied, visited him in gaol, and her father left his trade deals in Long Island to support them.[33]

Scott's trial in Hartford, Connecticut, lasted from 18–24 May. Before it even began, Winthrop's court had his estates sequestered.[34] Scott was brought to the bar in chains. He was a difficult prisoner and at one point the gaoler was ordered to load him with additional irons. But his complaints were of no benefit. He was found guilty of the ten charges, fined, and imprisoned.[35] The Duke of York, in whose name he had acted, whose future favour he had hoped for, and for whom he was now put in gaol, was probably not even aware of his name. No one in London was talking about John Scott as Governor of Long Island, because the Duke had kept the post for himself. His deputy governor, who would remain in America, was one Colonel Richard Nicolls. No thought was given to the man whose suggestion had started the ball rolling, and Scott's petition was entirely forgotten.

Colonel Nicolls set sail from England with a squadron of three small men-of-war and a transport, carrying ninety-two guns and 450 veteran soldiers. The Dutch ambassador in London watched it go uneasily, but Charles reassured him that its purpose was purely to settle disputes within his own colonies.[36] Nicolls, knowing the court's high opinion of Scott, was looking forward to consulting him when he arrived. He could not know that as he sailed, Governor Winthrop was celebrating Scott's prosecution with a triumphant trip into Long Island.[37]

It should have been a long imprisonment for Scott, but he broke out of his garret cell, let himself down by rope and fled Connecticut, his hopes for his life in pieces.

14

New Amsterdam

In the month he had been imprisoned, Governor Winthrop's court had impounded most of what John Scott owned. All he still had in the world was a hidden casket holding the Gothersons' jewels. He collected it, then he got out of America, making for Barbados to consider his options.

By some means, he got the Gothersons' son into the custody of an New England innkeeper as he fled. The boy had received nothing of the noble education he had been promised. Dorothea Gotherson, who received Scott's letters with undiminished trust, believed that Scott tried to take her son with him to Barbados, but the boy 'was afraid to go and ran into the woods', and was taken in and cared for at Scott's request. Others speculated that Scott either 'barbarously sold him or left him to shift for himself', and the man who later found the boy declared it the 'worst of all' Scott's crimes against the Gothersons.[1] If we believe Dorothea, Scott behaved gallantly. If we believe the rest, he needed some ready cash to supplement the jewels he had stolen from her.

Scott lay low in Barbados through the early summer of 1664, lodging with a merchant and keeping quiet about his recent history. Meanwhile, Colonel Nicolls's little fleet arrived on the coast of New England to conquer the Dutch and take their land for the Duke of York. To allay the suspicion of the anxious Dutch colonists, Nicolls blandly told them that he was just there to examine the English colonies.[2]

Scott heard of Nicolls's arrival, realised its true purpose and saw his opportunity. He had, after all, accepted the presidency on Long Island in the Duke of York's name and had hoped to be his servant. The Duke was about to become the new power in America; Scott could resurrect his tattered reputation through the Duke's man Colonel Nicolls. He returned to New England, the scene of his crime, to work his way into Nicolls's favour.

The fleet's target was New Amsterdam, the capital of New Netherland. It had started as a Dutch trading post in 1624 and grew slowly as the Dutch West India Company provided free one-way tickets and tax breaks to new colonists. By now there was an earth-walled fort containing the barracks, the Governor's house and a church. Outside its walls stood a windmill and some 350 houses, mostly stone or brick-built and covered in red and black tile in the Dutch fashion. It was a hopeless place to defend. The fort had no water supply and its walls were in some places as little as 10 feet high. The town contained only 150 soldiers and 250 civilians capable of bearing arms. Its sole defence, besides the fort, was the makeshift rampart along Wall Street. Invaders had only to climb a hill to the north of the town to command the streets below by pistol shot.

Nicolls, sailing in fog, had been separated from his other ships on the transatlantic passage. He had arrived in Boston and found Massachusetts (always the most rebellious colony) entirely unhelpful, fearing that royal domination over the Dutch might in turn lead to their own suppression. John Scott raced to Boston and wrote a flowery, effusive letter to Nicolls. It had no impact on the weathered, warlike colonel. Nicolls's men thought Scott's letter inflated and vacuous, and one described it as 'bombase stuff'.[3] So Scott rushed to New Haven, and asked permission to press men into his service, so he could help Nicolls fight the Dutch. That colony remembered how he had helped them in London, and disliked his enemy Connecticut. They believed Scott wielded genuine royal authority, and they provided him with men.[4] Armed, Scott set off for Manhattan.

Colonel Nicolls made his way to the western end of Long Island, gathering armed support from the colonists as he went. The Dutch at New Amsterdam had been fooled by false information coming from London about the purpose of Nicolls's fleet. They were not expecting any aggression. The Dutch governor, Peter Stuyvesant, had not prepared any defences and was upriver managing other affairs. When he realised that his vulnerable colony was under attack he hurried back to New Amsterdam, told the population to start digging and building fortifications, organised a military guard on the town, and called for ammunition.

The English ships anchored in the Narrows between New Utrecht and Coney Island, shutting up the mouth of the river. They captured the blockhouse on Staten Island. Scott arrived with his men from New Haven. The Dutch inside New Amsterdam had a sense that the gathering forces outside wanted plunder and bloodshed, but Nicolls maintained order.[5] He sent Stuyvesant a letter demanding generous terms. He wanted the inhabitants to submit. Those who did would suffer neither damage to themselves, nor loss of their property. Stuyvesant, worried his colonists would capitulate on hearing the terms, tore Nicolls's letter passionately to pieces. The word spread, the Dutch cried 'The letter! The letter!' and Stuyvesant was forced to reassemble it and have a copy made to avoid a mutiny.

When the terms were made public, the people begged him to surrender. 'I come with ships and soldiers,' Nicolls told him, 'raise the white flag of peace on the fort.'[6] Stuyvesant defiantly declared he would rather be carried out dead than surrender and on 25 August 1664 the attack began. English troops marched towards his town. Two English frigates swept up the bay under full sail and anchored opposite the town, intending 'if any resistance were offered to pour a full broadside into this open place and so to take the city by assault, giving up everything to plunder and massacre'.[7] Stuyvesant, standing on the wall of Fort Amsterdam with a gunner holding a lighted match beside him, watched the ships pass. The public drew up a petition urging him not to resist, since it could only mean 'misery, sorrow, conflagration, the dishonour of women, murder of children in their cradles, and in a word the absolute ruin and destruction of about fifteen hundred innocent souls'.[8] On 29 August, Stuyvesant gave up the fort and town. He and his soldiers marched out with all the honours of war, boarded their ships and sailed for Holland. Nicolls occupied the fort. In honour of his royal master James, Duke of York, he renamed it Fort James, and gave the town the name it bears today: New York. The project that Scott had set in motion back in London – to take America for the English – was complete.

Since England held Scott in esteem, Nicolls did too. Within three days, he granted Scott a pass to get him back safe to his estate without hindrance from Connecticut.[9] But Winthrop stepped in. He explained that Scott was a fugitive from justice and asked Nicolls either to return him to Hartford prison or fine him £250. Scott's friends persuaded him to pay the fine. He had to borrow the £250 from one of these, Major General John Leverett, who wanted security. Scott left him a locked chest containing, he said, the yellow wax seal and writing he had been given by the King.

Nicolls had every intention of consulting with Scott, thinking him 'one well acquainted with the place'. One of Nicolls's party, Edward Sackville, had a high opinion of Scott (it seems likely that their acquaintance dated from Scott's time in Whitehall) and Sackville 'once or twice' invited Nicolls and Scott to dine together with him. But Scott's train of cheats was beginning to catch up with him and both Sackville and Nicolls changed their minds about him within a month. Sackville learnt that Scott had cheated an illiterate man, by persuading him to sign a paper he could not read, and thought it 'very foul'. Nicolls also saw through Scott's façade of nobility and quality, and eventually 'found him so inconsiderable a fellow and so great a liar that he would not suffer Scott any longer to come to him'. As he felt his chance to ingratiate himself with Nicolls slipping away, Scott's stories became wilder and more grandiose. He pretended he had made a long journey in France, a country he did not know well. Nicolls, suspicious of the claim, asked him about his route. When Scott finished his tortured account of the fictitious journey, Nicolls told him he had travelled 1,500 miles further than he needed to and, turning to Sackville, cried 'God's wounds! What a fellow have you brought me here?'

Scott could never be Governor of Long Island, and now his chances of being employed in the Duke's regime seemed to be fading altogether. He went back and forth between Long Island and New York all that winter, but Nicolls's mind was made up and Scott could not ingratiate himself. Then Nicolls summoned a great meeting to introduce the colonists to their new government, and Scott saw a final opportunity.

Nicolls asked for two delegates from each English town to attend the meeting, which was to be at Hempstead on 10 March 1665. Scott, desperate now to find a way into the government, even at the lowest level, bought land in the town he thought would be most forgiving and got himself elected. But Nicolls also intended to resolve any land disputes at the meeting and as it approached, memories of the displaced townspeople of Setauket and the money he had taken from Southton and Southold began to haunt Scott. He 'developed a great apprehension that he would be attacked by the towns and people he had abused'. He set out for the meeting carrying a letter from Lord John Berkeley and Sir George Carteret praising his character. They had given it to him in London when life was good; he thought it might be enough to buy Nicolls's favour and protect him from attack.

It was so cold at the meeting that the beer froze in its barrels. Scott quickly realised that he and the other delegates would not be given any power. Governor Nicolls would head an unelected council, and there would be a new legal code, the 'Duke's Laws'. This was John Scott's first experience of the Duke of York's dislike of representative government, which fourteen years later would excite such a profound anxiety in England. When Nicolls turned to local matters, violent complaints did indeed erupt against Scott. Southton and Southold complained they had never received the Charters of Freedom they had paid him to get. The delegates from displaced Setauket told Nicolls of the trick he played on them when he built his mansion.

His brief 'presidency' also returned to haunt him; the Long Island towns complained about his armed rampage over the island. Other delegates shouted complaints. To defend himself, Scott whipped out Berkeley and Carteret's letter.

Endorsement from these powerful men helped him to quieten the complaints, which Nicolls mediated carefully. Scott's obligation to get Southton and Southold's charters was cancelled, to his relief. However, the last remnants of his time as a man of influence were taken from him. His swindled estate was confiscated and returned to the people of Setauket. He was ordered to sell the mansion he had built there to one of the returning inhabitants for a reasonable sum. It was all gone; he was plain John Scott again.

But Nicolls was not finished with him; there was a price to pay for his crimes. The governor demanded that Scott produce the document he had forged, the sheet of writing with the King's picture and great yellow wax seal that had driven the Setauket townspeople off their land. Scott was cornered. He had told his friend Major General Leverett in Boston that it was in the locked chest he had left with him, as security for his loan to Scott. Though Leverett did not know it, Scott had lied to him – the document was not in the chest. But Scott could not produce it because, although it had been convincing enough to fool the people of Setauket, his attempt at the King's signature would not fool Colonel Nicolls. He said he did not have it with him. Nicolls ordered him to produce it in court in October or face imprisonment.[10]

From the moment of that order, Scott's time in New England began to run out. He was under a legal obligation to produce a document that would expose him as a cheat. Within two weeks he was 'packing away', and had sold what he had left.[11] But he dallied, apparently uncertain where to go next, until his decision was, quite unexpectedly, made for him. In June, well ahead of the October deadline, Colonel Nicolls decided to arrest him.

It was the end of the American adventure for the miller's son. He had been brave, brazen, ruthless and inventive in the name of ambition. He had dressed himself up, persuaded England that he was that which he was not and had come so tantalisingly close to making a success of it that he had nearly been appointed Governor of Long Island. Now, everything, even his house, had been taken from him. He was not the type of man to explain the failure as a failure on his part. He could not see that he had built on the sand of lies and that the problem lay with himself. He felt in his bones that he had deserved what he aimed for. So he turned to fury and cast about angrily for the man responsible. The culprit was clear: it was the same man who had taken the governorship from him, and now held it in his place; the same man whose servant, Nicolls, had rejected his advances and driven him from America. It was the Duke of York.

Scott's fury at the Duke manifested itself in the most extraordinary way, and it was quite probably for this that Colonel Nicolls decided to arrest him (though he used the pretext that Scott had cheated a man out of £80). That month, news had reached Nicolls that Sir George Carteret and Lord John Berkeley, Scott's friends in London and close confidants of the Duke of York, had been given a huge tract of land west of the Hudson River. The lands under Nicolls's governorship were to be divided up. Nicolls's 'surprise was grievous', says one authority.[12] Only a few weeks earlier he had renamed Long Island 'Yorkshire' and conferred lands in a new 'Albania' to his associates. Abruptly, 'Albania' was no more; in honour of Carteret's defence of the Channel Islands, the territory was named New Jersey.

From the point of view of the colonists and the New York administration, the division was a disaster. In November, Nicolls wrote to the Duke to convey, in barely restrained terms, the enormous scale of the error. What the Duke had given away was the most 'improvable' tract of land he had, and of such a scale that it was 'capable of receiving twenty times more people than Long Island and the remaining tracts'. The land's fertility and potential for rich mines had been great attractions to settlers. Nicolls suggested offering Berkeley and Carteret a different stretch of land on the coast. He absolved the two men, saying they could not know how 'prejudicial' the grant would be. He had no doubt who the true criminal was: 'Capt. Scott, who was born to work mischief.' Scott's motive, Nicolls believed, was that he had 'aimed at the same patent' that the Duke received 'and has given out that he had injury done him by his Royal Highness'.[13] Nicolls's suspicions are borne out by the facts; Scott received a one-hundredth share of west New Jersey for his part in the affair.[14] Nicolls believed New York would become the pre-eminent town in America within five years, if it was not divided. His advice went unheeded. Throughout colonial times, the governors of New York protested about it. The existence of New Jersey meant that the state of New York controlled only some of the waters around Manhattan, and that the city could not incorporate its New Jersey suburbs, as it has with the rest of the urban sprawl. Scott's jealousy of the Duke, it seems, has shaped America's first city.

In October, Scott failed to appear in court with the yellow wax seal. His wife came instead and successfully sued to be put into the hands of trustees for the care of herself and her three children, for whom Scott had provided nothing in a year. He had tried to divorce Deborah by post. She had breached his faith, he claimed, by revealing his secrets.

In his absence, the flimsy life he had stolen for himself was dismantled. Colonel Nicolls made much of Scott's abandoned wife and provided her with a house. Trying to lay his hands on Scott's yellow wax seal, Nicolls wrote to Major General Leverett in Boston, who held the chest with it in. Leverett forced the chest open. It was stuffed with old clothes, shoes, stockings and broken bricks.

Accounts differ as to what had happened to Scott. He was either given a tip-off about Nicolls' intention to arrest him, or arrested and gave 'the sheriff the slip'. In the summer of 1665, disguised as a Quaker, he boarded a ship bound for Barbados. There he was looked after by an acquaintance from his last visit and, in token of gratitude, sold him land on Long Island for £200.[15]

He spent two years in the West Indies, and we have only his account of his activities. He describes glorious military successes in which he commanded attacks on Tobago and other Dutch settlements.* He took to making maps. He paid a short visit to burnt London at the end of 1666, then in 1667 came to the next great scene of his life.

The twin volcanic islands of St Kitts and the smaller Nevis faced each other across a narrow channel in the Caribbean. Colonists from France and England had lived peacefully there in close proximity. At the beginning of 1666, when it had become apparent that their mother countries would go to war with each other, the islanders came to a gentleman's agreement; they would refrain from hostilities unless specifically ordered to fight. It was well meant, but it failed. When France and England went to war, the English on St Kitts summoned reinforcements from Nevis as a precaution. The French suspected this was the prelude to a surprise attack and struck first, burning the English houses and cane fields, and driving the 8,000 English off St Kitts. These arrived as refugees on neighbouring islands, putting huge pressure on resources. The English were desperate to take St Kitts back and the governor of Barbados was more than willing to recruit John Scott as one of the officers to lead the attack.

On the morning of 8 June 1667, 1,000-strong force of English and Irish landed on the beaches of St Kitts, with Scott among them. They meant to land before dawn but they sailed late and by the time the ships began to cross the strait between the two islands, there was enough light in the sky for the French lookouts on the finger of St Kitts to give the warning that the English were coming. French forces got in place to trap the invaders on the landing beach. 'And now,' wrote Scott in a report afterwards, 'began the tragedy.'[16]

Unknown to the English, the French had garrisoned St Kitts with a veteran regiment from Picardy, a regiment of regular cavalry and 2,500 planters in arms. The attackers did not stand a chance. Penned up on the beach and under fire, the Irish panicked and broke away,

---

* There is also a version told by a Captain Byam, but the surviving copy of Byam's account is in Scott's handwriting and cannot count as verification.

attempting to climb a gully. Trapped in this unfavourable position they were quickly taken. In his description, Scott stressed that they had given up rather too easily.

The Irish desertion left the depleted English force on the beach to be shot, and what followed was a massacre. Of the 1,000 who had landed, 506 were killed on the beach, and 284 wounded, most of them mortally; 140 were taken prisoner.[17] However, a determined band of a hundred or so survived. Scott was one of them. From their vulnerable position below, these men continued to fire heroically at the enemy. The French charged at them with horses again and again, until the English, refusing to surrender, threw themselves into the sea and swam for the ships, which ventured bravely towards the shore to rescue them. Many drowned. Only seven men, Scott among them, were rescued.

That, at least, was the version of his conduct that Scott sent the English government a month afterwards. The captured Irish gave an entirely different account.[18]

They said that while the invaders were under fire on the beach, a lieutenant colonel found Scott's company without an officer. When questioned, the soldiers pointed to a low cliff. Tucked up as close as he could get to the foot of it was Scott. The lieutenant colonel drew his sword to persuade him out, but Scott refused to move. Asked whether he was not ashamed, Scott claimed that he had lost sight of his men. He was next seen stripped of his clothes urging his men to show a white flag. A soldier who heard that Scott intended to swim away to the boats warned Scott if he so much as stirred, he would personally knock his brains out. Scott hurriedly put his clothes back on and tried a new tactic. Claiming to be wounded, he was taken out to the *Jersey* frigate. Another soldier saw Scott come into the great cabin to report the hurt he had received to his shoulder. He was obliged to strip off to have the wound dressed, but when stripped there was no sign of damage.

Scott's account was a fudge. On 12 July, over a month after the attack, Scott was sent as an emissary to the French on St Kitts. His task was to negotiate the release of the captured soldiers. But he played a neat trick. He had no intention of freeing men who had witnessed his cowardice. So he behaved badly at the tense meeting, and used 'abusive language' with the French governor, to the horror of some of the well-bred Irish officers.[19] He got forty of the 140 prisoners released, but the Irish prisoners who had been witnesses to Scott's cowardice were left in French hands. The moment the negotiation ended and Scott left, the furious imprisoned Irish wrote their account of his behaviour during the attack.

That same day Scott returned to Nevis and (even as the Irish were writing theirs) wrote his fictitious account of the battle, casting himself as a military hero. The only men who could deny it were safely in French hands. Perhaps an account of his bravery while under fire would impress his old Whitehall associates into forgetting his American crimes. When he got to Nevis he complained that the Irish were inappropriately friendly with the French governor and four days later, he wrote to his old London friend Joseph Williamson to suggest that the imprisoned Irish were traitors, and not to be trusted.[20]

As a result, the governor of Barbados sent Scott to England believing he was a hero and an authority on the battle. On arrival in London, Scott sought out Williamson, gave him his fictitious account of the battle and handed him a letter from the governor recommending him as one who 'did his part better than some that may pretend to have done more'. The governor had no complaint, his letter said, against Scott, but against 'some others' – the fraternising, turncoat Irish.[21]

Then, on 3 January 1668, news that the war was over reached Nevis and St Kitts, and the French released their Irish prisoners. The Irish gave their account of the battle and Scott's behaviour in it. The next day the Governor of Barbados arrived and court-martialled Scott in his absence for cowardice.[22] The Irish prisoners swore to their account and the governor concluded that Scott was guilty and – had he not made off – could not have been saved by his 'smooth language'.[23] Two weeks later the governor again wrote to Williamson, sheepishly revising his original endorsement of Scott's account: 'perchance he has told you some truth,' he wrote, 'but not all gospel'.[24] But by this point, Scott was back in the fold in London, for the first time in four years.

He had begun to correspond with Sir Joseph Williamson and other court grandees again. But his old relationship with the Crown had been compromised. From late 1667, the government had been hearing about Dorothea Gotherson's non-existent land on Long Island. At the end of January 1668, Scott was briefly imprisoned for debt, and sent Lord Arlington a desperate letter detailing his good services to the Crown.[25] Arlington released him, but about the same time, the damaging news from Barbados arrived. By July, Williamson was openly displaying his dislike of Scott, leaving Scott scrabbling around to guess why.[26]

Among his possessions, Scott had a paper dated 29 August 1668. It was a warrant appointing 'our trusty and well beloved Major John Scott' to the position of Royal Geographer. In the context of Scott's declining relationship with the Crown it seems likely that the document was a forgery, and that Scott never held the position. However, when one bears in mind that Scott's friend Lord Arlington (who, long ago, had supported his petition to become Governor of Long Island) had recently been promoted in government, the matter becomes uncertain. Arlington may have helped Scott to the position, which was one Scott might well have coveted, and perhaps seemed well qualified for with his mapmaking in the West Indies and knowledge of the newly conquered land in America. It is impossible to be sure whether or not Scott ever had the job.[27]

He certainly had no opportunity to enjoy it. In October, Colonel Nicolls, having finished his term as deputy governor of New York, arrived back in London. He was still trying to undo the damage done to New York by the creation of New Jersey. His fervent campaigning put the recipients of New Jersey 'under a cloud'.* Lord Berkeley was 'out of all his offices' in February, and offering to surrender his claim

---

* Nonetheless, of course, New Jersey remained divided from New York.

to the land; it was thought Sir George Carteret would do the same.[28]

Nicolls was the last person Scott wanted to see in London. Nicolls knew everything: he had heard the charges against Scott on Long Island and he had seen through Scott's façade of respectability. Nicolls told the King, Queen and the Duke of York about Scott's crimes and his lavish, extravagant claims of having received their favour. His lies were completely exposed. It was more than he could bear. His last hopes of greatness in London were dashed. At the sight of Nicolls, he fled Whitehall.[29]

15

The Fallen Man

I must live.

JOHN SCOTT TO WILLIAM PERWICH, PARIS, 1674

Samuel Pepys knew nothing of John Scott's crimes in America, his flight from Whitehall or his hatred of the Duke of York. His only clue had come at the end of June 1679, when an informant wondered whether Pepys's accuser might be the same Scott who 'debased himself at St Kitts'.[1] But that was all Pepys knew.

John Brisbane's paralysis meant Pepys had very little from France, and Balty's first investigations had yielded only unripe and undersize fruit. The best harvest so far had come from the Low Countries, which were well stocked, it seemed, with Scott's crimes. It was hard to tell what kind of a criminal Scott was, however. At times he seemed petty, comical, even ludicrous. A Captain Platt related how, while he was garrisoned in a Flanders town, Scott had befriended him, then tried to persuade him to let French invaders slip in and take the town at night. Platt refused. Scott tried to involve him in a plan to con £100 out of a merchant at Bruges. Once more, Platt refused, so Scott, disgruntled, stole his scarf and ran off.[2]

The Low Countries information came to Pepys as fragments, peoples' individual encounters with Scott. Alone, they gave little sense of the whole man. But as they arrived and Pepys assembled them, the picture swam towards focus and then snapped clear; a portrait of the man Scott had been a decade before Pepys encountered him. Both Scott and Pepys had been in their late thirties then, but the difference in their lives could not have been starker.

Pepys, who had been on the verge of putting aside his Diary, was already thought the 'right hand of the Navy'. He had been master of a fine household; owner of a coach and a pair of black horses, and rich enough to retire comfortably if necessary.[3] At the same point in his life, John Scott had been a dissolute, fallen man.

Scott came to the Low Countries after his American crimes caught up with him in England and drove him from Whitehall. Exposed and rejected, he spat bitter words about England and the court to anyone who would listen. He seethed about the Duke of York casting him – as he saw it – out of his Long Island premiership. He claimed that he had killed one of the Duke's pages, and could not return to England for fear of being hanged.[4] This murder was Scott's revenge, violent but fictitious; he found refuge in fantasy. The greatest disaster of his life had been reinvented as a deep rivalry with the Duke who, he said, was now cruelly pursuing him.[5] Where he had once sought noble English status, he now tried to shed all remnants of his Englishness. He told people that he had been born in Leyden, Holland, and was related to a wealthy family in Zeeland.[6] In Harlem he associated with 'an ancient gentleman' called Colonel Wogan, as well as a Mr William Cole, a Dr Richardson and a Mr Ray, alias John Phelps. Pepys added a note to this particular attestation. Cole and Richardson were proclaimed traitors. Wogan and Ray had been members of the 'pretended High Court of Justice that murdered K. Charles I'.[7] Scott had sought out the regicides.

Financially, he was in a desperate state. His only skill was with his pen and he made a slender living drawing maps. He had no great cartographical skill, but he knew how to copy and decorate, and his elegant work ensnared inquisitive men. One of these, a London merchant called Edmund Custis, was particularly taken by a map of St Domingo, which he spotted in Scott's chamber in The Hague. Scott had brought many maps of towns, fortifications, coastlines and ports with him to the Low Countries. Among these (a detail which did not escape Pepys later) were several of the most important English forts and ports. Knowing, however, that it would be easier to sell local maps, Scott set to work. Custis walked into his chamber one day to find him copying a map of Brabant. Watching him, Custis realised that Scott was changing details of the original – distances, buildings, beaches – 'of his own brains', so that it would seem as though he had done the fieldwork.[8] He wanted to be thought an authentic cartographer. It was a cheap trick, but Scott pursued the work with the commitment of an artist. His room was tucked away at the back of his landlord's house. He called his workdays 'days of quiet'.[9]

The maps themselves earned him little, and it was not in Scott's nature to spend a lifetime collecting cockleshells when he could swap his 'cockleshells for jewels'.* To win jewels, some cunning was required. He told Custis that he intended to publish a book of his maps, and offered him a half-price copy if Custis would stump up in advance. Custis, a self-confessed 'lover and encourager of works of that kind', paid him the tidy sum of 100 guilders. He never got the book, nor his money back. The trick was humdrum, Scott's bread and butter, and before long he came up with a grander plan to raise himself in the world again.[10]

Holland was the most powerful state in the United Provinces. Its leader was Grand Pensionary Johan de Witt, a talented politician and intelligent mathematician. This was the level John Scott liked to aim at. De Witt received a note that 'one Major General Scott, one of the greatest engineers in the world', was in Holland with charts of all the islands and fortifications in the West Indies, and was 'capable to do much good or hurt to the States of Holland'. It was, the note instructed, 'most necessary' that Scott be courted.[11] Scott is surely the most likely author of the note. De Witt summoned him, and he came bearing maps showing the main English harbours and their depths, claiming that they would allow the Dutch to make a surprise attack on England.[12] De Witt swallowed this, promptly made Scott a lieutenant colonel and gave him a regiment of foot soldiers.[13]

It should be said, in Scott's defence, that the serious crime he now

---

* The phrase is John Brisbane's.

perpetrated while commanding this regiment was not his idea. A lawyer who had some private beef against the victim, Charles Dispontyn, was the real architect of the crime and it was the lawyer who first approached Scott.[14]

Dispontyn was the official responsible for paying Scott's regiment. In the spring of 1671, the lawyer, John van der Heyde, asked Scott if he would claim that the regiment's pay had never arrived and that Dispontyn had embezzled it. The lawyer told Scott he had powerful friends in government and they would get Scott promoted to colonel if he charged Dispontyn. There would be a financial reward too. Van der Heyde was an intimidating and perceptive man, and had chosen his target well. Though Scott confessed that Dispontyn 'had always done honestly by' him and that he held Dispontyn in high esteem, the dual temptations of wealth and promotion fired his restless ambition. He accepted van der Heyde's offer.

That Dispontyn was an impeccable bureaucrat and did pay Scott's regiment, as normal, is quite clear from the many subsequent testimonies he gathered in his defence. The payment was made on 15 May 1671, in the front room of a house in The Hague. A serving girl came in and out fetching wine, bread and cheese for the group of men. When Scott signed for receipt of the payment in a grey parchment-covered account book, the servant laughed at his spidery handwriting, saying, 'Sir, those are Polish letters which you write, I could make better.' She remembered it all vividly. The windows were open. She shut them in the evening. Two days after, Scott – his eyes on the reward – denied his signature before the aldermen of The Hague, and claimed Dispontyn had falsified the account and kept the money.

Eight years later, Pepys, reading the documents that told this story, cannot have failed to note the striking similarity between this case and his own: Scott had willingly lied under oath.

Dispontyn was imprisoned. One of the men who had been in the room in The Hague tried to persuade Scott to stop denying what was palpably his signature but Scott continued to pretend the signature was a forgery, in public at least. Privately, he was unashamedly open about the lie. His new money made it transparent in any case, for he loved to spend. Before long, someone noticed that he had become 'very magnificent in his habit'. When asked 'how he came to be so fine in Holland who went so plain in England', Scott replied with a bold smile that he got the money by a cheat.[15]

Scott and van der Heyde put pressure on the soldiers in the regiment to support their lies about Dispontyn, but the soldiers all refused. Scott was making mistakes, confessing his crime to too many people, not one of whom was as impressed with it as he was. But the decision that brought the affair down upon his head was his attempt to silence a woman called Deborah Egmond.

Deborah had drawn Scott's eye. She had come into contact with his regiment through a friend's brother, was twenty-five and unmarried. Scott was a strutting peacock from the moment they met, flamboyantly introducing himself as 'John Scott of Scot's Hall, Shield Bearer and Geographer to the King of Great Britain'. Quite possibly he was as attracted to her well-connected family, which served in the house of Orange, as he was to her. She returned little interest but Scott was proud of his powers of seduction (remember the married Quaker woman in England) and pursued her, even to the point of slavishly creeping around outside her house in The Hague. She continued to resist until, one day, he caught up with her wagon on a white horse and jumped in with her. This romantic display met with a cold reception. Deborah knew that Scott had been paid the money by Dispontyn, and she thought his lie despicable. She knew she was right, she said, because she had seen the money.

'What have you to do with that?' Scott asked, 'I would not have you say anything of your seeing that money.'

He tried to pretend he was not the criminal but the victim, and ranted about how Dispontyn was a rogue and a rascal and a liar. He was unconvincing, and she remained furious with him, so he gave up the charade (and any chance of romance) and offered her 400 guilders for a signed note retracting the claim, for his future security. She was wealthy already and did not need his bribe; she pulled the glove off her hand to show him a gold ring she wore. Scott's lie had affronted her profoundly. She told Dispontyn what had been said.

Scott's perpetual flaw, as Pepys had discovered from his cells in the Tower and King's Bench, was that he underestimated the depth of bad feeling that his cheats generated. What for him was a momentary thing, a means to an end, a rung on the golden ladder that carried him up towards the person he wanted to become, was for his victims an insult that was impossible to forget. He had abused Dispontyn, and self-confident Deborah Egmond counted herself among Dispontyn's friends. She would find a way to get justice for him.

As promised, Scott was made a colonel for his crime, and he clung to it proudly, for it was a legitimate and official promotion.* When his money ran out again he more or less disappeared from The Hague. Dispontyn remained in prison, gathering evidence against Scott, and visited by Deborah. From time to time, to keep Dispontyn locked up, Scott sent word that he would appear with evidence. Pepys, who by the time he was bailed had appeared in court four times without Scott prosecuting him, must have begun to wonder if Scott was doing the same thing to him.

Scott owed money when he left The Hague, to a shoemaker, a tailor and a sword cutler there.[16] He was somewhat anxious about coming back, for fear they would arrest him. Just in case, he timed his return to coincide with the arrival of the new English ambassador.[17] As the ambassador entered the town, Scott slipped through the crowd and joined his retinue, hoping for diplomatic immunity. He could still remember how to play the role of gentleman. But nothing could protect him from Deborah Egmond.

She was standing on a table to get a look at the new ambassador. When she caught sight of Scott she leapt from it, ran to him, took hold of him, swore at him, and demanded he come to answer the wrong he had done the imprisoned Dispontyn. He was having none

---

* He had awarded himself the title of captain before this. He was still using 'colonel' when he accused Pepys in the Commons.

of it, so she rushed to Dispontyn. Quick investigations revealed that Scott was not part of the ambassador's retinue at all. Deborah got a warrant for Scott's arrest and took it to the ambassador's house, where Scott was trying to ingratiate himself, but Scott made his escape out of the back door. He never reappeared in The Hague, reported Deborah, who was clearly ready to take action if he did. Dispontyn was discharged, but never got compensation for his long imprisonment. Deborah's fury at Scott brought her to Pepys's aid in 1679. She called him 'Squire Pips'.[18]

As for Scott, he was hounded and unable to penetrate into any powerful circles. He fruitlessly dedicated copperplate maps to a British diplomat, Sir William Temple, but in the end was reduced to stealing a bottle of sherry in his name.* He was a very long way from where he imagined his life might take him. He was at the end of his tether, addicted to the pursuit of greatness but exhausted by it, and a wanted man in every corner of the world he had spent time in.

There was a part of him that still wished to get back to England. He had raged against the country after he was driven out, but he had once yearned to be accepted there. (He would have been delighted to know that his promotion to colonel had been noticed.)[19] He was furious with the Duke of York, but at heart that was because he had been denied the opportunity to be the Duke's servant in America. England had been the scene of his greatest achievements; he had been a diplomat, confidant and policy-shaper. Only the narrow Channel separated him from it. At the beginning of 1672, he slipped back into London. The memories of his crimes in America and flight from Whitehall were still alive, so he was taking a risk. Unfortunately for Scott, his former friend, the Under-Secretary of State Joseph Williamson, had his ear to the

---

* Scott and an accomplice collected a bottle of sherry from a vintner, in Temple's name. Lacking a cork, the vintner stopped the bottle with a lemon. He had previously denied Scott a loan, and Scott, taking the opportunity to vent his anger, drew his sword. The story of Scott's outburst made its way back to Temple's table, but Temple had never asked for the sherry and Scott's accomplice trod on the storyteller's toe to silence him. PL, Mornamont MSS, vol. II, pp. 853–4.

ground. The cursory entry in Williamson's journal tells the story: 'Scott taken.' He was arrested.[20]

To the consternation of the Protestant English, it was becoming clear that there would be war with Protestant Holland – another shameful indicator of King Charles's Catholic bias. Joseph Williamson found himself confronted with a dilemma. Given everything that the man had done, Scott should be imprisoned. But on the other hand, here was an Englishman who knew Holland and was accepted there. Who better to keep an eye on the Dutch? Williamson sent him back to Holland 'for intelligence'.[21] Scott, let off the hook and, unexpectedly, a spy serving the Crown, embraced the opportunity. He had a page printed to be bound into an existing book called *The History of the County of Kent in the Kingdom of England*. The alterations showed him to be descended from the Scotts of Scot's Hall.[22] England was once again in his sights.

The third Dutch war began that March when England and France joined forces against Johan de Witt's United Provinces. Soon, wounded Dutch were carried ashore after the first sea-fights while people gathered silently on the quays and in the streets to watch. As the shock subsided, the Dutch began 'railing on the English'.[23] Scott was in an unenviable position, working for both sides – a Dutch soldier and an English spy. And while he was delighted to be back in the fold, the English government's embrace was not warm, for they were under no misapprehensions about his character. One government communication distinguished between Scott and 'honest Englishmen'.[24] Joseph Williamson kept a close eye on his movements, and asked for reports on him from other spies.[25] Wartime double-dealing made Scott understandably anxious. To allay any Dutch suspicions, he noisily told them that he intended to launch a private attack on the English.[26] He tried to avoid taking any active role in the fighting against the English – so much so, that the Dutch became aggravated by his frequent absences. 'Drums are beating all day for Col. Scott and for seamen,' Williamson was informed from Holland, 'and commanding those that are entertained to repair to their duties on pain of death.'[27]

It was an unsustainable position made even harder by the death of Scott's Dutch patron. The armies of the invading French almost reached Amsterdam. William of Orange, coordinating what seemed like a hopeless defence, opened the sluices to flood the surrounding land and stop the French. The Dutch got their courage back and switched their support from de Witt's defeatist republicans to bold William. They turned on the Grand Pensionary de Witt and his brother, dragging them out into the street and putting them brutally to death. Scott took the cue and left the Dutch services.[28] His stock was rising in England; he was spying for Williamson, and he had recently been befriended by the Duke of Buckingham, who was returning from a peace mission in Utrecht.[29] Scott had found favour in the circle of tricksters and criminals that surrounded the Duke, and was allowed to sit at Buckingham's table.[30] Confident that his star was in the ascendant in England, but not at all confident that he would be welcome if he moved back there, he made a professional decision: he would remain in Holland, a full-time English spy.

The English government had posted him to Bruges.[31] He received a yearly allowance for the work, but it was either insufficient, or he found it hard to get paid (a common problem for the Crown's servants abroad), for he came to be known as a dissolute figure among the English in Bruges. A captain there reported that Scott 'was generally hated amongst all the English because of his debauched life and false stories, inventing malicious lies against all such who would not respect him and furnish him with money'.[32] He seems to have been financially incontinent: his possessions included 'a silver belt, a fowling piece or two, two or three copper plates of maps, one great picture of great value and two swords' but he never had any cash and was forced to borrow small amounts.[33] He was staying in an Augustine nunnery when disaster struck. The Dutch caught him at work. He was discovered 'either without or upon the walls of Bruges' sketching the town's fortifications and given forty-eight hours to leave by town officials. In his hurry to get away, he abandoned his most unwieldy possessions and failed to pay the nuns his rent.[34]

Eight miles outside the town, he told local people that he had been robbed nearby, claiming that the thieves had taken his hat, some other belongings and one hundred pistoles (gold coins). The sympathetic locals gave him eighty pistoles as compensation. His hat and belongings were found 'industriously hid' in a hedge before he could collect them.[35] His relations with the Dutch were seriously damaged. He had left their army and been caught spying. His name was mud. His only friends now were the English, and even they were suspicious of him.

John Scott's final disaster followed fast; he made an enemy of the English too. It began in February 1673, when Englishmen in Holland began to disappear.

One was seized in Zeeland. Another was forced to flee Rotterdam. Someone had been telling the Dutch authorities that these men were English spies. Many genuine spies had to go into hiding; one Mr Paine did not dare return to his house. Scott, apparently worried that he would be the next to be picked up, sent an indignant letter to Williamson in London, asking him to find out who was behind it. Six weeks later there were further arrests. Williamson, distressed at this comprehensive attack on his Dutch network and already with some suspicion as to what was going on, charged his loyal agent James Puckle with discovering who 'the author of this mischief' was.[36] In Holland, Puckle made investigations and discovered that it was Scott.

Scott's anxious request for Williamson's help had been a decoy to colour 'his evil practice' – a childish attempt to cover up the crime. He had written to the State of Zeeland, claiming that he loved their country, to tell them 'that their enemies were the English vipers that were among them', and listing the names of men he said were English spies. Sixteen or seventeen of these were in fact not spies at all, but merchants. Quite probably, Scott, who no longer had an army salary, had given their names because he owed them money.

James Puckle brought the news of his discovery straight back home to Lord Arlington and Joseph Williamson at Whitehall. They had suspected that Scott was the culprit. He was the unreliable black sheep of their network. They removed him from his employment as an English spy.

He had fallen as low as it was possible for him to go. Though he had brought the disaster upon himself, John Scott was not above a display of regret. One evening in May 1673, James Puckle found himself outside the town wall at Bruges. Scott approached him, dressed as a milliner, disguised for fear of being recognised in the town he had been banished from. His high hopes for his life had fallen and shattered in pieces, and he was shattered too, a broken man. He accused Puckle of ruining him by giving his name to Arlington and Williamson. With cool professionalism, Puckle listed his sources. Cornered and unable to deny it, Scott fell into a thoughtful silence. He seemed sad. He was sorry, he said, that Arlington was angry with him. Then anger overcame him again and, casting furiously around for the culprit, he focused on the moment when everything had begun to go wrong – when the governorship of Long Island had been taken from him – and he raged against the Duke of York and called him his enemy. Finally, exhausted, he became contrite. He begged Puckle to intercede with the English government on his behalf. He wrote letters listing the ways in which his Dutch knowledge could be useful to the English, and Puckle carried them back to London. But Scott had destroyed his chances. In reply to the letters, Arlington said that Scott had so often abused the favour shown him and 'been so perfidious a knave, his Majesty could never trust him more'.[37]

His bridges burning behind him, out of his Dutch employment, and spurned for the second time in his life by the English, Scott turned to a country that knew nothing of his reputation: France, fast becoming the great enemy of the Protestant people. He took with him the asset he found most easy to transport, and which had proved most beneficial to his income – his maps. He also carried a desk fitted with 'conveniences' for pencils, instruments and paints. He got himself taken under the protection of the Prince of Condé, the veteran commander of King Louis's army in the field, who welcomed his maps of Flanders towns. On arrival in Paris, Scott sought out the best mapmaker in the city, who in turn directed him to the house of a maker of mathematical instruments. The gentleman was away, but his servant led Scott to an Englishman who introduced himself as John Joyne, a watchmaker. Joyne found Scott a room, and Scott set about drawing.[38]

In November 1673, an English agent in Paris was astonished to see Scott there, believing him to be in the 'quite contrary interest' of the Dutch. Scott pretended he was in France because the Prince of Condé had offered his patronage; he was trying to drive his Dutch defeat from his mind. He described his future, intending it to sound full of robust and energetic plans – but the listening English agent heard only a 'thousand chimerical projects'.[39] He made attempts to sell his maps of Dutch towns to the French government, but they would not pay the lump sum he wanted, and would only offer him a small annual pension. He refused; experience had taught him that no government would trust him for long.

In his lodgings, before the English agent and Puckle, he spread out his great many maps: of the East Indies, of Barbados and other English plantations in the West Indies, of Portsmouth, Plymouth and the 'comings in' of the Isle of Wight and Harwich, and draughts of the Thames and Newcastle. He showed them where the weak places were, and where the French should attack the English for greatest effect. The agent became intrigued by the maps and, in a letter to Arlington, recommended 'two which might be of great use to us', of the sea routes into Holland and Zeeland.[40] But he also asked Scott why he would sell English maps to the French king when it was prejudicial to his native country. Scott replied, 'I must live, and you hear from Mr Puckle my own prince rejects my services.'[41]

It was the same treason. The crimes Scott charged Pepys with in 1679 were crimes he had committed himself.

16

Pellissary's Household

Pepys walked out of Westminster Hall on 9 July 1679 free from confinement or close escort for the first time in fifty days. For a man who had acquired a great number of possessions in his life, he found himself in the peculiar position of not having his own house to go to. His comfortable apartment in Derby House, a three-minute walk away, had gone with the job and was no longer his to use. The finely decorated Admiralty barge that carried him on the river, with its damask curtains and cushions, had gone too. A loyal friend saved him from destitution. As a boy servant, Will Hewer had winked at him in the midst of one of Pepys's blazing rows with Elizabeth, and had grown up to be his adviser and confidant.[1] Now Hewer, showing the 'care, kindness and faithfulness of a son', furnished Pepys with rooms in his house in York Buildings, Buckingham Street.* 'God reward him,' Pepys wrote, 'if I cannot.'[2]

London was still thick with prejudice and anxiety, but now the doors of St Stephen's Chapel – the last place Pepys had been as a free man – were firmly shut; the prorogation of 27 May was still in place. The hostile Whig MPs were dispersed to the coffee houses and the political clubs. They were anxious to reconvene but had to bide their

---

* John Scott's patron, George Villiers, Duke of Buckingham, had developed the area after the Great Fire. With the comic self-aggrandisement which came naturally to him, he had named George Street, Villiers Street, Duke Street and Buckingham Street. There was also an Of Alley between the last two, sadly now lost.

time and wait for King Charles's coffers to empty. Then, when he opened the chapel doors and brought them together to ask for funds to maintain the Crown, they would pass the Exclusion Bill and drive his papist brother from England.

Naturally, King Charles was anxious to delay or prevent the meeting of Parliament, scheduled for 14 August. He had no wish to confront the Whigs' anger. In secret, he did the thing most likely to inflame that anger and approached the French ambassador, Paul Barrillon, to request money from Versailles. Louis now preferred to keep England's power divided between the King and an active Parliament. Barrillon, knowing that every snatched conversation with Charles would 'end in a demand for three or four millions', had learnt to coax, play and reject the English king.[3] Denied by the French, Charles was left with two options: to spend until he was forced to meet the Whigs, or dissolve Parliament and hope that the elections would return a friendlier Commons. The first was unthinkable; he would not have this Commons hold the Crown's descent to ransom and deny his brother's inheritance (he thought that his bastard son, the Duke of Monmouth, was Shaftesbury's favourite as heir). On the other hand, his advisers had warned him against dissolution. Whig sentiment was strong, the Plot was running high and the new elections were bound to return a Commons at least as hostile as the previous one – possibly more so, for the people had been deeply troubled by Charles's interruption of parliamentary proceedings.

Pepys's first morning in Hewer's house, a Thursday, got off to a misty start. It grew warmer as the mist burnt off and in the full heat of the day, the King dissolved Parliament.

England flung its arms in the air in fury and set about preparing for the election. It was clear it would be another Whig victory. Some anxious individual even tried to arm that figure of Whig hatred in the Tower, the Earl of Danby, with 'five cases of pistols, some double barrelled'.[4] When the Commons again clamoured for Exclusion and against popery, Pepys could expect the attack on him to redouble. Shaftesbury, Buckingham and William Harbord's cronies would doubtless find a second witness for Scott. The loyal town of Harwich asked Pepys to stand as their MP again, but he declined; it would be madness to excite the MPs by sitting among them. 'My adversary and his upholders,' he confided later to his ageing father in the Huntingdonshire countryside, '. . . shall receive fresh encouragement (as they seem to hope) from the countenance of some persons in the approaching parliament.' For now, he kept that to himself and turned back to building his defence.[5] Bail had not eased his cares.

On the day that Pepys had been pinning Scott in court, his two French merchant allies in Paris had been at work establishing that Scott had not been present at Georges Pellissary's dinner in honour of Sir Anthony Deane. The merchants had gone to the house with the black and white marble floors, and the orange tree and myrtle gardens, where Pellissary's widow lived with her staff in the rue de Cléry. They spoke to a servant who had worked in the house for twenty-three years. He shook his head in bemusement. He remembered that dinner, he said; there had been no stranger present. The same day, the merchants sought out the man who had been chief comptroller of Pellissary's household in 1675. He agreed. There had been no one there except those at the table. He had never met a John Scott; he said he thought that Pellissary had not known him either.[6]

The servant and comptroller's information contained another victory for Pepys. Scott – to explain away the delay between his discovering Pepys's crime and revealing it to the Commons almost four years later – had pretended that Pellissary and Captain Piogerie had sworn him to secrecy, and that he had waited for them to die. Yet Pellissary had died on 15 September 1676 and Piogerie in 1678.[7] Scott could have made his accusation a year earlier. The court would have some questions about that.

To Pepys, the Pellissary household was beginning to look watertight. Pellissary's secretary had said that, though he was trusted by his master, he had never shown him any English naval papers. He, the servant and the comptroller said that Scott was a stranger to them. Even if Scott had, for some reason, been in the house unknown to the servants, it seemed impossible that Pellissary would have shown him secret papers that he did not show his trusted secretary. Here was proof that Pellissary could not have shown Scott any maps. This fact was of 'mighty moment' to Pepys's case.[8]

His investigator, however, was tiring. After a month, the French adventure was wearing thin on Balty. Even his son's enthusiasm for 'the most beautiful town in Europe' might reasonably have started to wane from all the traipsing around it. Balty was pining for his wife; little, retiring Esther, who showed her spirit and wit shyly, and only after a time. Esther and Balty's financial fortunes were pathetically dependent on Pepys's, and had suffered as bail and the 'infinite expenses' of his foreign agents hit his reserves.[9] Will Hewer had taken Esther in too, and she and her other children now shared the palatial York Buildings accommodation. Pepys sent Balty regular reassuring updates on their health – but for Balty, it was a poor substitute for being among them.

It was in Pepys's interests to get Balty home as early as possible too, for it was expensive to maintain him. Pepys had sent Balty many elegantly phrased reminders of the necessity of 'good husbandry' and economy, to the chagrin of Balty, who was taking all the care he could.[10] As his defence began to gain strength, Pepys gave Balty encouraging signals. On 14 July he told Balty he should begin to organise his affairs for returning. A fortnight later, Pepys hoped that 'one post or two' would 'put an end to your absence from home'.[11] He felt that matters were coming to a conclusion: Balty, with the two French merchants, was diligently collecting notarised statements from the Pellissary household; and Pepys had the Marquis de Seignelay's reassuring word. John Brisbane had arrived back in London by 17 July, and took nearly two weeks to see Pepys, but they spoke at length about how best to proceed with the marquis.[12] Pepys would write a letter himself, but did not know who to ask to deliver it, frankly telling Balty that he might be thought too low a messenger. But he was confident of de Seignelay's help. His material defence was getting stronger all the time.

He had a new problem, however. He had plenty of evidence, in the form of witnessed written statements, but he had become unsure whether the court would accept these. At the beginning of June, the jovial barrister Edmund Saunders had advised him on how to have testimonies taken abroad, so that the court would accept the written document without the need for the witness themselves. The method required the help of a foreign court, an English ambassador and the King; for an investigation on the scale of Pepys's, it was impossibly complex. The statements Pepys had were simply witnessed by notaries. By the middle of July, Pepys was beginning to worry that this would not do. English law would not allow written evidence in court, but required that evidence be given *viva voce*, by the witness in person, in the courtroom – 'at least,' Pepys wrote to Balty in some confusion, 'I am as yet informed so; but will endeavour to understand it a little more distinctly.'[13] It might well become necessary to get some of Pellissary's household over in person.

For all Pepys's promises, Balty's return to his family might be far from imminent. Still Pepys continued to encourage him with hopeful little messages.

If witnesses had to appear in person, there would be other problems. The merchant Pelletier, who was helping Balty and whose name appeared all over the French documents, was a Catholic. Pepys, who judged the individual, not their religion, thought Pelletier 'a man of the utmost integrity, and one to whom I am infinitely bound for his generous offer of coming into England on my behalf, and I pray you to return him my most humble thanks accordingly, but such is the captiousness of our age against anything that is not Protestant' that Pelletier could never appear for him in court.[14]

On 14 July, Richard Langhorn was executed, his speech on the scaffold drowned out by the crowd's scorn. Four days later, the Queen's physician Sir George Wakeman was tried for planning to poison the King. Pepys's visitor in the Tower and King's Bench, the diarist and writer John Evelyn, attended the trial. He had no particular liking for capital trials; being an intellectual, he preferred the transcriptions published afterwards to the heat and drama of the courtroom itself. However, he recorded in his Diary, 'I was inclined to be at this signal one, that I might inform myself, and regulate my opinion of a cause that had so alarmed the whole nation.'[15] He was not alone. As for all the Plot trials, London had emptied into Westminster to watch; the Hall was packed with 'innumerable spectators'.

The famous Titus Oates took the stand. His main charge was that he had seen a letter in Wakeman's handwriting detailing a plan to assassinate the King. Oates had not mentioned this detail to the Council when he first told his story the previous autumn. Wakeman asked him why he mentioned the letter only now. Oates impudently asserted he was 'not bound to answer that question'. Scroggs told him that on the contrary, he must. Oates could not. The matter rested and the court turned to other details, but Wakeman wrestled the discussion back. Why had Oates not mentioned his treasonous letter to the Council? Oates answered that he had been up for two days and nights arresting priests when he went before the Council, and 'was scarce *compos mentis*'. Scroggs turned on him.

'What?' he bellowed. 'Must we be amused with I know not what, for being up but two nights? What, was Mr Oates so spent that he could not say, "I have seen a letter under Sir George Wakeman's own hand"?' [16]

In his summing-up, Scroggs ridiculed Oates's excuses and told the jury: 'Never care what the world says, follow your conscience.' After an hour's debate, the jury returned the verdict: not guilty. Discontent rippled through the listening crowd that had stood for nine hours to watch the Plotter brought to justice. That evening, Evelyn enjoyed a civilised supper with the judges, omitting to record anything of their conversation in his Diary. When the Portuguese ambassador attended Scroggs the following day to thank him, rumours flared on the street that Scroggs had been bribed to clear Wakeman. The mob raged and sang ballads condemning him, and a dead dog was thrown through the window of his coach.

Scroggs left London for the circuits, and in the capital the trials paused for the summer break. Wakeman's acquittal had done little to weaken Scroggs's belief in the Plot, however, and he presided over a murderous rampage through the provinces. Priests were executed simply for being in orders. That summer of 1679 was the 'great holocaust of the Plot';* between 20 June and 27 August, fourteen Catholics were executed.[17]

Pepys, at his liberty and with breathing space from the pressure of court appearances and parliamentary anger, was beginning to feel on top of things – and not just in France. Towards the end of July, a fascinating paper reached him from one Edward Sackville, containing allegations against Scott from respectable men in New York.[18] This was Pepys's first indication (apart from the mysterious reference to Scott debasing himself at St Kitts) of Scott's time in America. Pepys met Sackville, and took extensive notes of their conversation as Sackville told the story of his arrival in America with the fleet that conquered New Amsterdam, and his meetings with Scott. There was a rich new vein of Scott's life to be tapped for crime, it seemed.

Still the stories flooded in. In Mr Smither's coffee house, Thames Street; in Dutch towns; in the rue de Cléry in Paris, where Balty was digging through the maps, charts and globes in Pellissary's house; in Mr Pidgeon's barber shop in Covent Garden and before Brussels magistrates and public notaries in The Hague, merchants, clergymen, sword cutlers, tailors, sea-captains, secretaries, landladies and shoe-makers were discussing what they knew of Scott and doing their bit – as one put it – 'to add a little to the legend of Scott's life'.[19] Truth came rolling in alongside rumours, like the one that Scott had gone to New England with a person he then killed, and was taken to the gallows and the rope put around his neck, only to be reprieved at the last minute.[20] At the middle of it all, the hub of all the correspondence, the eventual recipient of all the papers (scrawled or painstakingly elegant), was Pepys at his desk in York Buildings.

By early August, Balty's homesick complaints had become voluble, and Pepys was promising him he would 'hasten all I can' to get him back to his family. Matters were drawing to a head, he promised.

Then he met two setbacks.

---

* The phrase is J. P. Kenyon's.

The first came from a man called Paul Le Goux. Balty's team seems to have got his name from someone in the Pellissary household – he was a neighbour, also living in the rue de Cléry. At three o'clock on the afternoon of 2 August, Trenchepain and Pelletier brought notaries to his house for him to swear his testimony. Le Goux revealed he had got to know Scott in June 1675 and after that 'saw him often at Paris'. Pepys's hope of proving that Scott had not been in Paris when Deane dined there vanished.[21]

The second setback was devastating.

The biggest disadvantage from Pepys's point of view was that every statement came to him second hand, in writing. He himself could form no opinions of the people being interviewed and assess their reliability. He had been meticulous in setting up a network of agents he could trust, or whom his close friends recommended. These, to a man, had worked diligently and solely with Pepys's interests in mind. But therein lay the problem. It was their tendency to want to believe information if it would benefit him, perhaps to the exclusion of other, darker truths. Pepys, aware of this, had taken to applying a healthy degree of scepticism to all the good news he received. Besides, if Scott had never been to Pellissary's house, how could he have known about Deane's dinner there? Hoping to discover nothing new, Pepys had pressed Balty to widen his investigations in the Pellissary house beyond the secretary, the servant and the former comptroller.

On 4 August, Trenchepain and Pelletier made their way through the black and white marble hallway to do Pepys's bidding by speaking to Pellissary's widow. Again the notaries accompanied them and turned her interview into a formal written declaration. On the day that her husband had entertained Sir Anthony Deane at dinner, she told them, she had dined alone with her sister and children in her own apartment. Sir Anthony and the others had paid her a visit after dinner to hear her play on the harpsichord. 'Mr Scott,' she said, 'did not dine in the house on that day.' It was quite clear that – contrary to what the staff had said – Mr Scott was both known to her and had dined there before.[22]

17

Wind and Smoke

John Scott had known Georges Pellissary. They knew each other well and this is how.

It was a question of cannon. King Charles's battling cousin, Prince Rupert, had spent the Civil War years as a royalist commander. In retirement he used his energy on a variety of inventions from new methods of mezzotint engraving to unusual forms of glass. The invention which caught the attention of Europe's masters of war, however, was his 'turned and nealed' cast-iron cannon. Conventional iron guns had to be awkwardly thick and heavy to stand up to the pressure of firing. Rupert's cannon had a much thinner casting, strengthened by a second heating process and then turned on a lathe to smooth out the rough patches which might make them burst when fired. They were light and strong, and cheaper to produce than the bronze alternative. The secrets of their manufacture were of immense value, and jealously guarded.[1]

During the 1670s France, keen to play a leading role in the growing international trade in exotic goods – spices, ivory, peacock feathers and so forth – turned its attention to strengthening its navy to protect its merchant fleet. Better cannon would give the navy sharper teeth. King Louis XIV poured money into developing the weapons, a project based largely in the iron-making town of Nevers, 120 miles south of Paris. The new guns promised a major leap forward in the arms race for any country that could manufacture them. Anxious to match other countries' progress, the French went recruiting for foreign experts. Prince Rupert's new guns were already on trial in England's navy. The *Cleveland* was armed with them when it brought Sir Anthony Deane and Will Hewer across to France with the two little yachts.

Prince Rupert held the patent to the cannon, and his English workers, who knew the details of the manufacturing process, were sworn to secrecy. One of them, however, had been turned out of his employment after several years in Prince Rupert's factory. In his own words, he was 'left destitute of a livelihood'. His name was Edward Sherwin. He had a highly marketable skill, he was broke and desperate.

At the end of May 1675, he received a letter inviting him to bring the secrets of Prince Rupert's cannon to France.[2] He threw patriotism and his promises of secrecy to the wind and accepted.

The letter came from another unscrupulous Englishman, Edward Manning, 'a fat and grave sort of man' who was looking for an opportunity to get rich.[3] Manning had teamed up with a young army drop-out called de Lavall, the son of a rich Yorkshire industrialist, who was supported by a generous allowance. They had two plans. Using Sherwin, they would make Prince Rupert's cannon for Louis. They also proposed a trip to the South Seas through the Straits of Magellan, to be made possible by possession of a rare map.

From its conception, the cannon project stank of conspiracy, fraud and quick wealth. It did not take long for Colonel John Scott to sniff it out. Scott found Manning in Paris, flashed his credentials as a French-speaker (Manning needed an interpreter) and one well connected with the French court to which Manning would sell his cannon, and climbed aboard.

Scott had been living on his wits since he arrived in France two years earlier. Seeing that the gun-casting project might make serious money, he set about hijacking Manning's idea, quickly and ruthlessly. Privately, he identified a trio of wealthy and well-placed French backers. He put a proposal them and on 27 May 1675, the three French signed an agreement with Scott that made no mention of the plan's instigator, fat, grave Edward Manning. Scott had cut him out.

The French partners were to bear the expense of bringing the cannon expert, Sherwin, over from England. The profits of the enterprise would be divided between Scott and the partners.[4] Their names were Mademoiselle Marie le Cocq des Moulins, a businesswoman (who, rashly believing that Scott set some value on his soul, insisted on taking communion with him at church before signing, to guarantee his trustworthiness); her neighbour and cousin, Louis Heroüard, known as the sieur de La Piogerie, a commander of Marines; and the treasurer of the French navy and owner of a house in Paris with black and white marble floors, Georges Pellissary.

Far from inventing a non-existent relationship with Piogerie and Pellissary, Scott had been tied to them in a clandestine business deal based on international industrial espionage.

As soon as he realised that Scott had hijacked his project, Manning took action. He found a new ally, Monsieur de La Tour, who was Governor of a town in Provence and a dabbler in alchemy.[5] Manning tried to set up a rival deal with de La Tour and another supposed cannon expert, one Stubbs.[6] Scott, who was anxious not to have Manning's new project as a rival to his, bumped into de La Tour in the street and, with characteristic ingratiating charm, set about blackening Manning's reputation. Manning, he said, was an impostor, a man who rowed a ferry-boat for a living and knew nothing about iron guns. Scott himself was the true expert. He was so persuasive that de La Tour arranged further talks and agreed to back him instead of Manning, as the agent for the cannonmaking. For this service, Scott agreed to pay him 1,000 crowns.[7]

Manning may have been fat but he was not soft. He was incensed. He found Scott in the street and challenged him to an immediate duel. Scott said he would meet him outside the city walls and Manning stormed off to a suitable spot. He waited, but Scott, always reluctant to engage in violence, never appeared. Manning sent a furious letter repeating the challenge. 'Colonel,' he wrote, 'I thought you would follow me because you bade me go before. I went out of the City and will do the like tomorrow morning and will be glad to see you beyond the Observatoire to play a game at bowls with you alone.'[8] The reference to a 'game at bowls' was because of the laws against duelling. Manning suggested a 4 a.m. rendezvous, 'for the Doctor finds the morning exercise to be wholesome.'

Scott was reluctant to engage in anything that might result in injury, particularly at that hour. Manning waited alone until it was clear that his adversary would not be coming. As the sun rose, Manning sent Scott another note written in frustration from 'hard by the place where I wrote to you I would be'. Scott had refused to settle the matter honourably, so Manning promised a different sort of revenge for the ruin Scott had brought on his cannonmaking plans. Manning demanded a quantity of money within three days, on pain of death. 'I and my friend have made an oath to destroy you,' he told Scott, 'and were you a prince you should not escape. Adieu, Edward Manning.'[9] Incidentally, it was Balty's discovery of this letter in 1679 that gave Pepys the first clue that Scott and Pellissary had been linked by business.[10]

Manning's fury at having been deposed by Scott from the captaincy of the cannonmaking business knew no bounds. As Scott and de La Tour were walking through the streets of Paris one night, Manning and a group of his friends, Irish mercenaries with a dangerous reputation, found them. Scott asked de La Tour to stay with him, as Manning's group passed and re-passed. While the respectable Governor de La Tour was there, nothing happened, but the moment he left, Manning set on Scott, wounded him 'and would, it may be, have killed him had they not been put asunder'.[11] Cowed and afraid of further violence, Scott signed a contract giving Manning a share of the profits from the guncasting.[12]

They were back in business and although they had come to blows, Scott and Edward Manning were birds of a feather. The potential profits to be had by working together outweighed their mutual acrimony. On the very day they joined forces, they began to conduct an expenses fraud on their new French business partners. Scott told Mademoiselle des Moulins that he had gone to St Valery, a port at the mouth of the Somme, in order to meet the cannon expert Edward

Sherwin, fresh from England. He arranged to draw down a large sum of money for his expenses on the journey, but instead of going there, he simply disappeared to a house in a Paris suburb and lay low with Manning, covering their activities by sending Mademoiselle des Moulins what purported to be a letter from the coast on 7 June. In it, he claimed he was waiting for Sherwin and eight others who were coming over in a pleasure boat provided by 'his cousin' Lord Winchilsea and he expected 'with much impatience' to have them in Paris in another week.[13]

Four days later Scott sent a second letter, this time purporting to be from Abbeville, just inland from St Valery. He concocted a new tale to suggest that he was providing a dangerous and valuable service by smuggling his cannon expert across the Channel against all the efforts of the English authorities to stop him. Sherwin, he said, had landed the previous day and just arrived in town. He had met trouble leaving England. Some of his people had been arrested at Dover and another in London by the King's order. Prince Rupert and others of the company owning the cannon patents had 'offered violence' to Sherwin.[14]

It was complete nonsense. Nonetheless, convinced by the account of Scott's fictitious journey, the French backers provided the cannon-casters with a bill for a hundred crowns for his expenses, which Scott's landlord, John Joyne, was sent off to cash. In reality, Sherwin travelled across to Calais without any difficulty at all. Scott and Manning then kept him – and themselves – out of sight for another week before visiting their backers, the better to convince them that they had all travelled back from the coast together.[15]

The French partners had paid Scott a lot of money to bring Sherwin over. Now, showing a certain overdue mistrust, Pellissary brought in his neighbour, Paul Le Goux, head of the Nevers cannon foundry, as an adviser. Le Goux was sceptical about Scott from the start. John Joyne, who had also been cut in as a partner in the deal, was there to translate because Scott's attempts at expressing himself in French left his partners shaking their heads. Le Goux was plainly not satisfied with Scott's answers and 'told Monsieur Pellissary aside

. . . that it was impossible for Scott to perform what he pretended to, laughing at Monsieur Pellissary for his easiness therein and giving him caution against trusting of Scott and his company too far'.[16] The hirelings then failed their very first test. To please Mademoiselle des Moulins, Scott had persuaded the French partners that Sherwin would make them a remarkable mortar, with its barrel decorated with red and white spots. This would, he said somewhat inaccurately, look like a leopard. The attempt to cast it with separate pots of molten iron and copper came to nothing.[17] Nonetheless, Sherwin's credentials as an expert in Prince Rupert's secret cannon were enough to keep the French backers' faith high.

The French had paid Scott through the nose for a specialist cannoncasting team. What they got instead was a motley collection of Englishmen recruited to make up the numbers. According to Joyne – Scott's partner in crime – their numbers included a pastry cook, a clerk and a bankrupt milliner.[18]

Their backer, the treasurer of the French navy Georges Pellissary, who was to feature as the recipient of Pepys's treasonous papers in Scott's account in 1679, never became friendly or informal with Scott; their relationship was purely professional. On 17 June 1675, Scott took four of his strange crew to Pellissary at his grand house in Paris. They were received in the public room paved with black and white marble and, as one of them later said, were 'treated very courteously by him as strangers but without the least appearance of familiarity either with the colonel or any other of the company, they receiving what was set before them as a breakfast.'[19] At that time Scott spoke so little French that Joyne had to interpret everything, though Scott was trying to learn the language with the help of a French grammar he carried in his pocket. Pellissary spoke no English. Scott and Pellissary's relationship was never as intimate as Scott was later to claim it was.

Some time in July, the cannonmakers set out southward from Paris for the royal cannon factories at Nevers on the river Loire, where the water provided the power needed for boring out the barrels of the iron guns. The foundries there had been struggling to make guns of sufficient quality. Scott had made up a carefully drawn picture book to explain the gunmaking process without having to resort to his faltering French. He and his team met a hostile reception from the French foundry men, who thought they would take their jobs. Scott and Sherwin got round them by plying them with drink and stayed with them for 'two days and nights together to see the metal in the furnace'.[20]

Scott sent an upbeat account of events to John Joyne a few days later. They had already cast four cannon and 'the iron is running for the fifth which will be cast at three in the morning tomorrow'. He had nothing but praise for the generosity of the local people. Sherwin was working wonders and had 'changed the nature and the colour of the metal in less than three hours'.[21] By his account, Scott was close to achieving his ambition. Pellissary's faith in him would be repaid. He would be showered with gold and glory, and France would be at his feet.

As more of Scott's crew of irregulars arrived in Nevers, however, the factional tensions between the English and the French got worse. Sherwin, on the lookout for what he called 'French tricks' saw plots and insults everywhere. He displayed a (possibly alcoholic) maudlin dependency on Scott, who described him flying into a rage and threatening to 'slake the fire and spoil the guns' because a visiting gentleman had taken off his hat to Scott and not to Sherwin himself. 'I was forced to humour that passion,' Scott told John Joyne, 'and before I was gone with him a quarter of a mile, he wept and told me he would die at my foot.'[22]

The cannonfounding scheme suffered from Scott's profound reluctance to share power or profit. Scott needed Sherwin's expertise, but had little desire to keep him on board for longer than was necessary. He was learning what he could from Sherwin about the casting techniques and at the same time playing a complex game to undermine Sherwin's credibility, so that he could eventually drive the expert out and take sole control of the enterprise. He had already fallen out with Sherwin as to which of their names should be engraved on the guns. He monitored what his crew was saying; one of them later swore that Scott made it his practice in Nevers 'to open people's letters and seal them again and to forge letters'.[23] He began a whispering campaign against Sherwin; he denounced him to the French backers as a rogue who would never perform the work properly. He intercepted Sherwin's incoming letters and when Sherwin consequently began to complain that he was not being paid, Scott suggested that he should refuse to work.

At the end of August, around the time of the crucial dinner when Pellissary entertained Sir Anthony Deane, Scott was back in Paris and had taken to visiting Pellissary rather more than was welcome. He took Captain John Browne on one such visit. Browne was the man Scott hailed in the Commons lobby almost four years later, just before he made his accusations against Pepys. He was a man of genuine skill but only as an engraver, a decorator in this case, of the finished cannon. On his nine-day journey from London to Paris, via Gravesend, Dover, Calais and Boulogne, Browne fell foul of the 'messenger' who had brought him to Paris; the messenger demanded £12, twice the agreed sum, to return Browne's luggage. John Scott took Browne and the messenger to Pellissary's house to sort it out. They were led through the reception room paved with black and white marble into a little garden adorned with myrtles and orange trees. Pellissary appeared, tore a strip off the messenger and ordered him to hand over the baggage for the agreed £6.[24] Scott was showing off his access to the corridors of power but his behaviour was to cost him. Pellissary did not like to be troubled in this way and, soon afterwards, he gave orders to his porter to let Scott in only if he had been specifically sent for.[25] It was not, as Scott would have the Commons believe in 1679, a relationship of close friends who confided in each other.

Poor Captain Browne must have wondered what he had wandered into. Drinking in a Paris tavern, Scott revealed the bitter streak that so often surfaced when events began to turn against him. He told Browne he would ruin Sherwin because 'this business of the guns was an undertaking of too great importance for such a rascal' and that if he, Scott, went ahead with the project by himself, he would be made a marshal of France. A burst of alarming self-aggrandisement followed. Scott told Browne that 'so little a rogue' as Sherwin should not get in his way, because he was so powerful that he 'could at any time set Princes and States together by their ears'.[26] It was the type of claim he was fond of making at the very moments when it was least true.

Browne stayed at Nevers for only three weeks before pulling out. Back in Paris, there was still more trouble. Manning and his Irishmen (reneging on the agreement to quietly accept a share of Scott's profits) were complaining to senior French ministers that Scott had hijacked the contract and was defrauding everyone. Scott turned to his forgery skills to manage the problem. He forged a letter from Sherwin to the French backers. In it, the cannon expert was made to say that Manning was telling a pack of lies, that Manning had never been in control of the project and that it was not Manning who had invited Sherwin to come to France. Rather, Sherwin had written to John Scott, his 'best friend in all the world', suggesting the cannon project before Manning ever contacted him. Indeed, the letter claimed, it was only because Scott had protected him from Manning's attempts to wreck the project that Sherwin had ever got to France at all.[27]

As the hawk-eyed Scott pilfered Sherwin's skills, he discovered the cannonfounder had a second secret art up his sleeve. Sherwin claimed to know a method for blanching copper, giving it such a convincingly silvery appearance that it could be used instead of silver for buttons and belt buckles. Scott began to experiment and soon, with Sherwin's help, claimed to have perfected the process. Then he hatched a grandiose and entirely illegal plan.

He intended to team up with his friend, the Whig MP Mr Wentworth. The Earl of Derby, now based in Paris and described as 'sovereign' of the Isle of Man, was to allow Wentworth and Scott to set themselves up on the island, each being made a governor of one of the castles. There they would make fake silver coins. The island being 'a place out of the reach of the laws of England', the Earl would 'wink at their coining of false money'. The coins would be dispersed in hundred-pound bags along the coasts of England, Scotland and Ireland, the Isle of Man being conveniently equidistant between those three.[28]

The plan proved their final undoing. A tradesman to whom Scott and Sherwin owed money threatened to expose them as forgers. They were forced to leave Nevers with their crew. Towards the end of 1675, they straggled back to Paris by river boat and hired wagon, bringing with them three small cannon.[29] His scheme in ruins, Scott broke off with his long-suffering backers, des Moulins, Pellissary and Piogerie, who managed to seize the best one of the three little cannon, beautifully engraved by Captain John Browne during his brief time at Nevers. It had been 'packed up in a box with bran for fear of spoiling of it' and the stylish carriage had been decorated by a skilled painter. It was all the partners were to get for their large investment. Scott now finally broke off with Sherwin too and took the two remaining cannon.

Against all the odds, Scott used his persuasive skills to get a new sponsor. He went back to de La Tour, Edward Manning's original contact from months earlier. Trading on the man's interest in alchemy, he dangled the copper blanching secret before him as bait. Scott offered de La Tour a huge annual pension for introducing him to Louis XIV's master of ordnance, the Count de Lude. Scott performed two demonstrations of his cannon. The small cannon worked well, fired off in the fields of the Faubourg St Antoine until Scott used up his limited supply of brass cannon balls. Larger cannon had been brought up from Nevers. They were test-fired outside the city gates. Three of the five cannon burst into pieces on firing and, as de La Tour ruefully remarked, 'the secret, my pension and the cannon have produced nothing but wind and smoke.' Scott, he concluded, 'was nothing but a bragging fellow [and] he had no other end but to get wealth and reputation at any rate, right or wrong'.[30]

Four years later, as Pepys began to understand Scott's Nevers farce, he constructed a day by day almanac of all the information on Scott's movements right through 1675. Covering twenty-six carefully ruled pages, it shows days and dates in both English and European numberings. It was intended to settle the question of whether Scott, who knew Pellissary and had been to his house, could have been there on the night of the dinner. Instead it is a document less notable for the information contained in it than for the long gaps in between, blank pages which Pepys hoped to fill with certainties but which left behind for posterity only that faint smell of wind and smoke.

For Pepys, the Nevers affair explained why Scott had chosen Pellissary and Piogerie's names; he had long been associated with them and, though he was not close to them, he knew them well enough to be able to describe crucial details like the lay-out of Pellissary's house. Crucially, too, the Nevers story proved that Scott had acted treasonously, by conspiring to use King Charles's gunmaking secrets for the benefit of a foreign power. When Edward Sherwin came to swear statements for Pepys, the cannonfounder was clearly aware of his own crime and made a risible attempt to rehearse a future defence, claiming he had told Scott not to reveal cannon-casting secrets to the French, and saying he had believed Scott to be a man of honour – 'but at length,' Sherwin told Pepys, 'I found by the workmen that he had betrayed his trust.'[31] Sherwin's attempts to make himself seem innocent were useless; he knew perfectly well that his willingness to demonstrate these methods was the only reason he had been hired. He was as guilty as Scott.

When Pepys finally understood the whole story and the scale of this particular treason, he sent his lawyer Mr Hayes off with Sherwin to swear the information against Scott. They appeared before Justice Jones in Fleet Street. The detailed allegations should have led to the immediate issue of a warrant for Scott's arrest but Jones ducked the issue, 'observing things in it very criminal to the king and government' and telling Hayes that Pepys should go and tell the King's Council instead. Hearing this, Pepys went straight round to see Jones and promised him the information would come out at his trial.[32] At last, it seemed, he could prove that the real traitor was not the accused, but the accuser.

18

The Serpent's Prudence

The implications of the discovery that the Pellissary household did, in fact, know John Scott worried Pepys a good deal, because Balty had cheerfully reported that they had never heard of him.

'I find . . . that Scott was not so entirely a stranger to that house, as your several letters heretofore lead me to think,' Pepys wrote with restraint to Balty on 18 August. The declarations claiming that Scott had never been to the house would all have to be disregarded. Balty's new instructions were to discover how well they knew Scott, 'for otherwise,' Pepys explained to his errant detective, 'it will be very easy for him to magnify his intimacy with Mr Pellissary and his family.'[1] Balty's optimism was perhaps his greatest failing. 'Be most slow to believe what we most wish should be true,' Pepys warned him on another occasion. The hostility of the court demanded total integrity on Pepys's part; one error exposed at trial would bring all his evidence into doubt.[2]

Pepys had an even bigger problem, however. All his witness statements were on paper but he now knew that, contrary to what jovial Edmund Saunders had led him to believe in June, he would need witnesses in court to give evidence in person, *viva voce*. All his carefully collected bits of paper, he realised, might be deemed worthless by the cantankerous judges. Balty began a tireless search for witnesses who could be persuaded to travel to England.

The evidence from Pellissary's household remained useful, for they were united in their certainty that Scott had not been at the dinner with Deane. To disprove Scott's charge, it would be essential to bring over one or two of the household, though given the expense, Pepys requested it be as few as possible.[3] The valet and the porter were settled upon, and Madame Pellissary generously agreed to part with them when the time came.[4] One of Pellissary's neighbours from the rue de Cléry, a former councillor to King Louis, agreed to come to England with them. He could prove that Pellissary and Deane had not had a moment alone for the private conversation about maps that Scott pretended.[5] Despite Balty's many conversations with them, the French were to be treated as strangers when they came to England. It would be lethal to be charged (like Richard Langhorn) with having prepared them.

Pepys still hoped to supplement his *viva voce* witnesses with the vast mass of paper evidence. The witnesses whose signatures appeared on these were the two French merchants, Trenchepain and Pelletier. Catholic Pelletier, Pepys had already decided, could not appear in court. Trenchepain was a busy man, and wrote to James Houblon explaining, with embarrassment, that he did not think he would have time to travel to England. The news put Pepys 'almost out of countenance'. If the witnesses could not swear to the statements, Pepys might as well have sat at home writing them himself, for all the weight they would carry.[6] Then a thought struck him. Balty had seemed to be hinting that an extra pair of hands was needed in Paris. Pepys knew a man who could replace Trenchepain and Pelletier as a witness; a gracious French merchant living in Long Acre, with contacts at the French court and in the French navy, who knew the Pellissary family personally.

His name was Claude Denise. It was infinitely more sensible (in the face of spiralling costs) to pay Denise's expenses for a quick trip to Paris than to retain the two Frenchmen in England for the indeterminable time before trial. Denise agreed to help. 'I commit my whole affair to you and my brother,' Pepys wrote to him on 29 September, 'and both you and it to God Almighty.'[7]

Courteous Denise provided Balty with letters of introduction to several illustrious French contacts. Though he was careful not to tread on Balty's toes, he gave him a list of suggestions of how Balty might further pursue his investigations – exactly the kind of thing that would insult Balty, who had been managing the affair for three months.[8] If Balty's pride was pricked, he kept it under control – but not for long. When he mentioned Denise, he thought he saw a shadow in Trenchepain's expression. Not knowing that Trenchepain was too busy to come to London, Balty misread the look. He leapt to the conclusion that Pepys was snubbing Trenchepain and, embarrassed for Trenchepain's sake, wrote a furious letter to Pepys, decrying his decision to send Denise. He thought that his team was being insulted. He went far too far, sneering at Denise's letters of recommendation to 'low' men, and saying that Denise was redundant, since the Pellissary family would not want to swear to their informations all over again before a new witness. He told Pepys that he had not hinted at needing extra hands and to reread his letters, this time more carefully.

This ill-advised tirade arrived in London on 2 October.* Balty's proud posturing earned him a great cuff to the head from Pepys, who commanded him to undo immediately any rudeness he had shown Denise. The simmering tension between the bossy bureaucrat and his wayward instrument boiled over. Balty's long-windedness took a hit, Pepys telling him that he had already read his letters, over and over again, 'as long as they for the most part be, and so ill as the condition of my eyes is'. So too did Balty's failure to spot Pellissary's familiarity with Scott. This was their lowest point.[9] Balty retreated. The new arrival's diplomatic touch soon calmed him down.

The autumn dragged on with little respite from their work. There were other tensions. Balty persistently failed to explain how he was

---

* None of Balty's letters from Paris is known to exist. Since Pepys was meticulous in collecting his correspondence, the fact is remarkable. Pepys advised Balty to make copies of his outgoing post in a letter-book; if Balty followed this, its whereabouts is not known. We have to infer the contents of Balty's letters by Pepys's replies.

spending Pepys's money. His failure to provide accounts of the money he drew from Trenchepain and Pelletier caused embarrassment for Pepys, who could not then repay them. Balty was getting through substantial amounts of cash, Pepys issuing him with £50 credit at a time on a regular basis.* All the while, he kept a watchful eye on Balty's propensity for extravagance and reprimanded him sharply when Balty planned to bring a tutor over from France for his son, a luxury afforded only by men 'in the uttermost circumstance of greatness', which Balty most certainly was not.[10]

Despite the tensions and misunderstandings, however, Balty came through for Pepys, and at no point did he earn Pepys's thanks more than when he discovered John Joyne.

Joyne was the English watchmaker who had taken Scott in when Scott arrived in Paris, fresh from his Dutch disasters, homeless, and clutching his mapmaking desk. Balty first knocked on Joyne's door on 19 August, and the watchmaker invited him in. He had known Scott very well, he said, for Scott had lodged with him for over two years and – since Scott owed him forty pistoles – he would be delighted to help.[11]

He later explained how that debt came about. Through the Prince of Condé, Scott had been paid 'fifteen hundred Crowns part in gold and part in silver' for showing his charts of the English coast to Louis's chief minister Colbert. Scott was fond of showing Joyne parcels of this money which he kept in the drawers of the cabinet. He used some of it to buy a suit 'garnished with silver buttons and a shoulder belt with large buckles of the same' but he spent lavishly and had to sell the buckles and buttons when he ran out of cash. Later on, when Scott planned to leave Joyne's house still owing him money, 'he did, for fear I should seize on his trunks, steal his things away by degrees and would call me up to his chamber, as if he had business with me and open his trunk that I might take notice that there was little value in them.'[12]

---

* As a guide, Pepys had a salary of £350 a year as Clerk of the Acts.

Joyne was everything Pepys needed from his witnesses: enthusiastic, communicative and available. Within a month he had located the men whom Scott had known through the cannoncasting business, and told Pepys that he should go to the sign of the Green Bear near Temple Bar, the gateway to the city at the western end of Fleet Street. There he should ask for Captain John Browne, the sealgraver, who would introduce him to the rest of the Nevers gang.[13] Browne proved amenable. Joyne meanwhile provided Pepys with papers in Scott's own handwriting which seemed to indicate that Scott had been in Nevers on the day of Deane's Paris dinner – a claim that Pepys tried fruitlessly to substantiate, but which turned out to be wrong. Pepys did a little research of his own and discovered that Joyne's father was 'a man of substantial credit in proportion to his quality'.[14] Joyne intended to make a trip to London anyway, so Pepys requested that he might arrive before the first day of the new court term. Denise would accompany him into England, while Balty stayed behind to tidy up any loose ends.

The remaining mystery was the motive for Scott's charge. If Pepys could supply that in court, he could destroy Scott. Again, Joyne seemed too good to be true; he knew why Scott had charged Pepys. He had heard Scott say that he intended revenge on Pepys because Pepys had accused him in the Commons of being a Jesuit and of 'running out of England upon the business of the Plot'.[15] According to Joyne, Scott then said, '"God damn me if I be not revenged of that rogue Pepys" and putting his nails to his mouth swore horribly, "God's blood, I will sooner eat these nails and have my flesh torn in pieces than live without being revenged of him."'[16]

So it was that, through Joyne, Pepys learnt that the Gravesend incident, when he had pursued Scott out of England as the murderer of Sir Edmund Berry Godfrey, was the reason for Scott's persecution of him.

A man called Foster revealed that he had heard Scott say the same thing. By Foster's account, Scott had known he was going into England to charge Pepys, and had sent details in advance to 'some duke or lord in England'.[17] As Scott prepared to leave for England himself, Foster had been struck by his fine clothing. Scott had always been short of money, yet he had begun to dress like a person of quality. Clearly he had been paid handsomely for his part in the plot against Pepys. It was entirely unclear, from Foster's account, whether Scott or his employers had first come up with the plan. Foster, who was known as a 'debauched idle rascal', refused to give fuller information. It would have been foolish to trust him; he was close to Scott and had written his 'Life' – a document of which sadly no trace survives today, though it was perhaps unlikely to be a paragon of objective truth.

It was an entirely disproportionate response on Scott's part. He had been chased out of Gravesend through an understandable and somewhat self-inflicted case of mistaken identity. Pepys had certainly pursued Scott but his arrest on his return was down to Henry Coventry and local officials in Kent; why had Scott fixated on Pepys? Buckingham and Shaftesbury were paying him, but that did not explain Scott's desire to be revenged on Pepys, nor the venom that Scott had displayed in court. Could that really be the full story of Scott's grudge against Pepys?

Captain Browne at the Green Bear introduced Pepys to the rest of the Nevers crew: one Mr Hastcote, 'sober' Mr Harrison and Browne's servant Thomas. Browne was not the only person who had had to rebuff Scott's attempts to recruit a second witness. Scott had also visited Harrison for the same purpose, at his house near Guildhall, just before Pepys's court appearance on 9 July. They were keen to be reunited with the watchmaker John Joyne, 'that they might together entertain one another with the histories of that fellow's villainies'.[18] Pepys was pleased with this rabble, thinking they would 'abundantly show the world the qualifications of this villain' Scott.[19] He doubted there was much honesty in their gunfounding enterprise, 'yet I find they all agree, that whatever the rest were to one another Scott was a villain to them all and to all the world'.[20]

There was also the cannon expert, Sherwin, whom Balty managed to find in Paris. Pepys wanted him as a witness, but Sherwin demanded money, which Pepys refused to give, 'it not being enough in this age, and in the company I am fallen into, to have the innocence of a dove, without some mixture of the serpent's prudence'.[21] To his astonishment, Sherwin appeared in London anyway, making all sorts of attractive-sounding claims, such as that Scott had been at Nevers, not Paris, on the day of Deane's dinner with Pellissary. Pepys, however, did not trust him; 'by what I see of him,' he told Balty, 'I had rather have been without his evidence, than by supplying him with the least sum of money.' Sherwin looked like the kind of man who might start talking about bribery.[22] As it happened, fate removed his evidence anyway: four days after his arrival in England he was taken ill and confined to his chamber. On 29 October, he died.

The long summer break drew to a close and the trees in St James's Park turned brown. Pepys had found little rest through the hot months, except for a day of guitar lessons with Morelli, out of town – a break from his 'molestations of mind'.[23] Now he expected to face a well-prepared Attorney General in court.

The political climate in London had changed too. August was always the great sickly season, and King Charles had succumbed. He had become ill, quickly and violently – an accident for which no one was prepared, for Charles had always been in excellent health. His fever was probably malaria, since it was cured by quinine. The Earl of Shaftesbury, taken by surprise and without a Parliament to excite, made no political capital out of it. Charles even refused to allow Scott's patron, the Duke of Buckingham, in to see him, saying that Buckingham had supported the election of Whig MPs who 'would cut his [Charles's] throat'.[24] For fear Charles would die, James, Duke of York, was summoned back from exile to England. He arrived fast. Though Charles was on the mend, his brother's presence was an indisputable display of royal right and inheritance. Nothing could have spoken more eloquently against the Whigs' attack on James and the Crown's descent. When it came to the crunch, the Duke was the man waiting to take control of England. Courtiers flocked to him.

Pepys was reunited with him. Before he left again, he was given assurance that the Lord Mayor would have proclaimed him king, had Charles died. It was no longer necessary to keep James overseas; he went to Scotland. In October, Charles turned Shaftesbury out of the Privy Council. The Whig cause had received a royal blow to the jaw.

In spite – or perhaps because – of this, Pepys was subjected to a rash of libels in the run-up to his autumn court appearance. He paid a visit to the recovering King at Windsor, and the next day an article appeared in the *Domestick Intelligence* newspaper claiming that 'as soon as ever his Majesty saw him there he frowned and turned aside, and walked away showing a dislike of seeing him there'. The Lord Chamberlain, the article claimed, told him he should not have come, being charged with treason.[25] Pepys came crashing down on the publishers, and the newspaper published a retraction calling the story 'altogether false and scandalous'.[26] Eleven days after the article appeared, arrest warrants were issued for three men for printing and publishing the libel. The savagery of what Pepys could do when cornered seems to have given John Scott pause for thought. Three days later he talked to an acquaintance with some legal knowledge, one Edward Wright, about the penalties for perjury. Wright told him that a perjurer would usually be put in the pillory, designed like the stocks for public humiliation. What if the perjury was against a man 'in great employment and authority' Scott asked. Wright replied it would be the same, but maybe with a fine as well. Scott sought refuge in disdain and answered, 'Is that all? Pox on't.'[27]

In October, a new libel appeared. *Plain Truth or Closet Discourse Betwixt P. and H.* was a knockabout dialogue in which Pepys displayed naïve delight at Will Hewer's cunning money-making schemes to make their fortunes by selling plum jobs in the navy.[28] James Houblon wrote the day after its publication saying, 'I see that the malice of your enemies increases. God forgive them for that villainous paper.'[29] His letter arrived as Pepys was finishing reading the thing. Pepys replied that his 'philosophy was never under so great a strain as at this moment'.[30] With a week to go until the court term,

Pepys's enemies kept up a sustained barrage of libel, and hardly a day passed without some fresh attack. The groundwork was being laid for his trial.

There is no doubt that, during the summer, Pepys's prosecutors intended to bring his case to trial in the new term. They were keeping his former butler, John James, on a retainer for this purpose. Around the beginning of September, a former clerk of Pepys's called Phelix Donluis (sometimes 'Lewis') spent a day rambling around the City with James. It was a hazy day spent in alehouses and the cheerful carnage of Bartholomew Fair in Smithfield, where they ate nuts and fruit. At the Blacked Boy goldsmith's on Fleet Street, James collected ten or twenty shillings.

'By God,' he exclaimed to Donluis in relief, 'I am mightily beholden to Mr Harbord, for he allows me ten shillings a week, and credit upon that Goldsmith to pay it me duly as I shall call for it.'[31]

He also revealed that Harbord – the great Whig ringmaster who had brought him to the bar of the Commons – and his friends were seeking work for him. He spent a good sum of it in the Derby alehouse, the Black Horse and the Axe in King Street with Donluis that night.

23 October dawned clear and bright, with the first nip of winter frost in the north wind. In Westminster Hall, the judges of King's Bench reconvened. Despite the barrage of libels and the money they were pouring into John James, the prosecution were not ready to press ahead. There was no indictment and no Attorney General, the old one having been removed and not yet replaced. Pepys and Anthony Deane's appearance was simply noted, and they left again.[32]

For the first time, Pepys was ready to take on his opponent. He had witnesses all set to come over from Pellissary's household, as well as a former councillor of King Louis XIV who had been at the dinner. He had the disreputable but eager Nevers mob, with whom he met in the Crown Tavern. He also had the indomitable Deborah Egmond (who, years before, had leapt off her table and chased Scott out of The Hague) on her way over to help 'Squire Pips'. After a long period of agony and paralysis about using Catholic witnesses, he had even written to the Marquis de Seignelay (though he had no intention of using de Seignelay's response at trial, but rather to prove his innocence to the King).[33] He had proof that Scott had sought revenge. He had combed through his case, and Balty in Paris had done the same, looking for omissions or mistakes.[34] The evidence, he thought, would render Scott 'of no credit among sober men'.[35] He was ready to appear in court with a clamouring group of the people Scott had wronged or infuriated; yet Scott was nowhere to be found.

It was Pepys's preparedness that had undone him. Scott had his spies on Pepys's work in Holland, and probably France too.[36] He knew how complete Pepys's defence was. He had seen how violently Pepys could hit back. So, at the end of September, he had fled to Paris with the Duke of Buckingham. Balty's security crossed Pepys's mind, and he wrote to warn and reassure him.[37] He suspected that Balty was safe, however, for he was beginning to get the measure of his opponent. He considered Scott's display of cowardice on St Kitts, the refusal to prosecute the imprisoned Dutchman, Dispontyn, and the refusal to duel with Edward Manning over the cannon business. For all his blustering and bold trickery, Scott was a coward. He would not stand trial because he was terrified of the characters Pepys could produce to testify to the 'several scenes' of his life. He was terrified of what Pepys might charge him with.

Despite that, he had Pepys squirming – a slave to his accuser.[38] Even King Charles had asked the Attorney General to press forward to trial, but the Attorney General could do nothing without evidence. Pepys was having to pay for Balty to stay overseas, explaining to Pellissary's servants why they were not needed yet. He was haemorrhaging money to maintain the witnesses that were already in England. It was an expensive thing, to fight a treason charge – and Pepys had done it on a grand scale. Slowly, crushingly, and without needing to do anything more to him at all, his enemies were breaking him.

By 15 November, the butler John James's income from the Whigs had gone dry. He poured out a torrent of complaints to his friend

Donluis. The promises made to him by Harbord's group had come to nothing. 'The Devil take me if I believe any one of them any more, for they are my Arse all over,' he said. He was heartily sorry for what he had done against Pepys in exchange for their 'encouragements'. Given the choice again he would see them damned before he would do it; although Pepys had used him unkindly he would not get involved with 'such rascally fellows as Harbord, Scott, Mansell and others'. Harbord, 'by God', had taken his allowance away. 'By God', he would take the first employment he could get and 'trust to no son of a whore of them all any longer'. They had got what they could out of him, and now, he complained, 'they slight me'.[39]

On 13 November, the new Attorney General, Sir Cresswell Levins, told Pepys's solicitor John Hayes that, without Scott, he could not draw up an indictment and as that day marked the last post by which witnesses could be summoned from France, there would be no trial before the next term, starting on 23 January.[40] Pepys could not continue to hold the fragile, tottering cathedral of his defence in readiness. He told Balty to put Pellissary's servants at ease, at least until the next term.* 'It seems too probable,' Pepys wrote, 'that we shall not have an opportunity of justifying ourselves to the world by a public trial.' He told Balty to find someone in Paris to act as a correspondent, to give or receive news or any urgent summons. Then he signalled that Balty's Paris work had drawn to a close:

Sir A D joins with me in recommending it to you now to be preparing with all convenient speed for your return for England, and with our kind acknowledgements of the diligence and successful industry you have expressed on our behalves through this whole affair, we remain,
Your truly affectionate
Friends and Servants
A D S P.

---

* The merchant Trenchepain came up with a devious plan to bring the witnesses over immediately, then delay them at Dover or Canterbury on the pretext of business, by which time they would find it was only two weeks to go before the start of the new law term and could probably be persuaded to go sightseeing until then. Pepys did not take it up.

Four days later, the Earl of Shaftesbury, expelled from government, flexed his muscles on the streets instead. In a fiery parade, a great wax pope attended by devils and nuns ('the pope's whores') was carried through London and consigned to the bonfire. For added realism the effigy was filled with cats which screeched as the flames took hold. The white-faced ghost of Edmund Berry Godfrey demanded vengeance, and spectators were provided with claret.[41] John Scott, drawn like a moth by this display of Whig revival, reappeared in London.

Scott's old landlord in Paris, John Joyne the watchmaker, had been in London since the beginning of the month, carried across the Channel under the wing of Claude Denise. On meeting him, Pepys found him a perfect witness – 'very ingenious' and 'very just'.[42] Joyne could not stand up in court this term if there was to be no trial but together, he and Pepys hatched a new plan. For Pepys's sake, he was prepared to refresh his old acquaintance with the colonel.

19

John Joyne's Journal

London was a compact city, and it took John Joyne little more than a week to bump into John Scott. They met on Drury Lane at eleven o'clock on Monday morning, 24 November. After warm greetings and shaking hands, Scott asked Joyne why he was in London. He had come to chase some debts, Joyne answered, and had business with the King's former mistress, Lady Cleveland.* They walked companionably to the house of a leading republican where Scott had spent the night. There they shared a crust and a bottle of ale, and Scott told the gentleman that Joyne was an old friend of his, an honest man and the best watchmaker in the world.[1]

This Scott was very much the same man that Pepys had got to know by reading about him. Within an hour and a quarter of their meeting, he had engaged Joyne to help him in his latest cheat.

Scott was trying to woo Lady Vane. She was the widow of the regicide Sir Henry Vane and some years older than Scott, but she combined the attractions of wealth and republican pedigree. It was reported to Pepys much later on that the match was Shaftesbury's idea, to reward Scott for services rendered. When, with Joyne, Scott reached the south end of Drury Lane, he stood 'a pretty while' contemplating a letter he was carrying. It was to Lady Vane. Scott

---

* This was probably true: Joyne intended to come to England for his own business as well as for Pepys's.

had written it, but it purported to be from one whose initials were 'I W'. Eventually, Scott put it into Joyne's hands, and asked him to deliver it on his behalf, then made off round a corner so as not to be seen. Joyne obliged, passing it to the lady's one-eyed porter, then asked Scott what was going on. The lady's daughter, Scott replied, seeing her mother's affection for him, had told her that he was another Colonel Scott, a man infamous for having the pox so badly that he had collapsed in front of his men. This letter from the fictitious 'I W' accused Scott of exactly that unpleasant history. Scott's plan was to disprove the allegation and undermine the malicious daughter completely. The grand manipulator was still pursuing a high place in the world and had, through long practice, acquired a subtle awareness of confidence and deceit. He appeared to be on the verge of success with the affectionate Lady Vane.

The ascent of the Whigs over the last year had come together with Scott's life in the most convenient way. It was a confluence of politics and personal resentment. Scott had been pointing his sword at the Duke of York for years. Now that the rest of England had unsheathed theirs to join him, he found himself a leader of men. He pulled off his periwig, hot from Ludgate Hill, and was chaffed for it on Cheapside by four or five cheerful young blades – all Whigs and Parliament men, he told Joyne. He served the sober men of Parliament by drinking with these 'young mad fellows' and influencing their opinions.

They called by at the house of the leading Quaker, William Penn, and at Scott's lodgings at the Dog and Dripping Pan on Fish Street Hill, and finished up at one of his regular haunts, Appleby's Tavern, at six o'clock for bread, cheese and Spanish wine. The landlord sat with them. Scott generously introduced Joyne as 'an admirable watch-maker'. He was capable of considerable charm, and wicked fun too.

'Now will I set this man a-talking,' he whispered to Joyne when the landlord was not listening, 'and make him cry when I please, and then make him think himself a great man and talk of his former affairs.'

Within minutes, the landlord was mourning the property he had lost when the Duke of York blew up his house in the path of the Great Fire.

Scott was pestered by a stream of men that evening. He had become a figure of authority, a politician of the street. A Doctor of Divinity asked how soon he thought Parliament might sit, 'the only salve of the nation'. An ancient Cromwellian captain sipped sweet claret and whispered in Scott's ear before lurching towards Joyne who, 'having some apprehensions what sort of man he might be,' made much of him, praising his choice of wine and even buying a bottle of it himself. Scott and Joyne parted with much ceremony and the watchmaker hurried straight back to York Buildings to tell Pepys about this first day in the colonel's vibrant company. His sister was waiting there, worried that he was out so late 'with this fellow Scott'. Under Pepys's supervision, Joyne began to write up his journal of their encounters.

Joyne gave such a full account that Pepys did not think to doubt him, nor to worry that Joyne's old friendship with the colonel might prove stronger than their own, very recent, association.

Two days later Joyne sought out Scott again and was directed to Newman's coffee house, where the air was alive with political discussion. Scott was drinking beer and sharing some small red herrings with a companion. They were talking about the great pope-burning parade the previous week, and passing around a transcript of the 'speech' the pope made as he was burned. Scott's companion, a lean-faced man in his twenties, was his friend, the searcher from Gravesend who had helped him escape the previous year – 'a rogue fit to be made use of some time,' Scott said later. Scott asked him to get money for the horse he had left behind, which had been confiscated in his absence.

In the street, more of Scott's acquaintances were anxious to discover the prospects for the recall of Parliament. Scott had once sought glory in royal circles, but with the thunderous Whig challenge to the Crown, he had found a new calling and set his sights on a parliamentary career. If elected he would 'do more there than ever was done by any one man yet', he told Joyne. He would have a seat in the Commons already, he said, if only he had a suitable estate.

With that, he set about getting one. He paid a visit to wealthy Lady Vane's house. Joyne, as instructed, waited until Scott would be comfortably ensconced, then delivered a new letter (in a 'painfully disguised' hand Scott had taken some time over) to an old porter standing by the Maypole in the Strand. Like the last, it denounced Scott as his pox-ridden namesake. An old co-conspirator of Scott's, a man named Benson, then conveniently arrived at Lady Vane's to confirm that Scott was innocent of the allegation and that it was all got up by her daughter.* Scott appeared vindicated, and the daughter malicious. His plan was falling into place.

Joyne spent the afternoon following Scott, out of sight, around the city's coffee shops and alehouses, and the night in Southwark, London's red-light district. He arrived at York Buildings the following morning dirty and unshaved. Pepys tetchily sent him home to change. Pepys was under some stress. The following day, 28 November, he and Deane made their way across the great flagstones of Westminster Hall to the benches of the court, only to be told – as they had feared – that they would have neither trial nor discharge. They would have to wait until the new year. By twelve noon Pepys was on his way back to York Buildings, where he found Joyne waiting for him.

Scott, Joyne said, still had every intention of prosecuting Pepys. Scott had been following Balty's work in Paris carefully, and had constructed an elegant little trick to undermine Pepys's evidence – he would claim Balty got it by bribery. Earlier that morning, he had shown Joyne a battered letter dated early September. It purported to come from a friend of Scott's in Paris, a language teacher called D'Allais. It claimed that Balty had offered D'Allais £2,000 to lie

---

* Benson was Shaftesbury's agent. Shaftesbury appeared to have many such agents, including a Harrington and also a Wilson. They were fewer than they seem: Benson, Harrington and Wilson were the same man.

about Scott for Pepys. The letter, as Joyne relayed it to Pepys, sounded convincing: Balty, Pepys knew, had indeed spoken to D'Allais; the letter warned that Balty had already got a statement from Sherwin, the cannon expert, as indeed he had; and Balty had allegedly told D'Allais that he could give security for the money by merchants in Paris who could cover it. That sounded like Trenchepain and Pelletier. Pepys was shaken. Scott had told Joyne that he would keep the letter until Parliament sat, then use it 'to claw off those dogs'. The phrase reveals how hunted Scott felt by Pepys. This was the kind of evidence that would bring the wrath of the court down on Pepys, if Scott could make the judges believe him.

As winter settled on the city, the fires were lit in the coffee houses, and the politicians of the street huddled up beside them. With no further court appearances until January, Pepys could only wait. Joyne continued to bump into Colonel Scott. Some encounters were mundane, others extraordinary. At the beginning of December, Joyne watched as Scott, dressed in a fine velvet coat, pulled a little bag from his pocket, out of which he took a brush and blackened his eyes and beard. He took a black periwig from a box in his closet and put it on. He was entirely disguised. Though Joyne was prepared for the transformation, it astonished him.

John Joyne was able to tidy up one small mystery for Pepys. When Scott fled from Gravesend and his rooms in Cannon Street were searched, one of the items recovered was a gold and crystal locket containing strands of human hair. Joyne explained it had belonged to a rich young Englishman – that same de Lavall who came to Paris with Edward Manning at the start of the cannonfounding saga. Scott hid the drunken de Lavall in a brothel after a gambling brawl and stole the locket, claiming a whore had taken it. With his watch-maker's eye for detail, Joyne recognised the locket on Scott's wrist. Scott insisted it was a completely different locket given to him by an old Dutch gentleman with a young wife for agreeing to lie with her. She had quadruplets as a result. Now Joyne was able to put things right. He wrote to de Lavall saying that he had discovered the locket and could help de Lavall get it back.[2]

If the figure Scott cut was sometimes comical, Pepys was nevertheless disturbed to hear that he had eleven witnesses ready to come over from France to finish him. Scott claimed he could produce the original papers Anthony Deane had delivered to the Marquis de Seignelay, and that he could prove that Balty had offered £2,000 to Foster and others to swear information to 'take away Scott's life'.[3]

Then, unexpectedly, his machinations against Pepys were driven entirely from the colonel's mind, and his ambitions for money, estates and, with them, a future in the House of Commons were dashed. On 13 December, in freezing weather, the target of his seduction, the prize that had driven him to tortuous duplicities, Lady Vane, died.

It was the latest addition to the patchwork tapestry of disasters that was Scott's life. It had all begun in New England, when Long Island, so nearly his, was snatched from him. It seemed that every time he got close to the success that he felt he deserved, everything fell to pieces at the last minute. It is clear from Lady Vane's surviving correspondence with Scott that she was (at least) extremely fond of him.[4] Scott believed that there were no fewer than three counties in which he might have been elected as an MP, with her estates to support him. Her death meant the collapse of this latest scheme for success.

John Joyne had been planning a trip to Paris when he heard the news. He went to the barber's shop in Bishopsgate where they handled the bookings for the Dover coach and asked if he could postpone his journey. The barber's wife told him she would make a note but he would only be able to change the booking if someone came along to take his place. He found Scott two days later in Newman's coffee house. The colonel, in a state of profound melancholy, said he had suffered the greatest loss in the world. Joyne offered him an orange from Portugal to cheer him up, and invited him to a dinner of calf's head and bacon the following day at his sister's tavern at St Clements on the Strand.[5]

It was less of a benevolent gesture than it seemed. After he parted from Scott, Joyne summoned Pepys to his sister's tavern. They examined the dining room on the first floor, and a closet in an adjacent room. Over a tankard of warm ale, they hatched an astonishing plan.

The following day, 17 December, Scott arrived for his dinner. It would be wrong to assume that his seduction of Lady Vane had been a cynical exercise. He was quite heartbroken. No man had ever had such a loss, he told Joyne, speaking at length about the excellence of the lady's wit, spirit and extraordinary love for him. She had told him (he remembered her words) that 'the very light of him fed her soul'. On and on he went, pouring out his grief.

Pepys, crammed into the closet nearby, heard every word.

Until now, everything Pepys had learnt about his adversary's life – with its great hopes and attendant disappointments – had arrived on bits of paper. The old desire to be a first-hand witness – the same desire that had driven him to walk through the streets as London burned – returned. Inside his closet, for the first time, he encountered the private Scott, in the full flood of despair.

The colonel had with him a favourite letter from Lady Vane and was reading it to Joyne. They had had private nicknames for each other; she called him 'the Grand Artaban', and referred to herself as 'Constantia'. She had evidently been willing to subscribe to Scott's old fantasies of nobility; Artaban, Scott explained to Joyne, 'was a person that lived a great while as a private man, but afterwards proved a prince'. Time, the lady had written, would do Artaban great right. She knew 'the grandeur of his mind and his true zeal for his country'.[6] Therein, no doubt, lay part of the reason why Scott had felt so enamoured; the lady had been willing to see him as he saw himself.

As the wine flowed he spoke of a 'well-turned whore' he had seen, and who he hoped would take away his melancholy. Joyne agreed that if anything would cure melancholy, that would. With the fury that often accompanied his disappointments, Scott swore and said he would marry Lady Vane's widowed sister. He had the affection of the people of England – now he simply needed an estate to get into Parliament and all the MPs would flock to him. But first he would make love to the dead woman's daughter, and if he could marry her, then by God that he would poison her; she was a bitch who looked as if she would put crooked pins in children's bread and butter. If one of her children died, he would bring witnesses from France to swear that she poisoned it.

All afternoon, Scott sat and drank, lamenting the money he had lost, proclaiming his importance to the people of England for his vast knowledge of foreign princes, and fuming at the roguery of former colleagues such as Sherwin the cannon expert, 'a fellow that was made of soft wax'. He spat insults at the Nevers gunmaking crew, who 'were mere tools'; he could not help it if his tools had failed him. His talk was of love, politics and popularity. Women liked him, not only because he was a 'beau garçon', but because he was of good humour and more sense than most. If he walked into a coffee house packed with a hundred people, he boasted, they flocked to him to hear him speak. He spoke of a petition he had written demanding Parliament be allowed to sit, and of the Duke of York, whom he loved as little as anybody and had 'much reason to do so'. The Duke had cheated him in New England, and had but few friends. Joyne asked him who those friends were.

'That rogue Pepys,' answered Scott, 'and the officers of the navy.'

Scott became more and more in drink, calling freely for both wine and tankards of ale, and his swearing and cursing grew until it was excessive. Returning to the matter of Lady Vane, he said she had seemed very well before she died, and that he would 'have her body opened, swearing that the bell that rang for her, rang murder'. He asked Joyne to help him set fire to the Vane house and pull it down about the daughter's ears. Joyne tried to guide him towards confessing that he had received 'many sums of money from the Court of France', but the colonel kept singing snatches of a French song at him in reply. He had drunk himself to a high pitch and 'began to be very full of love' and to kiss Joyne's sister and her maid. Around six o'clock, he heaved himself to his feet and staggered off to a ball at Newman's Court.

Pepys extracted himself from his closet.

'If an angel from heaven had recounted this,' he told Joyne, 'I would not have believed it,' and he thanked him for the 'horrendous revelations'.[7] But it was not only Scott who had unnerved him. Listening to the way Joyne had agreed with Scott, and the two old friends' easy conversation, Pepys began to feel very nervous of Joyne, and deeply suspicious that he was being betrayed.[8]

It was, as it turned out, a legitimate anxiety. Some time after these events, Pepys received a piece of information from a third party, Edward Wright – a straightforward man and a reliable witness. On Thursday 27 November, Wright had encountered Scott and Joyne in Fleet Street and mentioned that he had heard of no new witnesses against Pepys. Scott said that, to the contrary, Mr Joyne could prove that Pepys's brother-in-law Balty had offered him £2,000.[9] Joyne omitted the conversation from the journal he was writing for Pepys. On 7 March the following year, Scott told Wright that he had sent 'Mr Joyne, a jeweller, to Mr Pepys to give him some information'. Joyne had had £100 from Pepys, which Pepys would find 'would cut his throat'.[10]

The watchmaker from Paris, caught between loyalty to his new master Pepys and his old friend Scott, had been playing a double game. He was not a brave man. Moving openly between Scott's haunts and Pepys at York Buildings was a hazardous affair. It seems likely that Joyne elected to tell Scott at least part of the truth, while at the same time passing Pepys any information he could glean. Altogether, the months Joyne spent with Scott told Pepys more about Scott's state of mind than they contributed to his defence. Pepys would have to wait until the court convened again in January to discover whether Scott's claims of fresh evidence and witnesses against him were true, and whether Joyne had betrayed him to Scott.

20

Habeas Corpus

As the new term approached, Pepys, embarrassed by how he had kept Pellissary's household waiting, decided to bring his French witnesses over regardless of whether there was to be a trial or not. The goodwill and justice that he had met from these strangers stood in stark opposition to the attacks he had received from fellow Englishmen, and he wanted to thank them, regardless of the cost. On 5 January 1680, he told Balty to return, and to bring his two witnesses with him. He hoped that 'the lowness of their quality', being servants, would mean he could entertain them cheaply.[1] At the last minute, Pellissary's valet got cold feet and pulled out. Madame Pellissary's nephew stepped into the breach. To his chagrin, Pepys had an expensive gentleman to look after.[2]

On 9 January, intending to apply a little back-door pressure for trial to the new Attorney General, Pepys visited his chamber in Gray's Inn. The man's name was Cresswell Levins. He heard Pepys, then told him politely that he could do nothing to hurry his trial. Pepys complained about his expensive foreign witnesses. Levins said, with regret, that given 'the malignity of the age, which begot a great many other evils', he thought that witnesses from France – regardless of their religion – would be of very little credit in court. Besides, he said, Harbord had a new witness. The crimes, if proved, would be capital.[3] It must have been a sober ride home to York Buildings. The Attorney General seemed anxious to see them convicted, and whoever the second witness was, Pepys had no defence prepared against them.

When Pepys and Deane walked into court on the first day of the new term, 23 January, they did indeed come under a fresh attack, one for which all Pepys's diligence, correspondence, investigation, expenditure and energy had not prepared them in the least. It was not, however, an attack by Scott, Shaftesbury, Buckingham or a new witness; it was an attack by the Attorney General.

Levins had run out of options. Despite his claims, Pepys's accusers had failed to supply him with a second witness to support Scott's charges. With only one witness, he could not draw up an indictment. He could do nothing to prosecute Pepys.

He could, however, make sure that Pepys was not allowed to go free, and he turned his attention to this. The judges of the court came to his defence. It was entirely natural for them to do their best to prevent the release of a man who had been charged with treason. The operational principle of English law was to convict the accused traitor if at all possible. It was, therefore, anathema to the court simply to allow Pepys to go free. The personal opinions of the row of judges on their high wooden bench about his guilt or innocence were entirely irrelevant; habit compelled them to hold him for as long as possible.

Without trial, the most effective tool at Pepys's disposal to win his freedom back was the Habeas Corpus Act. The Act had been passed by the furious, Whig-filled Commons on 27 May, one week after Pepys and Deane were imprisoned. That Parliament had been almost barren of legislation, because the Whigs had focused their energy so completely on excluding the Duke of York, but the Habeas Corpus Act was the one big, beautiful fruit. *

---

* The Act was only passed because, as a joke, one of the parliamentary officials counted one particularly fat peer as ten. Shaftesbury leapt to his feet and spoke for an hour to prevent any recount until enough lords had entered the chamber to make it impossible. The work of A. S. Turberville in 'The House of Lords under Charles II', Part 1, in *English Historical Review*, vol. XLIV (July 1929) has given credibility to this unlikely story.

Habeas corpus had been established legal procedure in England for centuries. It was the bedrock of individual liberty, and has since, by export, been carried to all corners of the world. First and foremost, it was a safeguard against arbitrary imprisonment. It allowed any imprisoned person to request a court appearance, and it compelled the gaoler to bring them to court and give a reason for the imprisonment (the phrase in full, *habeas corpus ad subjiciendum*, means 'you should have the body brought [into court]'). If the reason given seemed insufficient, the court discharged the prisoner. If the charges were acceptable, and not thought to be bailable, the prisoner was kept in prison.

This was only one half of habeas corpus practice; if that had been all there was, a convincing-sounding charge like Scott's would have been enough to keep a man imprisoned for ever. There was a second component: the prisoner could not be detained indefinitely. After two terms without trial (there are four in a year), they had to be released.

The new Habeas Corpus Act superseded the old established practice in 1679 because there had been loopholes which made the old practice ineffective. Faced with a summons to court, a gaoler could (for example) move the prisoner to another gaol to invalidate the summons. Sometimes prisoners were taken to the Scilly or Channel Islands, out of reach.[4] The 1679 Act closed all those loopholes. It was passed for purely political reasons; the hostile Whig Commons was trying to stop King Charles throwing his political enemies in the Tower. Shaftesbury, who had experienced the cruelties of arbitrary imprisonment firsthand, was one of the authors.[5] Nonetheless, it was perhaps the greatest blow ever struck for the freedom of the individual.

The attack that the Attorney General launched when Pepys walked into court on 23 January was to deny that Pepys came within its remit. Only imprisonments after 1 June were covered by the new legislation; Pepys had been charged in the Commons on 20 May. However, Pepys's team quickly reminded the court that he had been imprisoned anew on 20 June, when they moved prisons. He and Deane were therefore protected by the Act.[6]

Scroggs demanded that the Attorney General explain how he intended to proceed, telling him Pepys and Deane might expect trial or discharge this term. The Attorney General explained that he had no second witness to support Scott's charge, but reiterated that the charge, if proved, would be high treason.

Pepys went on the offensive. They had been in the hands of the court nearly a year, he said. It was the fourth term since their arrest, and the third since their most recent imprisonment – either way, the two-term limit set by habeas corpus was well past. The court shifted uncomfortably. When Pepys began to deplore the great cost of holding foreign witnesses, the court forced the Attorney General to promise that he would say next Tuesday what he was prepared to do in their prosecution. For the first time, it looked like their ordeal might be coming to an end.[7]

The prosecution, however, had barely begun.

On Monday Pepys sent his lawyer, Mr Hayes, to the Attorney General to discover whether there would be a trial, since he would need to send for his witnesses by the next post.[8] That night, in a state of some excitement that trial was imminent, Pepys sat down to write to James Puckle to leave Flanders immediately – but then the answer came back; the Attorney General did not think there would be a trial this term, nor could he foresee whether they would ever have one.[9] The letter to Puckle was never sent. Disappointment again.

As Scott moved into the background, it was the Attorney General who emerged as Pepys's enemy, and his tactics were puerile. Back in court on Tuesday he pretended to forget completely what had already been established, and declared again that Pepys and Deane had been imprisoned too early for the Habeas Corpus Act to apply to them. Again, Pepys fought this off. This was only the opening gambit. A comprehensive attack was being made on their right to habeas corpus, and some of the judges were complicit. Justice Francis Pemberton came from a family that had supported Parliament in the Civil War. He had himself been a victim of the past inadequacies of habeas corpus and he knew the new law inside out. He tried to get them on technicalities. Perhaps, he mulled, Pepys did come within habeas corpus, but he had forfeited his right to it by neglecting to demand trial on the first day of the previous court term.* Pepys and Deane immediately vowed that they had indeed demanded it, but had not insisted that their demand be recorded, since the letter of the Act did not require it. They were having to be quick on their feet.[10]

They were immediately hit again. Justice Dolben joined with Pemberton and together they made a spectacular claim about the Habeas Corpus Act. Quoting the language of the Act, they argued that it was intended to protect the rights only of people who were committed by the King's Council. Pepys had been imprisoned by the court; the Act, they said, did not apply to him.

The English legal system shuddered. The practice of habeas corpus had been evolving for over 200 years. It had developed, quite organically, into the best available defence against arbitrary imprisonment by any malicious party – king, Parliament, court or private enemies. Under its benevolent power, any persecuted creature in any freezing cell could get their case heard in court. It was, in short, the great bulwark against cruelty and injustice. The Whigs, by formalising it into an Act, had put it in writing. Their intention had been to improve its efficacy, but Dolben and Pemberton, in pursuit of Pepys, were interpreting the words in a way that disempowered anyone not imprisoned by the King. They were departing altogether from the spirit of habeas corpus. If they managed to win the point and set a precedent, it would be a crushing defeat for the safety of all English subjects.†

To his eternal credit, the Lord Chief Justice William Scroggs stepped in. History, with good reason, has not been kind to Scroggs. During his life, he had a reputation as a lover of wine and women, a

---

* It was a requirement of the Act that the defendant ask for trial in the first week of each term of his imprisonment.
† Since the principle of habeas corpus was later exported worldwide by colonial expansion, it seems reasonable to remark that world legal history was at stake.

man whose rough beginnings were evident in his unrestrained tongue and his ambition. In retrospect, Scroggs's support of Oates, his bullying of his juries to return 'guilty' verdicts and his abuse of the Catholic defendants cowering at the bar seem obscene. Of Catholics, he famously declared that 'they eat their God, they kill their king and saint the murderer'.[11] However, his ruthless prosecution of the Plot stemmed from a belief that the majority of Englishmen shared; he believed the Plot was real.

For all his failings and the miscarriages of justice he presided over, Scroggs knew a dangerous precedent when he saw one. He slapped down Dolben and Pemberton's attack. Although the Act had been intended to relieve those imprisoned by the Crown, he said, he did not doubt that it was also intended to help anyone imprisoned indefinitely. By the normal course of the court, he reminded his over-zealous colleagues, no man was to be denied a trial within two terms after he first asked for it.

Scroggs turned to Levins, demanding to know his plans. The Attorney General answered that Deane might expect to face the *Hunter* charges at the next assizes in Winchester. As for the treason charge, he had no evidence but Scott's and had not 'to this day' seen any of the witnesses.[12] The Whig MP William Harbord, in court at the Attorney General's request, was called up to explain where Scott and the rest of the witnesses were. He raised his hands helplessly. He bore Pepys and Deane no ill will he claimed, disingenuously. His job as chair of the naval miscarriages committee had been simply to deliver the committee's papers to the Attorney General; he had no concern in it himself. It was a massive step down by the man who had promised to prove Pepys 'an ill man'.[13]

Scroggs was bewildered. No one seemed willing to take responsibility. He turned back to the Attorney General and asked him where the witnesses were. Had Levins sent for them? Were they ready to give in their testimonies? The Attorney General replied he was completely ignorant of their whereabouts. He had been given nothing but their original declarations. That, he said returning the buck, was why he had asked Harbord to come. Again Harbord shrugged. He had seen the witnesses, he said, but they were resolved not to give any evidence except when Parliament was sitting. Parliament had been prorogued until November. He had no idea where they lived.

Baffled silence in the hall. The judges blinked, then turned inwards to murmur among themselves. Pepys spoke up. He offered Harbord an olive branch. He told the court that he believed Harbord's vehemence against him in the Commons had arisen from a belief that the evidence had been good. But the evidence, Pepys pointed out, had not been proved nor, he was sure, comfortable in the results of his investigation, ever could be. Harbord knocked the olive branch away, snarling that Pepys and Deane were unfit for any government position of trust.

'We know what you would be at,' muttered Justice Pemberton to Pepys's counsel, seeing how the wind was blowing, 'you would put us upon difficulties, by pressing for a discharge.'[14] Pepys leapt in to say that they had never asked for a discharge though it was the fourth term since their commitment. Both he and Deane wanted trial more than discharge, 'by how much our reputations are more valuable to us than our liberties'. He asked for trial again, but failing that he thought he and Deane should not be kept in bonds, 'without knowing when we shall be quit of them'.[15]

Despite his association with the Whigs, Scroggs was a royalist at heart, and like Pepys had worked his way up the professional ladder. Pepys's quick, eloquent displays in court had impressed him. He listened attentively, then decided to bring the thing to an issue. Pepys's request, he announced, was 'very reasonably and very modestly demanded'. He directed the Attorney General to appear on the last day of term with details of how he intended to proceed. If there was to be no trial, Scroggs said that he wanted to hear a good reason why not, 'I say a very full reason.' He was beginning to realise that mud had been flung.

'I do not say this as any rule or resolution of the court,' he continued cautiously, 'but as an intimation of the opinion of this court, that those gentlemen should not be kept in this condition under bail and with the imputation of treason over them, which was very grievous indefinitely.'[16]

Harbord left court laughing heartily and saying that he had kept Pepys and Deane bound over for another term.[17] But Pepys and Deane walked out with a light step.

Two weeks later, on the eve of the last day of term and this final court appearance, the King stepped in at Pepys's request. Charles spoke to Attorney General Levins in the Council Chamber. He suggested, with the light touch of royal power, that Levins might either try the men or discharge them.[18] Scroggs and Justice Dolben received similar messages. Thus, the great royal hand finally reached down to help Pepys when Pepys no longer needed help. Through the King, the word came back that as of six o'clock that evening, the Attorney General still had no new witnesses.[19]

It was the depths of frozen February, and the 12th was the last day of term. At King's Bench, Pepys and Deane's counsel moved for discharge.[20] Scroggs asked how long they had stood committed and was told four terms.

'Mr Attorney General,' said Scroggs, 'what have you to say?'

'Truly, I have nothing more to say to them than what I had at the beginning of term,' replied the helpless Attorney General, 'only this,' and he pulled a very tatty rabbit from his hat – a letter delivered to him the previous night. It contained extracts of several letters from beyond the seas relating to this business. It had been brought by an attorney, one Richard Goodenough, who had told him that John Scott had been waiting nearby.* Levins had told him to bring Scott to court. The court called both men. Only Goodenough appeared.

'Have you brought Scott, or not?' demanded the Attorney General.

---

* Goodenough was soon to show his true republican colours, being accused of participating in the Midsummer riot at the Guildhall in 1682 and then in the Rye House plot, an unsuccessful plan to assassinate the King on his way back from Newmarket in 1683. C. S. Knighton, *Pepys's Later Diaries* (2004), p. 63, note.

'I spoke to Scott to attend the court,' said Goodenough, apologetically, 'but his answer was that he would not come.'

A great murmur of dissatisfaction arose from the judges. The Attorney General, trying to salvage the situation, asked that the papers should be read but Scroggs indignantly forbade it because they were not signed and there was no one in the court to take responsibility for their content. Pepys's lawyer, who had brief sight of them, later confirmed that these 'letters from beyond the seas' were in fact in Goodenough's own handwriting.[21]

Scroggs, eager to clear the decks for more serious matters, applied himself to Pepys.

'Why Mr Pepys,' he said, 'would it be much inconvenient to you to appear again here next term?' Justices Jones and Dolben seconded the question with a great deal of respect and gentleness. Pemberton sat scowling. He never said another word about Pepys's case.

Pepys boldly replied that it would be very inconvenient. His friends were struggling under the huge bail they had put up. He himself, being now wholly unconcerned with public business, had plans to go to the country to sort out family affairs. The judges nodded their heads in understanding. They offered to discharge both men's bail and said that, if next term was too soon for Pepys' affairs to be properly settled, he could return the term after.

'My lords,' said Pepys, 'give me leave to demand what assurance we should have then more than now of being fully discharged.'

Scroggs poured forth a stream of fresh expressions of respect.

'As for any assurance,' he said, 'we can give you none, but from our present proceedings you might very well judge what the inclinations of the court would be.'

Later, Pepys recorded the stream of thoughts that went through his head at that moment. It would be ill-advised, and probably unsuccessful, to press the court for more when it was treating them so well. They had achieved their principal aim of having bail discharged. He thought about the prorogued Parliament; he did not want to be brought into court 'in the very beginning of their heats', nor did he want to seem afraid to appear in court while they sat.

'Take it, take it, take it,' urged Deane beside him.[22]

Pepys looked up and told the court that he would be content to appear on the first day of Trinity term, 12 June. The court seemed pleased with his compliance. Pepys's and Deane's suffering supporters were returned the vast sums they had put up for bail, and the two accused were given back all but £1,000 each, to guarantee their appearance. They thanked the court and turned away into Westminster Hall.

The London mob, dismayed and suspecting Scroggs had been bribed, had a new song to sing:

Since Scroggs for Pepys and Deane took bail,
And on the good cause did turn his tail –
For £2000 to buy beef and ale,
Which nobody can deny.

Our Juries and Judges to shame the Plot
Have traitors freed to prove it not,
But England shall stand when they go to pot,
Which nobody can deny.[23]

Two weeks later, on 4 March, Pepys sent his French witnesses home again.[24] Outside the courtroom, meanwhile, another part of the plot against him was falling to pieces.

21

The Confessions of John James

By January 1680 Pepys's accuser and former butler, John James, was beginning to unravel.

James saw himself as a professional. After employment in the navy, he had served a string of great masters, among them Sir William Coventry, Sir Richard Mason and the Prince of Orange. His mother's fond opinion that he was very 'able in his trade' need not be doubted.[1]

James had been in decent employment and about to leave for Spain in the service of a knight when William Harbord and the other plotters against Pepys first approached him.[2] The butler would be looked after, he was told, if he gave them information. He refused, thinking it wrong to say anything against a master whose bread he had eaten.[3] The offers escalated. The promises of good money and free accommodation enticed him to Harbord's house in Covent Garden.[4]

To begin with, he was treated well. The day after his Covent Garden meeting, at which he and Harbord discussed his memories of working for Pepys, he was given twenty shillings.[5] Accepting that made it hard to reject the second payment a fortnight later. Harbord's shady go-between, Colonel Mansell, let James know he was a 'made man'.[6]

The industrious James took advantage of his new contacts. A month after he charged Pepys, he heard that the storekeeper's job at Woolwich was available. John Scott's patron, the Duke of Buckingham, scribbled a line endorsing James's application for the job; the rest of the letter, which commended James's honesty and his service in the navy, was written out by James's sister.[7] To supplement his income, James got Harbord to write a letter to the Earl of Essex recommending that he be rewarded for his part in discovering a 'cheat' involving a lieutenant and two bales of silk.[8] Harbord also wrote to Sir Henry Capel to try to secure James the purser's job on the *Jersey*.[9] All these failed, but Harbord made sure James was kept funded and (once, when he was arrested for debt by his tailor) out of prison.[10]

Several months of fading hope followed, and by the late summer of 1679 James was scraping by on the bottom of his resources, reliant on Harbord's allowance of ten shillings a week and surely wishing he had gone to Spain in the first place. It will be remembered that Phelix Donluis had had to buy him nuts on their drunken ramble around Bartholomew Fair and the City. Then, Harbord stopped the allowance and on 15 November, James swore and damned Harbord, Capel, Scott, Mansell and the rest, who despite their many opportunities to get him a job had completely failed to do so.

Pepys, James now realised, was the major obstacle to his finding work. It was Pepys who had unfairly sacked him for the slight crime of sleeping with the housekeeper and failed to supply him with a reference. Then, in the House of Commons, Pepys had blackened his name in front of his regular pool of employers, not only telling them about the housekeeper but also claiming that James had robbed his house – a particular affront, since James had been abroad in the service of the Prince of Orange at the time of the robbery.[11]

By January 1680 James was living in poverty at the house of his mother and sister. All three now shared the same bed.[12] From being the dapper butler in the houses of the great, he had become utterly dependent on his family. It was essential he remove the block between him and employment. If Pepys was the cause of the problem, he might also be the solution. Slowly, inevitably, James began to gravitate back towards his former master.[13]

The first Pepys heard of James's fall from grace was when his former clerk, Phelix Donluis, gave him the Bartholomew Fair information on 12 January. On the 24th, Pepys returned home to find

Sir Anthony Deane waiting for him. Deane told him he had just missed two most unlikely visitors. The Harris brothers had come to call. Deane sent a boy to summon them back.[14]

Alexander Harris was the messenger at Derby House, the building which housed the Admiralty Office and Pepys's private lodgings. John Harris had been the porter until Pepys dismissed him on suspicion of playing, with James, a part in the robbery.[15] John's dismissal had 'put a brand upon him', and he could not get the arrears of pay he was owed. The brothers had already shuffled in to see Deane two or three times, asking for John's pay and claiming they could give information that would do Deane and Pepys 'more good than any body else could'. John was benign. Alexander was a full-blown rogue who had given false evidence against Pepys in the Samuel Atkins case.[16] Pepys had not forgotten the betrayal.

Only Alexander came back with Deane's boy. Pepys summoned him into the Great Parlour below. He demanded to know Alexander's intentions but his firmness covered his anxiety. The Atkins experience had showed him that words with Alexander Harris could be turned to 'ill-use'. It was for this reason that Pepys, ignoring the cost to his eyes, began to write a diary again that night.

Alexander replied with a list of accumulated grievances, the 'long' unkindness he had received from Pepys, such as 'his being pinched in the profits of his place' – he thought Pepys had done nothing to secure the twelve pence owed him for every Admiralty pass issued. Pepys answered Harris with characteristic authority, 'shortly and calmly' telling him he had never done him wrong, nor ever would.

Confronted with this impasse, Alexander delivered his bombshell. A great deal of wrong had been done to Pepys, but he knew details of what else was still to come. Deane was to suffer further and Will Hewer was to be accused too. They had a witness; a Mrs Wood had confessed that large sums of money had passed through her hands. Alexander had decided to do Pepys all the right he could in the future. In return he expected that he and his brother would receive Pepys's help in getting them paid.

That was not all, and Pepys might have suspected what was coming. Alexander asked him to promise to forgive one other person. He would not name this person, declaring earnestly that he would rather die than bring them unnecessarily to Pepys. Alexander's friendship with John James had not escaped Pepys, who replied that he would be sorry if it was he, but Alexander would give nothing away. They reached a compromise; Pepys promised forgiveness on condition that this man provide the justice he said he could. Alexander would return with him in two or three days.

Sinister Alexander was in fact not interested in the money and – suspiciously – asked for less than was owed him. The money camouflaged his true intention. He had been one of the three men who had persuaded John James to bring charges against Pepys in the first place.[17] With so many Catholic plotters on the gallows it had seemed the route to success in the new Whig regime. Pepys should have been dead but instead he was alive and fighting, and James was turning. Alexander wanted to save his own skin. He knew that James's desire to be reconciled with Pepys might lead to a full confession; then he would be vulnerable to Pepys's wrath. So he had paid Pepys a visit to recast himself as the midwife of Pepys's vindication by James.

Alexander was not the only rat abandoning the plot's sinking ship. The second man instrumental in convincing James to bring the charges was the Derby House clerk, Phelix Donluis. Donluis, who knew Alexander well, had learnt of James's desire to be reconciled with Pepys and, like Alexander, sought to defend himself pre-emptively. Out of the blue, he had sent Pepys the account of the Bartholomew Fair adventure with James, proving that James was receiving an allowance from the Whigs, and describing James's fury when the allowance was cut off. Like Harris, Donluis had concluded that it was best to curry as much favour as possible as the plot against Pepys collapsed.

When Pepys and James met, the tension was high. Pepys privately feared accusations of bribing witnesses; James risked the wrath of his co-conspirators.

It was 27 January and Pepys had spent a successful morning in court listening to Scroggs insist that the Habeas Corpus Act applied widely enough to cover their case. He celebrated by going to the theatre to see Etherege's *She Would If She Could*. On his return home, Will Hewer told him Alexander Harris was waiting in a nearby coffee house with the man he had refused to name. When Alexander walked in with James, Pepys ducked into the little parlour and summoned Alexander to him. He was not happy to talk alone with James. Could Hewer sit in as witness to what was said? The downtrodden James was 'very willing' that the meeting should be witnessed. The four men sat down in the parlour, and James poured out his grievances. It was a slight thing to have slept with the housekeeper; it was a worse thing to be denied references and to be wrongly accused before the Commons of theft. He complained that Pepys had 'bespattered' his name and hindered his employment. Pepys studiously gave him very sparing answers and, seeing James's emotional state, gently pointed out the great wrongs James had done him.

After stumbling through an account in which he elevated himself to a central role in the plot, James offered his help. There was more 'mischief' brewing, he said, and he was to meet Scott and the merchants 'to carry on their further designs' against Pepys and Deane next week. He could stop this, but only in exchange for the Harrises' arrears and, which he wanted most, his own employment in the navy. He would give Pepys three or four days to think it over.

The offer was difficult. Any employment Pepys got James would look like a bribe. He told James curtly that he could not make promises of employment but if James helped him of his own accord, Pepys would give him 'all the just offices of kindness I can'. After they had left, he aired his doubts to Will Hewer. They agreed that the men had enough villainy to make ill use of the meeting. Pepys decided to let them take their course 'without ever desiring any further communication with them'.

Pepys's confidence unnerved Harris and James, who had seemed blustering and unconvincing against it. After three days of silence from

Pepys, their nerve broke and they came up with a new ploy to frighten him into promising James employment. Before church on Friday 30 January, Harris, feigning alarm, came to warn Pepys that James's commitment to aiding him had become 'unsteady' because James was not sure he would benefit from it. Pepys, uncompromising, told Harris that his innocence would stand without bribery. The obsequious middleman answered that he had said much the same to James – they must expect no reward but must trust Pepys.

Despite the game-playing, each side needed the other. When Pepys missed Harris's next three visits by being away from home, Will Hewer found himself taking a trip to Derby House where he just happened to fall into conversation with Harris and arrange a meeting.

That second meeting, at six o'clock on 6 February, was a much more congenial affair. A fire was made in the parlour where the four men sat. James was no longer full of recrimination – his disclosures took the form of naïve questions. Was it usual for a parliamentary committee to adjourn regularly in order to hold private meetings in other places? Harbord's committee, he said, had met in the Mitre in Fenchurch Street. Here the merchants who gave evidence for the *Hunter* charges were told that their losses from the *Catherine* would be reimbursed from the estates of the executed Pepys and Deane. Was it due method for Parliament men to give money to witnesses? James could refer to his black pocket-book for dates and amounts; his last payment was the biggest, at £3.

As James talked, the shady characters behind the scenes were starting to become clearer to Pepys. Mr Garroway, who had seemed outraged to hear the charges in the Commons, had been a key player in formulating them and was one of Pepys's 'greatest enemies'. It was Colonel Mansell, a man who Pepys did not know, who 'first began all the mischief'. At this stage, he knew only that Mansell was Harbord's 'associate'. Promising that he would come again soon, James left with Harris.

All that Pepys needed now was a signed and witnessed information from James and for him to tell the court the truth, but he heard nothing more until 10 February, when word reached him that

James's doctor had confined him indoors. A second silence lasted two weeks, then news came that James was dying.

He had tuberculosis. The disease infects the lungs and begins with an unrelenting cough. As it progresses, the patient coughs up phlegm and blood, suffering night-sweats and weight loss. On the 10th, he had wanted Pepys to know that his doctor had 'charged me not to stir out this week, for my cure wholly depends upon this five or six days'.[18] By the 25th, James's body was being ravaged by the later symptoms, he was 'sick to despair of life', and Alexander Harris concluded privately that he had at most forty hours to live.[19]

James had not told Pepys the complete truth. His partial confession had given him great 'quiet of mind', for his lies had weighed heavily on him, but now, facing death, he wished to make a full one.[20] He did not send for Pepys directly, but addressed a note to Will Hewer, a gentler confessor.[21] Harris, the middleman he would betray, took it to York Buildings, but Hewer was away in Chatham for several days so Pepys opened the note himself and learnt that James was in his last hours.[22] It was now vital to secure a written confession from James, and quickly.

In Hewer's absence, Pepys decided to ask Thomas Povey to witness James's confession. Pepys had a low opinion of Povey – whom he called 'simple Povey (of all, the most ridiculous fool that ever I knew to pretend to business)'.[23] Povey had a good reason to dislike Pepys; Povey had transferred the position of treasurer for Tangier to Pepys in exchange for a four-sevenths cut of the rewards that Pepys had consistently failed to deliver to him. Povey was also a friend of Harbord's. Despite all this, it was an excellent choice, since Povey could not possibly be seen as Pepys's stooge. His impartiality was assured and by using him, Pepys demonstrated his confidence that objective truth would vindicate him. Pepys wrote him a terse letter appealing to his public-spiritedness and, when Harris delivered it early the following morning, Povey readily offered his help.[24]

John James was proud and ill and ashamed, and Mr Povey was a man of great quality. He had once impressed Pepys by giving a supper at which he playfully challenged the guests to name any food they desired him to produce, and had prawns, swan and venison instantly brought forth at their request.[25] James hated the thought of any such person seeing him lying in the one bed at his mother's house. Besides, by the following morning James was sufficiently better to hope that he might write his confession himself, then keep it in his possession until he was dead. Pepys forbore to send a less imposing witness to James, a risky move given the possibility of James's further decline. Instead, Pepys made Harris promise to 'be watchful' and keep him informed of James's condition daily.

Three nail-biting days passed during which Harris strikingly failed to keep that promise. James's sickness had put pressure on Harris. Afraid that the dying man might abandon their friendship, confess all and implicate him, Harris told Pepys nothing about James's deterioration, and Pepys could enter only 'Nothing stirring' and 'Nothing' for whole days in his Diary. Then Will Hewer returned from Chatham and, on 1 March, found an excuse to tag along with Harris to James's mother's house. John James 'fell passionately a-weeping' when he saw him. He asked his other visitors to withdraw and so, free from Harris's watchful eyes, began to 'discharge his mind' to Hewer for the next half hour. When Hewer returned the next day he brought Povey and Pepys's lawyer John Hayes, for James was now ready to have his confession turned into a legal document. With his mother and sister beside him, James finally told the whole truth. Conscious of those who were not in the room he asked 'that A H might not be acquainted with what he had declared concerning him'. All of Harris's machinations had not been able to overcome James's need to meet death with a spotless conscience.

The confession was everything Pepys could have wanted. James told how he had first been approached by Harris's lodger Colonel Mansell on 26 April 1679, six days after the Whigs had taken over the navy board and two days before William Harbord's Committee of Enquiry into the Miscarriages of the Navy was established; how James had initially turned the offer down but how the promises of good treatment, combined with pressure from Harris and Mansell, had eventually got him along to Harbord's house in Covent Garden. There, Harbord flattered James, confirming he could rely on the rewards promised and would be safe if the plot failed. James told the listeners how Harbord had pressed him for what he knew of Pepys's religion; how he had delivered invitations to the merchants to dine with Scott; how at this dinner Harbord promised the merchants Pepys and Deane's estates and then gave James a guinea and – here we sense James was much more on the fringes of the plot than he had pretended to Pepys at their first meeting – James left Mansell, Scott, Harbord and the merchants dining 'and went away'.

Then, James told the listeners, a day or two before he brought the charges against Pepys in the Commons, Mansell summoned him to the Mitre tavern in Fenchurch Street. There he had found Harbord and his Whig supporters on the Committee, with Captain Moone and the merchants. Harbord pointed to John Scott, sitting by himself in a little room wearing a velvet coat and embroidered belt, and said that he was one who would hang both Pepys and Deane.

James related how the cash dried up and how, when he wrote saying he had been damned by depending on his promises, Harbord sent him a dismissive final sum. After Pepys was bailed, Mansell put James on to writing what he had collected against Pepys and Hewer. Mansell supplied the title, *Plain Truth*. James sold it to Benjamin Harris the bookseller. There was a second paper, he said, which Mansell had drawn up, but James would not permit it to be printed. This was an obscene libel, and the contrite James put it into Mr Povey's hands. Pepys cannot have enjoyed reading it. It included a passage saying Pepys – who was the son of a tailor – was

so cheap a soul that he would have squeezed a poor cripple out of 12 penny worth of farthings . . . [to allow him his] pension which by the king's allowance he was to have for the loss of his limbs in his majesty's service. I hope this tailor-like person with his hypocritical designs and Judas-like face may be a warning not to trust one of so poor a descent so puffed up with pride through the advantages of his preferment which swells him more than the wind colic with which he is sometimes troubled.[26]

James charged Alexander Harris, Colonel Mansell and Donluis as the 'great instigators' who persuaded him to bring the charges. He did not point the finger at Harbord in the same way; Harbord had only promised a reward.

'I do not believe,' he said finally, 'that Mr Pepys either is or ever was a Roman Catholic.' Morelli was just for singing and playing the lute and 'I do not believe he kept him for any such purpose as I suggested' – a marvellously understated word – 'in my Information.' That Information had been written by Harbord, and James could never justify it to any person or Parliament if he lived 'a thousand years'.

It was done. The witnesses by his bed signed their names at the bottom of what had been written. It seemed that this part, at least, of the charges had lifted.

For eight days, the anxious record of the James business disappeared from Pepys's journal. His days filled with action as he supervised his visiting French witnesses, swearing their information about Scott. He threw the last dinner for them on 3 March with Deane and Povey in attendance then sent them home. He sent James 'charity' anonymously, and when the James family asked the messenger where the money came from, they got no answer. He now called James 'the poor sick man, for whose soul's health I am truly concerned, however he has been misled, to the occasioning me much evil', and he engaged the Canon of Westminster, Dr Adam Littleton, to provide the sacrament to him. That took place on the 6th, beside his mother, 'she and her son in tears', and James again confessing all, which the vigilant Pepys had Littleton write down in full.

Pepys's confidence in his case soared. This short diary shows that he was enjoying the finer things in life once more. He dined with old friends, received visits from his flirtatious friend Lady Mordaunt and watched a new play by Otway.

Alexander Harris now let slip an extraordinary piece of information, wrongly thinking that James had already confessed it. James and the Harrises had planned to kidnap Will Hewer. For £5 they had bought the services of a coachman whose foot-boy was to come to

Hewer's house at night dressed in the Houblon livery, with a message that James Houblon wanted to see him. 'By fair or foul means' they were to get him into the coach waiting at the corner of the street. Should anyone disturb them they would pretend it was an arrest. They planned to move him between one hiding place at 'Marrow Bone' (Marylebone) and another at Hyde Park Corner as the 'counter-designs' of Hewer's friends necessitated. Their intention was to get from Hewer a bill 'upon his Goldsmith' for £500 or £600, pick up the money then flee to France leaving a message for Pepys telling him where Hewer could be found. The plan was to cost £20, but John Harris did not receive his wages as soon as he expected and the design 'wholly fell'. This plan must have been born out of the desperation that followed the cutting-off of James's allowance. Will Hewer confronted James who, embarrassed, confessed to the plan but 'imperfectly and with trouble'.

On 10 March, this period of calm ended. The great coordinator of the plot against Pepys, William Harbord, discovered that James had confessed and arrived 'very hot' at Alexander Harris's house, demanding Harris meet him that afternoon. Harris insisted on neutral territory and they chose the cloister of Westminster Abbey. On his way, Harris was intercepted by a very shifty Mansell, who mentioned that there was no need to visit James. It took no great skill to decode this incompetent deception, and Harris went straight to James's. A disastrous scene greeted him. Harbord, Dr Spratt, two JPs and a clerk were crowded around James's bed. Spratt, who was Dean of Westminster, was clutching a document, stopping the others signing it because it concerned Pepys who was absent, entirely unaware and dining on lobster pie with Lady Mordaunt. The frustrated Harbord sent Harris to fetch Pepys to come the following morning.

When Pepys heard the news that evening he feared Harbord had been forcing the sick man to sign a reaffirmation of the original charges, undoing all his work. First thing next morning, Hewer summoned the lawyer Hayes and set off to James's while Pepys chased round trying to find out just what had happened. They met at Povey's where Hewer told him that James was this morning valiantly 'persevering to assert the truth' of his confession of eight days before. Pepys and Hewer arrived at James's together a few minutes before ten o'clock.

The tiny house was empty of visitors. It was the first time the great Mr Pepys had visited his former butler, and the first time he had seen him ill. The abbey bell was tolling in the distance and it was clear that James had little time left. Pepys stayed just long enough to ask him how he was, then he and Hayes escaped from the oppressive sickroom into the fresh air. They wandered aimlessly around the new buildings in the area and when they got back to the house, there was 'much company at the door'. Hewer, Harbord and others were in the chamber and Harbord had brought an arsenal of witnesses. There were too many for the room and after a stiff greeting, Harbord persuaded Pepys to come to Sir William Waller's nearby house. Povey was there along with many of Harbord's supporters and the mysterious Colonel Mansell whom, Pepys recorded, 'I never saw before.' Dr Spratt was there too. Alexander Harris, a weathercock spinning to the strongest breeze, concluded that Harbord was now in the ascendant and spoke 'very scurvily' to Pepys.[27]

What happened next brought Pepys huge relief. Dr Spratt explained that Harbord's paper was not a revised confession from John James. It was only intended to clear Harbord from James's charges of bribery. Spratt had resisted its being signed because it concerned Pepys, who had been absent. Harbord, who had a parliamentary reputation to consider, rattled off his defence. He had indeed given James money, but only in imitation of the King's own practice of 'allowing dinner of meat to the Lords in the Tower', not to make James swear anything falsely. Pepys, concerned only with clearing his own name, signed the paper and let Harbord off the hook.

James's confession showing Pepys's innocence was read again. At the part where Harbord promised the merchants satisfaction out of Pepys and Deane's estates if the charges succeeded in having them executed, James 'cried out aloud'. He was not without bravery, and for the first time he accused Harris and Mansell to their faces of having brought him into the 'roguery' against Pepys. All present agreed that in signing, James cleared Harbord of bribery and Pepys of popery. The advantage was Pepys's for the first time in a year, and he recorded delightedly that Harbord publicly declared that 'he did not believe me to be a papist or popishly inclined'.[28] The company all followed suit. Later that day, Harbord asked Pepys for a copy of the paper James had signed. Pepys told Harbord he could have a copy only if Harbord gave him the papers he had against Pepys. There was triumph in the words.

When the meeting broke up, Harbord suggested they both give James two guineas, then came to Pepys privately. 'What rogues are these,' he said, for Alexander Harris had come to him the day before to brief him. Neither side could trust him. Harris was not the only rat leaving the sinking ship; Colonel Mansell walked with Pepys as far as Westminster Abbey, 'declaring that he was able to do me a great deal of right in this matter' and claiming he 'had long observed this John James to be a rogue, and had advised Mr Harris and his wife to put him out of their house'. Three days later, Harris tried to win himself some credit by telling Pepys that Mansell was 'very great with my Lord Shaftesbury', whose fire he liked to sit beside. By now it was no surprise to Pepys to hear that the thin-lipped Whig lord's hand was at the helm of the plot against him.

Harbord's two guineas were just for show. The next day he took his physician to attend James in the hope, Pepys learnt later, that he might keep him alive long enough to sue him.[29] On 13 March, a news sheet published the first mention of James's confession and Will Hewer was mobbed by acquaintances at Whitehall who wanted full details.[30]

Faced with political humiliation, Harbord fought to keep his tottering plot from collapsing. On the 14th, Harris surprised Harbord and his brother-in-law Captain Russell interrogating James about the early meetings with Pepys. They had a paper claiming Harris bribed James to speak to Pepys. From his bed the sick man cried no, the idea to speak to Pepys had been his own. They read it to him in parcels of three or four lines. To each parcel, James, lying weak in bed, said to them, 'no, no, that is not as I spoke it. You write quite contrary to what I say.' They then pretended to alter it. When it was finished they read it to him but 'brokenly and imperfectly' so that its sense was unclear and it was impossible to judge whether it accorded with his corrections. Harris tried to leave immediately, but Russell took hold of him and pulled him over to where a paper was lying, saying he must sign it. Harris said he would not sign. Russell insisted he must. Again Harris refused and the furious Russell cried, 'God damn this rascal, for eighteen pence he shall swear anything.' James, too weak to read it himself, and desperate to be left alone, signed. This obliged Pepys and Harris to go over the facts of their meetings very carefully the next day.

James's mother and sister willingly shared the poisonous air James breathed out. His comfort and discomfort were theirs too. They hated these violent visits. Harbord 'always came in like a lion' or 'in passion', Mrs James told Pepys, which made her son 'afraid and troubled'. Whenever Will Hewer came, James was delighted and 'to the last hour of his life he did speak of it as a matter of great joy to him that he had eased his conscience and made his peace with his master'.

John James died in a flurry of paperwork. On 14 March he was light-headed and losing strength. On the 17th a news sheet wrongly called his original information to Parliament against Pepys and Deane a sworn affidavit. Pepys and Hewer hurried to him. He had been delirious in the night but was clear-headed enough to confirm that the news sheet was wrong. By the 19th he had grown visibly worse and in the evening Pepys brought a paper for him to sign, confirming that he had not sworn to his information. It had to be read over deliberately to him, and twice to his mother so she would remember the contents. She could not write, and he did not have the strength to sign, so it was signed by his sister. Hewer rushed it to the printer, but found him too late to get it printed in time for the following day's issue. The next day, Pepys dined with Lady Mordaunt, then travelled by water to Vauxhall 'and so home' where James's mother and sister were waiting with the news that James was dead.

22

The Road to Oxford

On 30 June 1680, Pepys and Deane appeared before the court in Westminster Hall. Neither the Attorney General nor the judges had anything to say against them. They were discharged and told to depart.[1] The immediate legal proceedings against them were over but there was only a little comfort to be gained from that. Courtroom triumph over John Scott had been denied them, their names were tainted and they were completely exposed to fresh attack.

The strings of the plot against Pepys had been pulled by Parliament men, but Parliament had barely met since Pepys was charged. His enemies had had no opportunity to finish their attack. King Charles's coffers were emptying into the expensive African outpost of Tangier and were not being filled again. He would have to call a Parliament, and then strident Whig indignation would again fill St Stephen's, emboldened by the voice of the London mob outside. Pepys's fate rested entirely on King Charles's ability to either placate Parliament or find a way to rule without it.

Pepys had constructed his defence. All he could do now was bring order to it. He gathered up the accumulated bundles of letters, memoranda and witness statements, and his neat scribe Paul Lorrain began to copy them into two large books. The pages were numbered and the contents indexed. It was the practice of a good bureaucrat, brought into the home. The story of Parliament's movements against him, of his imprisonment and of his duplicitous accuser's life was a shield against parliamentary wrath and a record for posterity. In France, during the cannonfounding escapade, 'looked on as an undertaker or workman' by the great Georges Pellissary, John Scott had cast about for some elevating nobility and feverishly declared himself 'Lord of Ashford and Mornamont'.[2] Ashford was his birthplace. Mornamont, he claimed noisily, was his castle near Dover. The castle seems to have existed but, like Scot's Hall, it was merely a part of the Kentish landscape that Scott knew; it did not belong to him.[3] For Pepys, Scott's absurd posturing was delightful and appropriate to a life built on grandiosity and delusion. He had his title: 'my two volumes of Mornamont'.*

Only a fool laughed long at a man like Scott when a Parliament was looming and Pepys was no fool. Poor Henry Coventry – driven into retirement by his gout – still wanted to make amends for setting Scott free on his return from France. The moment Pepys was legally in the clear, Coventry told him Scott's story about the Earl of Berkshire's deathbed confession. As he lay dying, Scott had claimed, the Earl had summoned Scott to him, commanded his servants out of the chamber and then warned him about the 'giddy madness' of the Catholic lords and the 'foolish and ill design' of their Plot. He begged Scott to find some way to warn King Charles.[4] Scott, it will be remembered, had touted the Berkshire confession when he returned to England to charge Pepys. Coventry had released Scott in exchange for the evidence – then watched in horror as Scott pointed a finger at Pepys. Now Coventry risked a little exposure for his friend's sake and Pepys was guided towards the servants who had attended the Earl in his final misery.

The servants admitted that Scott knew the Earl but said he could not possibly have had a private conversation with him on his deathbed. One of them had been beside the Earl every waking moment because of his incontinence or, as one put it, 'a constant looseness . . . that was very offensive'. The Earl had been so extremely

---

* They are now in the Pepys Library, Magdalene College, Cambridge.

deaf for the final month of his life that anyone who wanted to speak to him had to shout in his ear. Thus Pepys established what Coventry had come to suspect: Scott's account of Berkshire's 'confession' was pure fiction.[5] Of such stuff was the Popish Plot built.

Pepys thanked Balty by getting him a naval posting in Tangier, after failing (perhaps unsurprisingly) to get him the top position of Admiralty Commissioner. Pepys's old influence had evaporated in the hot Whig sun. Balty had heard too much about the horrors of Tangier to feel at all pleased by the prospect of living there. Pepys had a rosier view of the African outpost, derived from the joyful experience of putting a tithe on its huge running costs into his own pocket. A humiliating disagreement over salary left Balty feeling underpaid and highly aggrieved.

At the end of September, thinking himself 'sacrificed and torn from the bowels of my sweet little family', Balty set out from London with a heavy heart. 'After all my youth spent in his Majesty's service in ever and all dangers and troubles,' he complained, he had 'no other recompense than to be sent to the Devil for a New Year's gift.'

Balty, a stranger to conciseness, wrote a highly dramatic narrative of his attempts to sail for Tangier. After having to say farewell to his family in London 'and leave them (perhaps never more to return) desolate which burst my heart to think of their precious tears both of mother and babes', he missed his boat downriver. Eventually arriving in Gravesend that afternoon with just time to grab a piece of bread and cheese, he was rowed out towards the buoy of the Nore, an anchorage not far out in the estuary, where there was a ship that would take him round the coast to Deal. Such a fog and storm arose that, Balty reported, 'our cockle shell took every sea over, and we like to perish not seeing one inch before us nor knowing whither to steer.' They rowed around in the storm for three hours with their boat filling with water until, at 11 p.m., they found the shore again and collapsed on to a bench in their soaking clothes. At 4 a.m. they tried again. This time they reached the buoy of the Nore. The ships had gone. Balty, at a loss and in danger of missing his ship from Deal, was saved by the arrival of a small ketch which plucked him out of the sodden barge. Hungry and wet, he made Deal and the Downs, caught his ship to Tangier and, overjoyed that his exploits were over, described himself as 'like a woman in labour after her deliverance'.[6] Disasters liked Balty. We can only wish his letters from Paris had survived.

It was far from the end of Balty's troubles. He had such a hard time in Tangier that he was to return without permission a year later hoping the Navy Board would be sympathetic. The Board deliberated for two months then, at seven hours' notice, put him on a ship back to Africa. One of Pepys's correspondents who happened to see Balty at Plymouth reported that he was 'the thoughtfullest and melancholiest man I ever saw'.[7] It was scant reward for his work in Paris. Pepys generously thanked his fine friends and the strangers who helped him, but dependent, melodramatic Balty would never be treated so well.

Grimly for Pepys, the King called Parliament for 21 October. He had no choice. An expedition to save Tangier from collapse had drained his resources. More acceptably to the Commons, he also needed money to reinforce a new agreement with Holland and Spain against French expansion.[8] The Whigs gleefully went to work. They picked a rival successor to the Duke of York and spread a rumour that the (conveniently dead) Bishop of Durham had a black box containing proof that Charles had married the Duke of Monmouth's mother and Monmouth was therefore legitimate heir to the throne. In late summer, Monmouth made a triumphal tour of the West Country. John Scott, the politician of the coffee houses, softened the ground ahead of him with the black box story. The proof bore the Bishop's signature, Scott told his listeners. King Charles had sent out word that Monmouth was not to be encouraged and Scott's rumour-mongering landed him in Lyme Regis gaol for five days. The country was again entrenching against the Catholic heir to the throne and no witnesses were prepared to come forward against Scott. The authorities had to release him.[9]

Any new Whig charges against him would break Pepys. After the vast cost of dealing with Scott, he could not afford to construct another defence. The Crown, however, owed him several thousand pounds. At the end of September he joined the court at Newmarket to retrieve arrears for twenty years' service; the sum was too considerable to be lost, he thought, 'considering what is approaching'. The strain of the moment produced some sharp words about the merry monarch's court. He wrote to James Houblon after several fruitless days:

Our ministers are here; but not a word of business nor (one would think) so much as a thought of any, there seeming nothing now in motion but dogs, hawks, and horses; so that all matters look as if they were left to God Almighty to look after, and much more happy it might have been for us all had they been long ago so.[10]

While there, he was obliged to take down in shorthand (and thus preserve for posterity) the well-worn drama of the King's escape from Worcester in the Civil War.

He left Newmarket on 4 October for Brampton, his family home in Huntingdonshire, intending to spend the day with his eighty-year-old father. He found the community in the grip of illness. His father had been buried earlier that day. His sister Paulina was sick and her husband John Jackson had died a few weeks before. After a quick trip to London, Pepys rolled up his sleeves to get to grips with the Brampton estate, bringing his scribe Paul Lorrain and the part-completed volumes of Mornamont back with him.[11] He threw himself into these projects, removed from the political storm gathering in London as the meeting of Parliament grew close, but always watching the weather by the frequent letters and news sheets Will Hewer and James Houblon sent.

Houblon had been a sturdy friend throughout, though 'one of so tender a memory,' Pepys wrote to him, 'that there is no good deed of his own that will stick in it, for he shall do you twenty good offices before he will think them one.' Pepys had his portrait painted as a gift to make it impossible for Houblon to forget 'his errands on my score to Westminster Hall, his visit to the lions [the Tower], his passings over the bridge to the [Golden] Patten in Southwark, and a thousand other things.' Pepys suspected that Houblon, if he knew the intention of the present, 'would turn his head a' one side every time he comes in sight on't'. To avoid that he sent

a small bribe to every one of his family, to get them, in such a case, to be putting in some word or other as he passes by, to make him look upon it; as thus: 'Was Mr. Pepys in these clothes, father, when you used to go to the Tower to him ?' Or thus: 'Lord, cousin, how hath this business of Scott altered my poor cousin Pepys since this was done!' Or thus: 'What would I give for a plot, Jemmy, to get you laid by the heels, that I might see what this Mr. Pepys would do for you.'[12]

In London Charles, hoping to dispel the gathering storm clouds, sent the Duke of York back to his Scottish exile and welcomed his Parliament. He tried to explain away the long delay in meeting and promised them that he would 'give them the fullest satisfaction your hearts can wish for the security of the Protestant religion'. They applauded him but even in the same sentence Charles defended 'the succession of the Crown in its due and legal course of descent'. The old battle lines were not redrawn; they had never been erased. One MP declared that the life of every Protestant in England was threatened, and the Commons threw themselves into passing the Exclusion Bill to keep the King's brother out.[13]

At Brampton, the Mornamont volumes filled up with Lorrain's neat hand. Pepys had Hewer send some blank-paper books he had absently left in his writing desk beside a secreted volume of the Earl of Rochester's erotic poetry (written 'in a style I thought unfit to mix with my other books,' he explained, unruffled).[14] Pepys's investigations had put him in a strong position. He had presided over the total exposure of John Scott. Rather than wait for the attack, he could publish details of Scott's life, or disclose Scott's crimes to the Commons. Deane's nerves were frayed by the sitting Parliament. Using the pseudonym P. Bayly he urged Pepys to make a pre-emptive strike through two sympathetic MPs. '[I]f it had been in my power it should have been done,' he wrote.[15] But Pepys and Will Hewer counselled against it. Their evidence was their great asset and Harbord was not above undoing it with a bribe here or there. Pepys did not believe that attacking Scott's character at this moment would 'prevent their purposes, who had use of his testimony'. He warned Deane that Scott might choose simply to confess to the offences, secure a pardon and put himself out of their reach forever, in the manner of Oates and Bedloe.[16]

In November 1680, England came horribly close to civil war again, with Shaftesbury and the King locked in a duel of wits. The outcome would depend on whether the mob could be incited to exclude the Duke of York at any cost, even violence (as Shaftesbury hoped), or would baulk at going to war with the monarchy (as Charles was beginning to suspect). On the 4th, when the Exclusion Bill had its first reading in the Commons, the tide was running strongly Shaftesbury's way. Only a handful of MPs dared to speak against the bill. The mob was being prepared to march on Whitehall Palace if it passed both Houses. Will Hewer took all Pepys's chests and hampers of papers from York Buildings to the relative safety of his large house to the north of Clapham Common.

The bill was stopped in the House of Lords after a debate in which Lord Halifax took on his uncle, Shaftesbury, in fifteen or sixteen separate speeches, answering him point for point. Charles was present in the Lords throughout the debate, listening intently as it wore on into the night. He ate his meals hurriedly in an adjoining room but otherwise he stood by the fireside, or stalked round the benches to lobby individual lords as candles were brought to light the chamber. It ended after ten o'clock, the Whigs losing sixty-three votes to thirty. Their attack in Parliament seemed to have been halted.[17]

On the streets there was no such pause. Shaftesbury was assiduously cultivating the London mob as a political force. On 17 November, two days after the Lords' vote, Queen Elizabeth's accession day came once again, to be marked by another great pope-burning parade. Charles, with the fear of a London rebellion in his mind, told the Lord Mayor to do what he could to stop the procession but the Lord Mayor said he might as well try to stop the tide flowing through London Bridge. This time, the effigy of the pope had his feet on the body of a prostrate king, whose crown he was kicking off.[18] An effigy of the Duke of York was consigned to the flames with the word 'Ninny' written in huge letters above it.[19]

That same day, Pepys set out for London and the heart of the storm. It was a brave move and he was following Will Hewer's advice that it would be a good idea to be seen in the city.[20] Pepys had taken great care throughout the Scott affair to show the public a face of determined innocence. Now his absence in the country was leading to malicious talk that he feared to appear in London while Parliament sat. He returned, so bound up in the approaching danger that he hardly seemed to mind when six highwaymen stopped the coach and robbed him.

The city to which he returned was in a most dangerous mood and the Plot now gained another victim, the weakest of the five Catholic lords still held in the Tower. On 29 November, Lord Stafford, old and sick, was finally put on trial before his peers. After more than a week of legal torment in which his voice had been too feeble to make himself heard when trying to ask questions, he was found guilty and broke down in tears. Charles, present at the trial and angry at the verdict, could not prevent the execution. All he could do was protect Stafford's body from being drawn and quartered. The blood lust of the politicians had, for once, outstripped the mob. There was a quiet unease in the crowd at Stafford's beheading. It was a straw in the wind.[21]

In the run-up to Christmas, Edward Wright, the man who had already told Pepys that his trusted John Joyne was in league with Scott, contacted him again to say that Scott was back from France and planned to bring new charges against him in that session. Wright told him Scott was claiming Pepys had been betrayed 'by his pretended friends'.[22]

At the same time, the Commons were turning on some of Charles's ministers and tried to impeach Lord Chief Justice Scroggs for having the temerity to give their star Plot witnesses a hard time. On 8 January 1681, Shaftesbury made a mistake. He told Justice Warcup, thinking him a sympathiser, that he planned to take control of London and execute Charles, not realising his words would get straight back to the King.[23] Two days later, Charles prorogued Parliament. He forecast correctly that the Whigs would grudgingly accept this. They needed a short break so that they could reintroduce the Exclusion Bill in the new session. Eight days after that, with no MPs in St Stephen's to protest, he played his trump card and dissolved Parliament, announcing that, after fresh elections, the new Parliament would sit not in London but in Oxford on 21 March. By that means he took the next session out of the reach of the London mob. He had been worried for some time that the Whigs' grip on London had become too strong for safety, that if he tried to dissolve Parliament while it was sitting, the opposition might simply move elsewhere and carry on the session despite him, a rebellion that would lead to civil war. Quiet Oxford, where the university authorities were supporters of the Crown, seemed a safer bet.

For Pepys, life still seemed far from safe. Ever since John Joyne had returned to France, they had been exchanging coded letters. Joyne outlined fresh conspiracies brewing in Paris and asked for large sums to buy off new French witnesses who, he alleged, were about to cross the Channel to accuse Pepys.[24] In the end, the watchmaker went too far. Believing the furore in London offered a chance to get rich quick, Joyne and a Portuguese accomplice invented another plot which, because it predicted King Charles's assassination by his own queen and the Portuguese ambassador, brought him to the attention of Charles's Committee for Foreign Intelligence. This transparently absurd story finally destroyed Joyne's credibility with Pepys and his friends in government.

Pepys's safety was entwined with Charles's political manoeuvres against Parliament, and Charles had something up his sleeve. He had played his international cards well. In France, King Louis guessed that Charles might be forced to defuse the crisis by choosing William, Prince of Orange, as regent to rule in place of James in the next reign. Fearing that this might lead to a Protestant alliance of the English and Dutch against Catholic France, Louis lost his nerve and decided he had to support Charles. In the first ten weeks of 1681, the two kings negotiated a verbal cash deal which promised Charles £375,000 over the next three years in exchange for him not allowing Parliament to sit. By the middle of March, Charles knew he could get by without the Commons.[25]

Thus was the stage set for the most dramatic political *coup de théâtre* of that age. Charles tightened the screw by removing his remaining opponents from the Privy Council. In March, three Oxford colleges were prepared for the arrival of the royal household. Shaftesbury, finding it hard to secure the right accommodation in the (largely royalist) colleges, had to settle for a small house in the narrow confines of New College Lane. On the Friday and Saturday before the opening, the town began to fill up, Charles diverting to take in some horse racing at nearby Burford, and Shaftesbury stage-managing his entry into Oxford on horseback surrounded by 200 well-armed men. Both sides suspected the other of planning violent action.

Charles feared violence. Shaftesbury, with his pope-burnings, incendiary literature and coffee house propaganda had built an army for himself: the London mob – untrained and unreliable, certainly, but fired by the anxiety he had poured into them and perhaps capable, if it came to it, of taking the capital. If Charles denied Shaftesbury his Parliament, he risked civil war.

So Charles came to Oxford. Some Whigs hoped that he might be willing to concede. In his opening speech, Charles criticised the Whigs for generating 'unnecessary fears' about religion in order to change the foundation of government. Though he stood firm on the succession issue, he said, he wanted 'to remove all reasonable fears that may arise from the possibility of a Popish successor's coming to the Crown' by ensuring a Protestant administration, and would 'hearken to any expedient, by which the religion might be preserved'. In the Commons, Tory MPs offered the Whigs a string of concessions. The Duke of York, though he would be a nominal king, could be banished, and his daughter Mary could reign as regent in his place. But the Whigs, hoping for victory, rejected all compromises and pushed for James's full exclusion.

The canny monarch had known his concessions would not be accepted. He watched his opponents entrench. All the while, he put on a show of wanting to placate them. They had complained about their poor accommodation so he offered to re-house them in the Sheldonian Theatre and took a personal and convincing interest in the rapid building alterations required. But on the afternoon of Sunday 27 March he consulted his council, now containing only trusted supporters. They agreed a strategy. That night, his coaches were quietly taken a short way out of town. On Monday morning, he joined the House of Lords in the hall of Christ Church College. He was dressed in his ordinary clothes, but had the robe and crown necessary to dissolve Parliament tucked away in a side room. When he sent for the members of the House of Commons to join them, the MPs came in confidently, expecting to hear Charles's final surrender. They pushed in through the narrow entrance to see that the King had changed into his robes. He dissolved Parliament in a single sentence: 'All the world may see to what a point we are come, that we are not like to have a good end when the divisions at the beginning are such.'[26] Only then did the Whigs realise that their own intransigence had ruined them.

Charles quickly left town, under cover in Sir Edward Seymour's coach, along roads guarded by his soldiers. He was expecting a violent reaction and instructions had been left to delay the post so that no word could get out before he was safely back at Windsor. In the next weeks, he mounted a propaganda campaign to reassure the people that, when the time was right, he would meet Parliament. In fact, it never sat again in his lifetime. He had opted instead to survive on his modest French subsidy. The parliamentary war against the Duke of York and his servant Samuel Pepys ended with that dissolution, and John Scott's power ended with it.

At some point, an addition was made to one of the early pages of the Mornamont volumes. The deft, confident strokes look like the scribe Lorrain's. Inside the 'O' of the 20 May 1679 order that the Commons should investigate the charges against Pepys, there is a tiny smiling face.[27]

23

The Leman and Ower

During the early summer of 1681, King Charles's men heard that Shaftesbury had planned an armed uprising at the Oxford Parliament. On 2 July Shaftesbury was taken from his bed at 6 a.m., examined all day by the Privy Council with the King present then sent to the Tower. He fought off the allegations, winning his release in November with the help of a Whig-dominated jury, but emerged into a changed world where many former radicals, seeing the King recovering his strength and his powers of patronage, had slipped over to the royalist side. A tough new policy dried up the flow of Popish Plot informers by refusing to give them pardons ahead of their testimony.

In March 1682, the King cautiously called his brother down from Scotland to Newmarket. The Duke of York met an enthusiastic welcome when he landed at Yarmouth, and Newmarket bulged with the crowds who had come to see him. Reassured by the public's enthusiasm, Charles brought his brother to London where the welcome continued. Bonfires burnt around Whitehall but now the fuel for the flames included effigies of Shaftesbury and copies of the Exclusion Bill. James's exile was over and the King cleared the way for his permanent return. James's pregnant wife was waiting in Edinburgh. At noon on 3 May, James set sail from the south bank of the Thames in the largest of the royal yachts, the *Mary*, to collect her. He had eighty people on board with him, and 500 more crossed the river from the city to see him off. The *Mary* sailed triumphantly out to sea where she was joined by six frigates, the flagship *Gloucester*, commanded by the vastly experienced Sir John Berry, the *Happy Return* under Captain John Wyborne, the *Lark,* the *Ruby,* the *Dartmouth* and the *Pearl*. With these were three more yachts, the *Katherine*, the *Charlotte* and the *Kitchen*. The Duke and his close entourage boarded the *Gloucester*. Over two hours, the rest of his party and all their luggage was transferred into the other frigates, then the flotilla set sail for Scotland, in what Captain Gunman of the *Mary* described as 'dourthy' (dirty) weather.[1]

Samuel Pepys was with them. He had rejected an invitation to travel in the *Gloucester* with the Duke, and had hoped to get aboard the *Happy Return* after deciding (rather at the last minute) to accompany James on his triumphal sail north. 'I shall, I am sure be more at ease,' he wrote to its captain, Wyborne, 'than in the *Gloucester* by having your conversation and succour, for I mean to be very sick.'[2] Captain Wyborne turned him down and Pepys wound up aboard the *Katherine*, an old friend. She was regarded as the Navy Office's particular yacht and she had come to his rescue once before, providing the alibi which saved Samuel Atkins's neck when the Whig plotters first turned their attention to Pepys.

It was over 400 miles to Edinburgh by sea. Off the Norfolk coast lay a series of dangerous shoals and sandbanks: Haisborough Sand, Hammond Knoll, Newarp Sands and beyond them, 30 miles out to sea, the parallel ridges of the Leman Bank and the Ower. The Newcastle coal boats heading for London used the 'collier's route' inside the sands, hugging the coast to save time, but more cautious sailors stayed well off-shore. On this occasion, with a wind blowing mostly from the east, towards the inner sandbanks and the shore, there was all the more reason for caution. These frigates were not designed to beat closely into wind.

On the evening of 5 May, around 7 p.m., the ships were six miles off the Suffolk coast, almost level with the port of Lowestoft. The main sandbanks lay ahead. The yachts *Mary* and *Charlotte* were sailing ahead of the *Gloucester*. The Duke, clearly concerned about the easterly wind, had them called back. The smaller boats came up under the stern of the *Gloucester* and the Duke asked their captains, Gunman and Ralph Sanderson, for their opinions of the pilot's course. They were unanimous that the present course would take them on to the Newarp Sands and they must tack south-east to gain some sea-room. Gunman bluntly told the Duke that he thought the pilot 'mad if he did not tack off'.[3]

The pilot had come aboard and taken over responsibility from Sir John Berry for the *Gloucester*'s safe navigation through the sandbanks. His name was Captain James Ayres and he was held to be one of the most experienced and able navigators of that coast.[4] He was clearly annoyed by Gunman and Sanderson's doubts, and insisted they could safely weather the sands. The Duke of York, however, had always trusted the sober Gunman. In his career Gunman had surveyed the coast of Britain and mapped its harbours. He kept a diary, which emerged in the 1950s from the storerooms of Doddington Hall, Lincoln. This little-used document provides a full description of the events that followed.

For another hour the *Gloucester* stayed on the same course, sailing into danger until Gunman, watching from the deck of the *Mary*, could stand it no longer. He turned his yacht and ran up under the stern of the *Gloucester* and asked why they had not tacked. The *Gloucester*'s officers asked him again if she could not weather the sand, to which Gunman (by his own later account to his wife) replied, '"No" and stamped and flung my hat on the ground like a madman, saying I would not adventure the king's yacht to follow them.' The Duke, persuaded, swung round to the pilot and commanded him to tack. The pilot protested angrily, but obeyed.[5]

The *Gloucester* altered course southwards. The Duke had told the pilot to keep to this course for four hours, until midnight, but after an hour and a half, the pilot demanded 'very urgently' that he be allowed to tack back to the original course. The Duke thought they should stand off for longer but Ayres exclaimed vehemently that he would stake his life that by tacking now, they would weather all the sands. The Duke compromised. They stayed on course for another half hour, then tacked as the pilot wished, sailing north-north-east to stay out to sea, all sails trimmed to point as close into the wind as possible. At 4 a.m. with the first signs of dawn in the sky, the pilot confidently asserted that they were in the clear, well past the Leman and the Ower banks and they came round a little more to the west.

It was blowing hard and there was a big sea. Captain Gunman, still not trusting the pilot's decisions, had taken the *Mary* out ahead of the *Gloucester* again, staying a little inshore of the frigate to put himself where he thought the danger lay, anxiously scanning the sea ahead for signs of breakers. He had a man in the bows sounding with a lead-line and he went below to get some rest after the long night, leaving his mate William Sturgion in charge with instructions that if he met shoal water he should bear up into wind and call his captain.

At half past five, the unwelcome call came. Gunman shot up on deck to hear the soundings falling sharply from fifteen to seven fathoms. He looked back to see the *Gloucester* half a mile behind and coming on fast. She needed much more water than the smaller *Mary*. Two minutes' work with a lead-line showed Gunman on which side the bulk of the sands lay, and he signalled the danger. It was so windy that a warning gun would not be heard, but it was getting light so he told his gunner to fix a flag to a long staff in the time-honoured way. Bearing up into wind, the gunner waved it at the *Gloucester*, weaving it around five times to indicate five fathoms' depth. It was too late.

The *Gloucester* ran full-tilt on to the bank. The impact did terrible damage. The ship, driven by the wind, beat along the edge of the sands, hammering its hull as it did so. The helmsman and crew tried to turn her but the violent waves now breaking over the ship tore off her rudder. She lurched off into deeper water, firing guns to warn the other frigates, while reports came up from below that an entire plank had been torn off. The crew pumped, but the water was rushing in.

There is a painting of the wreck by Johan Danckerts in the National Maritime Museum. It is an accurate representation of a three-master of the time, the sails still set on the mainmast and the foremast and the royal standard flying. The cannons have all been run out through the gunports, and there any resemblance to reality ends. The ship appears to have run gently aground on a friendly looking beach. One member of the crew is walking on the sand. Two more appear to be praying, while another is caught in the act of plunging into the choppy waves to try to reach a heavily laden open boat a few yards away. It is a peaceful scene, far removed from what really happens when several hundred tons of timber hit an immoveable object at seven or eight knots.

Captain Wyborne's *Happy Return*, coming up behind the *Gloucester*, dropped anchor to avoid the same fate. Panic broke out on the *Gloucester* and the command structure collapsed. The sailors cried for help. In the *Katherine*, Pepys was roused from sleep by the shout that the Duke was aground, and went up on deck in the cold, gusty dawn. Gunman in the little *Mary* yacht did his best to inch as close as possible to the stricken ship while avoiding the waves breaking around it. Sailors were spilling into the water, naked so that the weight of their clothes might not drag them under. Gunman saved as many as he could. It took a great deal of precious time to persuade the Duke that he should abandon ship. This same stubborn streak had made him so intransigent about his impolitic Catholicism. He seems to have believed that the *Gloucester* could still be saved if he remained on board to encourage the crew. Eventually, wearing only his coat and breeches, he was persuaded into the ship's barge.

Afterwards Sir John Berry idealised his men's conduct, writing that despite the chaos, they made sure the Duke got off safely by dutifully allowing his barge to be hoisted out and lowered into the water, not one attempting to jump in. 'In the midst of all their affliction and dying condition,' Berry wrote, they 'did rejoice and thank God his Royal Highness was preserved'.[6] Sir James Dick, a down-to-earth Scot, described, probably more accurately, how James got into the barge through the great window of the stern cabin without the crew seeing him. John Churchill, the future Duke of Marlborough, went with him and two or three more flung themselves in. The Duke of York shouted for the (rather severe) Lord President of the Privy Council of Scotland to jump for the boat, but the Lord President fell short and the Duke pulled him from the water. Those in the boat drew their swords to hold the other seamen off.

When the Duke was safely away, Dick, in his nightgown and slippers, helped swing out the ship's boat and there was a scramble to get into it. The Earl of Middleton jumped on to Dick's shoulders as the *Gloucester* sank lower. As Dick's boat pushed clear, twenty or thirty seamen leapt into it, so overloading it in the crashing surf that a hundred more did not even try but instead climbed higher into the ship's rigging as it went down. Halfway between the wreck and the yachts, a great number of swimming sailors, crying for help, caught a dead grip on the boat to keep their heads above water. Those in the boat shouted that they would all be drowned if they did not let go, and their hands were loosened.

By the time the ship's boat had made it through the quarter-mile of violent sea and strong wind to the yacht *Charlotte*, only the royal standard flying from the *Gloucester*'s topmast remained above the water. The Duke of York came aboard the *Mary* with Gunman. Those sailors that could had swum to the nearby yachts, and the *Katherine*, with Pepys aboard, had taken several exhausted souls from the water including Sir Charles Scarborough, nearly dead after a competition for a floating plank of wood with the Duke of York's dog, Mumper.[7]

There had been some 330 people on board, 250 of them seamen and the rest nobles, gentlemen and servants of the Duke's entourage. Nearly half of them were drowned. The sombre list of the dead included Lord Roxborough, Lord O'Brien, Sir Joseph Douglas and the *Gloucester*'s lieutenant who was the brother of Laurence Hyde, First Lord of the Treasury. In an apologetic letter to Hyde, Sir John Berry said his brother was missed 'in the general disorder' and that he was obliged to give up the search for him to save his own life 'as the rest of the common men did'. Plate, linen, clothes and money went down with the ship, worth some £5,000.

The Duke was determined to press on to Scotland, and Gunman scurried around providing for him on the underprepared *Katherine*. He lent the Duke his own clothes, and was relieved that the yacht was more than ordinarily stocked with liquor and provisions. He was able to serve two or three dishes of meat each meal, but lacked enough suitable tableware and had to resort to fast footwork, always washing one of his two silver-plated dishes while the other was in use.[8] The diminished flotilla straggled into Edinburgh, the *Kitchen* yacht arriving last having spent longest at the wreck. From dry land, Pepys wrote to Will Hewer about what would, as he put it, soon be 'the talk of the town'. Age had made him portly and he was profoundly thankful that he had kept to the yacht, 'for,' he wrote, 'many will, I doubt, be found lost as well or better qualified for saving themselves by swimming and otherwise, than I might be.'[9] The *Katherine*, the provider of Sam Atkins's alibi, had saved him again.

Blame, unsurprisingly, fell upon the pilot. He had swum to the *Charlotte* and was immediately put into custody. Later, he was court-martialled and sentenced to life imprisonment.

He had headed straight for one major and well-known marine hazard, given way with very bad grace when ordered to change course, then demanded another course change that took the ship straight on to the bank. Sober Captain Gunman believed that 'the ship was deliberately wrecked by Ayres'.[10] Pepys thought the same. Ayres, he said, had pretended to be asleep at the time of the impact 'to show his security', and should be hanged.[11]

Ayres's intention had been to hit Newarp Sands earlier in the night when it was still dark, sink the *Gloucester* and drown the Duke. As Pepys said, if the collision had occurred 'but two hours sooner in the morning . . . the Duke himself and every soul had perished'.[12] Ayres had 'made a provision for his own escape'.[13] He was an exceptionally strong swimmer and intended to make for another ship as the *Gloucester* went down.

Ayres was a known republican. The Duke of York was in fact aware of this but, 'having a particular knowledge of his ability and having done him many signal favours, trusted him'.[14] Ayres was not acting alone but 'as an agent for a party of conspirators who desired the death of the Duke of York'.[15] The exact identity of these conspirators was shady. The Whig parliamentary opposition must, however, come top of the list of suspects. Shaftesbury had shown no scruples about pushing the Duke's servants on to the gallows, and had equally few about killing the Duke. The Whigs had no other tools at their disposal. After Oxford, they had been denied an effective parliamentary voice. The King's cause seemed to be strengthening. Under such circumstances, they were willing to resort to violence to remove James from the succession. They chose a sailing accident.

The conspiracy had failed. What went wrong? Gunman's opposition to the pilot's chosen course had delayed the wrecking until it was light, and the Duke could more easily be rescued. Furthermore, as a result of Gunman's concerns, the yachts were much closer to the *Gloucester* than they should have been, sounding the depth. The 'provision' that Ayres was later reported to have made for his escape may have been a friendly reception (and perhaps a subsequent and secret disappearance) when he hauled himself, dripping, on to one of the other frigates, which under normal conditions would have been closest to the *Gloucester*. Instead he had to swim to the yacht *Charlotte* and Captain Sanderson, who had thought his course dangerous, put him into custody. The Duke's rescue boat, meanwhile, reached the nearby *Mary* yacht.

In the aftermath of the wreck, the conspirators, in a ham-fisted attempt to deflect the blame from Ayres and silence his most outspoken critic, fell upon Gunman. Their initial target was his first mate William Sturgion, and when Gunman arrived at Sturgion's hearing aboard the *Charlotte* to defend him, he was denied entry. The panel were busy trying to get Sturgion to incriminate Gunman. Pepys, there as 'one that had barely escaped bearing a share of the consequences', was also prevented from entering.[16] As he waited to hear Sturgion's fate, Gunman was summoned into the room, read several contradictory statements then told, to his utter astonishment, that he had been found guilty. He was not aware that he had been tried, nor had he been charged with any offence, nor even required to attend the court that day. He was sentenced to dismissal from the navy, an indeterminate gaol sentence and the forfeiture of his last year's pay.

The president of the court martial was Sir Richard Haddock, and the pilot was (in Gunman's words) his 'particular bosom creature'. Captain Wyborne of the *Happy Return* helped Haddock try to pin the blame for the wreck on Gunman. Wyborne's lies about Gunman's behaviour at the time of the wreck were so extravagant that Gunman said Wyborne 'might as well have sworn I did kill a man at the Barbados at that very time and hour'. Wyborne and his pretty wife were friends of Pepys, but Wyborne's behaviour in this affair was most peculiar. His frigate would have been one of the closest to the *Gloucester* in the normal course of events. Could he have been the planned escape route for the swimming pilot?

The Duke of York – recognising a set-up and refusing to allow Gunman to be vilified – sped to his rescue by persuading the King to step in. Charles demanded the details of Gunman's case from the Commissioners of the Admiralty. He ordered that Gunman should be taken out of the Marshalsea and imprisoned in his own house in Deptford, and that they should keep the command of the *Mary* open for him.[17] Six days later Charles pardoned Gunman and gave him his job back.

The wreck had backfired massively on the conspirators. Captain Gunman's reputation was restored after the ill-conceived attack on him; he was to die of gangrene after falling off a pier at Calais in 1685, and John Evelyn, at his funeral, reflected that Gunman was an excellent pilot and seaman who had proved to Evelyn's complete satisfaction that he was in no way responsible for the *Gloucester*'s sinking.[18] The Duke became a popular hero. Medals were struck to commemorate his escape, and Nat Lee wrote a flowery poem declaring him 'too precious for the deep'.

An hour after sketchy news of the wreck arrived in Whitehall on Wednesday 10 May, all London knew the story: the Duke was dead; the Duke was saved; all were saved; all were dead and only the ship was saved. When names of the dead arrived, the families made 'a great cry', and withdrew to grieve.[19] It was assumed Pepys had drowned, for it seemed impossible that he would have travelled anywhere but on the Duke's ship. At James Houblon's house, the women and girls were beside themselves, Houblon reassuring them but anxious himself until Will Hewer arrived two nights later clutching a letter from Pepys. Houblon's relief burst out of him. 'What it is to leave us on that sudden as you did without either asking or, for all that I know, having our prayers,' he wrote back. 'We were all so angry at your going.'[20] Hewer also took the good news to the affectionate widow in Portugal Row, Lady Mordaunt, that night.

Pepys saw the sights of Scotland and was impressed by Glasgow, 'a very extraordinary town for beauty and trade', but much less by the Scots themselves. In an offensive aside which was apparently greeted as hugely witty by his London coterie, he said, 'the truth is, there is so universal a rooted nastiness hangs about the person of every Scot (man and woman), that renders the finest show they can make nauseous, even among those of the first quality.'[21] He put in at Berwick upon Tweed on the yacht trip home, taking his time and doing some more sightseeing at Lindisfarne. He was in no hurry to return to London. This was a break from the debilitating strain of the previous three years. At Newcastle, a letter from Hewer brought the most extraordinary news.

On 1 May, three weeks after his enemy James, Duke of York was welcomed back by the people of London, Colonel John Scott had been drinking at the Horseshoe Inn on Tower Hill. The Whig cause was on its knees and all that was left of the Exclusion Bill was the ash in the streets where the bonfires had been. Scott's hopes of the Duke's demise and his own glory had, despite the promise of the last three and a half years, come to nothing. He was in a foul mood. At the end of the night he sent a messenger to fetch a hackney carriage to carry him back to his lodgings. There were none nearby and the messenger had to go as far as Aldgate, where he found George Butler and his hackney. When Butler came into the Horseshoe, Scott argued with him over the proposed fare. They could not agree and Scott told him to go away. Butler wanted money for his trouble in coming down from Aldgate to collect Scott.

'Come down with me,' said Scott, 'and I'll give you something for your pains.' They went outside the inn and Scott drove a five-shilling rapier deep into Butler's belly. Butler died six days later.[22]

It was a cowardly, uninspired act. It had none of the scale, inventiveness or sheer audacity of Scott's other crimes. Those qualities had raised him above the common gutter rogue, promised some form of redemption and inclined the historical eye to be generous in its treatment of him. It was a murder; dank, calculated, pointless, cold and totally unoriginal. There could be no sympathy for John Scott now. The coroner, Will Hewer's letter told Pepys, had found it wilful murder.

Not for the first time in his life, Scott faced the prospect of a long imprisonment. Pepys would be free of him. However, under the practice of the time Scott could arrange to be forgiven the murder. First he would have to buy the widow's forgiveness for some sort of compensation, then go to court to secure a royal pardon. He or his cohorts were already trying to buy off Butler's widow and her three small children. Pepys, knowing Scott had information the King might want to hear about Shaftesbury and other senior Whigs, feared he might find a pardon. From Newcastle he wrote urging Hewer to stop the court acting until he and Deane had been heard. Hewer told Charles's government he had been 'credibly informed' that Scott had been taking part in dangerous correspondence with foreign powers.[23] They need not have worried, however. Scott was not seeking a pardon. He had done what he usually did when things went wrong: he had fled.

The word was out. The news sheets were full of the murder, 'Thompson's Intelligencer' described Scott as lusty, tall, squint-eyed, thin-faced and sometimes wearing a periwig. London was on the

lookout for this 'great vindicator of the Salamanca doctor' (meaning
Titus Oates), who was a friend of the increasingly discredited Plot
witnesses and manipulators.[24] Readers were told of Scott's life of
crookedness in Holland and France, his attempts to sell maps to
foreign powers so they could 'burn all his Majesty's navy in their
harbours', how he had pretended Pepys and Deane had wanted King
Louis to burn the ships and had 'played a thousand pranks more'.
Deane and Hewer had been busy sharing some of the choicest bits of
Pepys's findings. With a sneer, the papers relayed 'how valiantly
Colonel Scott killed Butler the coachman'.[25] Meanwhile, government
officials were going through the possessions Scott had left in his
lodgings, including a letter from Scott to the King from America in
1664, a map of Kent and a paper entitled 'That a King ought to be
Instructed to Reign Well'.[26]

On 27 May, the *Katherine* arrived at Scarborough where Pepys
found a letter waiting for him in Hewer's hand, posted only two days
earlier. It scared the daylights out of him.

There has something happened . . . of great consequence, and very ill both to you
and my self and some other of our friends, which I dare not communicate to you
with pen and paper, and therefore wish for your speedy return, which I hope in
God, you will defer no longer than bare necessity requires. Your humble servant,
Wm Hewer.[27]

This letter, Pepys wrote back,

puts me (by its obscurity) into an inexpressible pain to arrive at the ground of it,
a thousand things running in my head but without knowing which to pick upon,
or what kind of misfortune it is, that could so suddenly surprise you.[28]

He had to get home as fast as he could. The quickest land route
would take nine days; it was better to stay with the yacht. He was
deeply troubled.

When he arrived back in London, apprehensive to hear the
disaster, he learnt that the letter had not come from Hewer at all. It
had instead been sent by one (he explained in a memorandum):

who in a sportfull revenge for my taking this journey without their knowledge designed to interrupt the pleasure of it and hasten me back before my time by a feigned letter from Mr Hewer wherein his hand was so well counterfeited that I was easily imposed upon to give credit to it.[29]

Fond Lady Mordaunt, perturbed by Pepys's hasty and unannounced departure with the ships, thought his disappearance into Scotland unforgivable, and had forged Hewer's hand to bring him quickly home to the seat in her salon, where she liked to be amused by his wit.

Sadly, we have no record of the conversations between Pepys, Hewer and the malicious Lady on his return but we might perhaps suppose that he let her off lightly. Scott was gone, after all, and he had survived.

24

Gravesend Unravelled

Had he not concerned himself with me first
I had never meddled with him.
JOHN SCOTT TO EDWARD WRIGHT (ABOUT PEPYS), 27 JANUARY 1680

Samuel Pepys and John Scott were born a year apart. The similarities between them are striking. One was the son of a tailor, the other of a miller. Both felt the stirrings of ambition, sought favour through the patronage of the powerful in Restoration England and claimed kinship with a great family. Both had pinned their early hopes on the Duke of York.

Their differences however, set them far apart. Pepys built his career methodically and he became a close (though not uncritical) associate of the royal family. He had honed his skills in England's bureaucratic heart where success came from being one step ahead of other powerful intellects. Scott's approach was forged in the frontier land of the new America where cunning and quick wit were at a premium and his career was marked by a series of dismal failures. These failures, which were often of his own making, inspired his profound personal dislike of the Duke of York and compelled the English government to reject him. A perfect Whig was born, for his anger at duke and government aligned with Whig preoccupations. When the Popish Plot and Exclusion became the great motivating forces in English politics, Scott found his movement, and he and Pepys faced each other from opposite sides of the political battlefield.

Scott had the peculiar mentality of the egoist who believes his desire for a thing is simultaneously his right to it. Because he desired power and status, he expected to be given them. If they were not forthcoming, he would acquire them by any means. Truth was usually the first victim in this process, but Scott may even have come to believe some of his lies himself. How else could he have persisted for so long in the claim of descent from Scot's Hall? There is great authority in such a personality and Scott's success was that he managed to get away with conning so many people for so long.* But there is also tragedy. Scott threw together extravagant, fictitious lives for himself, then watched in horror as the sand shifted and the whole thing collapsed. When that happened, he fled elsewhere and began again. He lacked method and application, but became very good at being convincing. This served him well with the Whigs, whose cause he could sell in the coffee houses. The search for power was perpetual. It was the motor of his life. The key to understanding Scott is that – though he changed his allegiance frequently – his ambition never diminished. It was his ambition that first brought him into direct conflict with Pepys after Gravesend, though Pepys never knew it. Before we unravel Gravesend, however, there is a little more story to tell.

For killing George Butler, Scott became a wanted man again, evaded the hue and cry with his usual mastery of the unguarded ways and fled to the Low Countries. By an intermediary, he pleaded with his old patron Lord Arlington, hoping that his intimate knowledge of the Whig leaders might buy him a royal pardon.† Arlington's cool response came verbally, and a familiar chill of exile ran through Scott. 'I had hoped', he wrote flatly to Arlington on 26 June 1682, 'for . . .

---

* He even managed to seduce his biographer from beyond the grave. In Lilian T. Mowrer's eyes he could do no wrong.

† The intermediary was probably his son. By the time Scott made this plea, an old acquaintance had already written to Pepys from New York, expressing joy that Pepys and Deane 'are out of the pernicious power of that villain Scott, whom doubtless the hand of justice one day will reach for all his horrid contrivances and practices' and telling him that Scott had a son who had gone 'from hence' into England to look for his father, hearing that he was 'famous in that kingdom'. Scott had two sons, John and Jeckamiah. This was probably John. PL, Mornamont MSS, vol. II, pp. 861–2. Wilbur C. Abbott, *Colonel John Scott of Long Island* (1918), p. 81.

such an answer as might have encouraged you to favour me with two or three lines.' He offered up tantalising titbits. There had been 'a black design' a few months earlier, he wrote, possibly referring to Shaftesbury's planned coup d'etat, 'which was of worse consequence than was imagined'. He himself had been a restraining hand. 'I wish as great security to the government as I wish to my own soul,' he claimed, '. . . I was never for overturning and my moderation may one day appear to have been of some service.' He had been mis-represented to the Duke of York, and it was 'my misfortune more than my natural inclinations' to adhere to the Whig cause. But he could say no more unless he was pardoned.[1]

Arlington believed not one word of it, and Scott remained in exile, moving from Holland into Scandinavia.

In January 1683, the Earl of Shaftesbury died. His chance of power irretrievably lost, he had fled from England the previous November, apparently disguised as a Presbyterian minister.[2] Passing under the well-used republican alias of John Johnson, he found an inn in Amsterdam, where a valet tasted everything he ate or drank. By the end of 1682 he had a serious stomach disorder, probably due to a stoppage in the drainage from the tube in his side which had kept him alive for the previous twenty-five years. His usual physicians were out of his reach, the Dutch doctors did not know what to do and the old wound finally killed him.

That July, Scott was spotted in Norway by John Gelson, who was supervising shipments from there (Norway was a key supplier of masts to the English navy) and was a cog in the wheels of intelligence-gathering.[3] Predictably, Scott had claimed a grand background for him-self, and was dismayed to see Gelson, who knew otherwise. Gelson attacked him for his villainous behaviour. Scott defended himself as 'a tool much used', and seemed ready to turn against his former masters. The failure of the Whig movement had left him out in the cold once again, and – his loyalty to the cause all used up – he began to confess.

Scott had not devised the attack himself, he said, but had been put upon contriving Pepys's destruction by 'one that hoped to be a successor in the secretary's employment', meaning William Harbord. Harbord had led the Commons attack to seize Pepys's job for himself and designed to take Pepys's life to secure it.

Scott claimed the Plot's focus on the Catholics was entirely cynical. '[T]he Protestant cause,' he told Gelson, 'was used only to make a party of the zealously blind.' The Plot-movers 'struck the Government through the side of the Romanists [because] . . . they had no other way to destroy or wound it'. The English, 'a giddy and unthinking people', had been deluded by fictions into becoming violent defenders of the Protestant faith. The Plot-movers had sought power. They wanted to make themselves 'kings, or rather tyrants'. Shaftesbury had promised Scott great rewards for his services in stirring up Whig support. In this and subsequent meetings with Gelson, Scott claimed Shaftesbury had offered him the Governorship of the Isle of Wight, a yearly pension of £1,200 and the hand of Lady Vane.[4]

Scott, in short, blamed Shaftesbury for the Popish Plot and Harbord for the specific plot against Pepys. However, when he said Harbord had put him on contriving Pepys's destruction, he was lying. As we have seen, Harbord chaired meetings of the bit-part players who pointed their fingers at Pepys but when Scott, the male lead, arrived on their stage, he arrived as a stranger. At that meeting in the Mitre tavern on Fenchurch Street, just a day or two before the charges, when Scott was sitting alone in a side room in his velvet coat and embroidered belt, Harbord barely knew who he was and had no idea whether he could be trusted. Harbord did not recruit Scott to destroy Pepys. Scott was handed to him by Shaftesbury and Buckingham in order to make the charges capital. Scott's appearance in the Mitre turned Harbord's somewhat paltry plot into one that would send Pepys to the gallows.

Scott's Norwegian confession was disingenuous. First, contrary to Scott's claims, Shaftesbury had been motivated by genuine anti-Catholic feeling. He always had Protestant England's interests at heart, however unscrupulous and terrifying his tactics for preserving her. Second, Scott completely failed to mention his great patron, that other key player in the plot years, the Duke of Buckingham. Unlike Shaftesbury, Buckingham lusted after power and was prepared to treat with the Catholic French for his own political gain. The cynical Whig plotting Scott described, in which the Catholics were to be used as a convenient camouflage for attacking Charles's government, reflected Buckingham's opportunistic approach, not Shaftesbury's more genuine concerns. Scott had sat long at Buckingham's table. By the time he met Gelson in Norway, Shaftesbury was dead and an easy target for his confession. Buckingham, greatly reduced and retired from political life, was still alive, so Scott protected his real master by omission. He and Buckingham together were surely the originators of the plot against Pepys.

Scott had relished his role. A conversation with Edward Wright at another time makes clear how instrumental Scott's resentment at Pepys had been. Scott demanded:

What a pox did Pepys concern himself with me for to represent me to the Parliament to be a man squint-eyed, thick-shouldered, fat and lean, and a man that could put himself into any shape and a Jesuit beside, to rifle my lodging [and] seize my money.

Then, crucially: 'Had he not concerned himself with me first I had never meddled with him.'[5]

He was talking, of course, about his flight from Gravesend when Pepys had pursued him out of England thinking him the Jesuit murderer of Sir Edmund Berry Godfrey. It had been an honest mistake by Pepys and Scott's anger at it was beyond all proportion. But talking to Gelson in the cold exile in Scandinavia, with one eye on a pardon and a return to England, Scott heightened Harbord's role and played down Buckingham's part and his own fury at Pepys.

Pepys got Gelson's letter relaying all this at Portsmouth.[6] He was due to sail with a convoy for Tangier. He did not know why. It was the first time since Scott charged him that he had been given official duties. On 11 August, as he was about to depart, Pepys wrote thanking Gelson for 'the frank declarations and confessions of Colonel Scott, whom God has followed so closely with his justice for the villainy of his practices, not only against me but against his King, the best of Princes, and his country'. Pepys had no personal wish for revenge, but he thought that Scott should give the King a full confession, as long as it proceeded 'from a real sense of his guilt, and a hearty inclination to the making of his peace with God, the King and us for his past iniquities'. If Gelson suspected Scott was just after a pardon he should leave him alone, 'for his reward he will certainly have soon or late from heaven's hand, however he may think himself by flight secured against it from mine'.[7]

Pepys was back on top, a government official again. Scott, on the other hand, was in exile. The wheel had come full circle. From Scott's condition, Pepys deduced that it was 'most certain that to save himself he will tell all', and suggested Deane discuss with Houblon the possibility of getting Scott back to confess who 'his fellow rogues in the intrigue' were. It should be kept very quiet, because Harbord ('the other party') still had enough highly placed friends to hear about it and would immediately give Scott a life-pension to stay overseas.[8] Pepys had entirely swallowed Scott's claim that Harbord was the main plotter. At a subsequent meeting in Larvik, Scott told Gelson he knew all the Parliament men who had attended 'consults for overthrowing the government', and would put it in writing. That, Gelson thought, would keep them out of office when Parliament sat again. But that is the last we hear of him and his dealings with Scott.[9] There is no more in the records.

Pepys, meanwhile, had learnt that his trip to Tangier was not to sort out the troublesome affairs of the expensive, beleaguered English base, but to destroy it. Tangier had been a place of hardship and a futile waste of lives and money, overlooked by surrounding hills and impossible to defend. Great explosions got rid of the mole and fortifications. After dinner, on a quarterdeck, Pepys saw Balty among a throng of officers, 'mightily altered in his looks – with hard usage he tells me'. The line tells us all we need to know about Balty's experiences in Tangier. It was Pepys's only reference to Balty in the record he kept of the trip.[10] On 30 March 1684, Easter Sunday, Pepys got back to England, after getting stranded in flooding in Seville and beating through a gruelling gale in the Bay of Biscay. The first stage of his naval rehabilitation was complete. One month later he was made Secretary for the Affairs of the Admiralty of England and he started on the task of rebuilding a navy that had fallen into sad disrepair, many of the finest ships simply rotting at their moorings.[11]

King Charles died on 6 February 1685 after four days of excruciating treatment in which his doctors threw every known cure at him. He had been in the midst of his concubines, 'profuse gaming and luxurious dallying and prophaneness' just a few days earlier.[12] Despite the Whigs' efforts over the Exclusion years, James, Duke of York, came to the throne. His opponents tried, and failed, to depose him almost immediately. Charles's illegitimate son, the Duke of Monmouth, landed at Lyme, gathered a ragged army equipped with improvised weapons and marched to defeat at Sedgemoor. Monmouth was killed and George Jeffreys's 'Bloody Assize' sought his supporters, but otherwise King James satisfied only the milder end of Whig fears. The Marian bonfires were never rekindled in Smithfield. The majority of the bloodletting against good Protestants was political not physical. James filled his top posts with Catholics but made an exception of the Admiralty where Pepys was allowed to keep a tried Protestant team around him, bringing Sir Anthony Deane back on to the Admiralty Commission and finally rewarding Balty the same way.

James's obdurate, unsubtle rule did not go down well with a people who had learnt that a heady slice of political power was theirs. Shaftesbury and, by now, Buckingham were gone, but this was the legacy their carefully orchestrated popular politics had left behind.* In autumn 1688, news came that an invasion fleet was massing in Holland. Pepys, at the Admiralty, sent orders to Lord Dartmouth's fleet to intercept it. They misjudged the Dutch fleet's destination and failed to stop them. On 3 November, crowds watched from the cliffs of Dover as 500 Dutch ships sailed westward past them, heading for Devon. On 5 November, that most symbolic of anti-Catholic festivals, Protestant William of Orange, husband to James's daughter Mary, landed at Torbay to the delight of a large section of the people of England, and James fled the country.

Though John Scott had failed, his cause had ultimately been a success. The Whigs of the Exclusion years had asserted their right to approve the succession, and things would never be the same again. Parliament, announcing that James had 'abdicated the government', invited the invader and his wife to reign in his stead. The crucial constitutional precedent was set that the sovereign rules not in defiance of Parliament, but by its grace. Over the next years, Parliament legislated to prevent a Roman Catholic from coming to the throne, a law that still holds today. The people stood above a diminished Crown. The road to modern England was paved.

With the fall of the Stuarts, Samuel Pepys's naval career came to an end and his old enemies were back in charge. William Harbord was promoted to high office. In May 1689, England was about to declare war on France where James was in exile and it was thought Pepys and his friends might tip him off. Pepys and Deane, suspected of 'dangerous and treasonable practices against his Majesty's government', were arrested again and committed to the lowly Gatehouse Prison. This time, Will Hewer was sent with them. They were held for six weeks and released when the danger passed.[13]

A year later, rumours spread that a French invasion fleet was in the Channel and Pepys was once more arrested as a Jacobite sympathiser, nipping in the bud his plan for a return to Parliament. Once again he spent over a month in the Gatehouse but it affected his health badly. On 14 July 1690, he was released on bail after urgent intervention by Dr Richard Lowther who certified that he was so ill with an ulcer on his kidneys that he was in danger of death. His team of friends, with

---

* Buckingham had retired to his house in Yorkshire to take shelter from a blizzard of debt. He died in 1687 from a fever contracted after his horse dropped dead under him while hunting on the moors.

James Houblon at their head, rallied round to bail him again and he was eventually discharged on 15 October.[14]

There is no record of whether Samuel Pepys's name figured in John Scott's mind after this. Scott was more amoral than immoral. As a result, the memory of his crimes did not eat at him, but dissipated with the fresh breeze of time and travel. There is no evidence that he ever felt remorse for his crimes against individuals: the trusting Gothersons in his early days in King Charles's court; Dispontyn in Holland; or the host of other people he cheated for money. If he did experience remorse, it certainly never stopped him doing it again. It seems unlikely that Scott gave Pepys much thought in later life. He had lied in the Commons because he was angry with Pepys and had resented Pepys's royal master for a long time. The lie had failed to finish Pepys, but it dealt him a heavy blow. Scott had taken his revenge. He moved on.

For Pepys, however, the story was quite different. The memory of Scott never left him. Pepys's prominent position made him a target in the turbulent cycle of kings and religions, and he kept an eye out for Scott, in case his old enemy should return. Fortunately for Pepys, King William's arrival initially did nothing for Scott's fortunes: Scott's friendship with William's enemy in the Low Countries, the republican de Witt, was held against him and kept him in exile. But in 1696, when Pepys was sixty-three and Scott slipped back into England disguised as a Dutch skipper, Pepys's loyal informant Edward Wright thought it necessary to let him know. Scott was going around in good clothes and a periwig, and claiming that he had been given a pardon for killing the coachman. Wright referred to Scott as 'your prosecutor', as though he had never gone away.[15]

Anxiety coursed through Pepys. He asked Wright to make urgent enquiries about the pardon.[16] Wright reassured him that King William did not usually give pardons before conviction, and that 'the Colonel has always been obnoxious to him', so the claim seemed unlikely to be true. But Scott had been showing off 'a parchment with a broad seal to it', and planned to get a silver box made to keep it in.[17] Scott was, Wright said, 'not a bit altered, not as to his person and carriage'. The news was like a knife. He did not know, or at least, did not tell Pepys that Scott had indeed been pardoned for the murder. State papers show that his pardon was approved on 29 April, at Kensington, and his sentence of outlawry was reversed.[18]

Pepys, in fact, was safe. He had spent the years since his last imprisonment in an altogether slower and more contemplative way of life, filling his time with a gentle correspondence with his learned friends. He was now far away from the world of politics, power and responsibility and that world had moved on a long way from the Stuart era. Nonetheless, the Mornamont volumes were in his bookcases as a enduring reminder of how dangerous and unpredictable Scott could be. Scott persistently claimed that Gravesend was when Pepys had earned his wrath. But in pursuing Scott from Gravesend, Pepys had made an honest mistake; Scott's fury at it seemed disproportionate. Because Scott's attack on him had seemed irrational, Pepys never felt secure against another assault. He had the measure of the man in everything except what lay at the heart of Scott's vindictiveness, which was a mystery to him.

Pepys never solved the mystery. For all his copious investigations, there were some things that were buried too deep in the secret workings of the seventeenth century even for him. They had to come to light slowly. In the very first years of the twentieth century, Winifred, Lady Burghclere, researching a book on the Duke of Buckingham, was going through the *Affaires Étrangères* section of the French archives in Paris when she found the key to this story (though she did not know it). It was a document dating from the same day John Scott rode on a lathered horse into Gravesend, where the fair was in full swing. Sir Edmund Berry Godfrey was dead and Scott was about to be mistaken for his Jesuit murderer and chased out of England by Samuel Pepys. She had found the letter Scott was carrying.[19]

In the hysterical aftermath of Godfrey's murder, when England thought King Charles's assassination was imminent, Scott's patron the Duke of Buckingham went to the French ambassador to ask for a large amount of money. He had an audacious scheme. He intended to use the Lord Mayor of London to raise a militia, under the pretext of assuring the safety of the town. By calling all citizens to arms, Buckingham planned to create a powerful civic force, outside royal control, which would 'demand many unforeseen things'. It was to be the start of a coup to topple Charles. The crisis of those days, Buckingham knew, was the right moment to take the government of England for himself. He could claim he had saved it from a Popish tyrant.

Barrillon, the ambassador, knew Buckingham's wild side all too well and recognised his potential for creating mischief. He later wrote to Louis that Buckingham showed it was 'not the most regular minds which always strike the most considerable strokes'.[20] The ambassador played for time and Buckingham – desperate not to let the moment be lost – decided to deal directly with King Louis. He gave his trusted servant John Scott two letters and sent him to France. One letter was to the Marquis de Pomponne to get Scott access to (as Buckingham described Louis) 'the person in the world whom I honour and love the most'.[21] The second was a note to Louis himself. It begged him for the money. Time was short, the note claimed, as 'is shown by a new incident which the bearer (Mr Scott) is charged to inform you'.[22] It is dated only 'Saturday', but as this comes after Godfrey's murder and before Scott sailed for France, it can only be Saturday 19 October 1678, the day Scott rode into Gravesend on a black horse. To cover his tracks in Gravesend, Scott claimed that he had spent several days on the road. In fact, he had come directly from Buckingham's house – which was why his horse was lathered and his clothes clean.

The verbal message that Scott was to give to Louis was this: the Duke of York and the Earl of Danby (Buckingham had learnt) 'had resolved to shift the government of France into other hands'. Several persons had taken the sacrament on it to assassinate Louis. Buckingham thought it his duty to communicate this, and begged Louis to 'beware of strangers, and in particular of Irishmen'.[23] Buckingham's intention is clear. He would terrify Louis with the prospect of his assassination by the Duke of York's agents, then promise to safeguard him against it by toppling Charles II and the murderous Duke. To protect himself (Buckingham hoped) Louis would fund the coup. Scott was, however, denied access to Louis, and wrote the message down in a note in French, described by Lady Burghclere as 'curiously illiterate and ungrammatical'. Scott's French was never very good.

Marooned in Paris, Scott predicted to John Joyne that a militia would be raised in England, Parliament would vote to disband the army, and the King would soon be joining his brother in exile.[24] Because of Pepys, however, Scott was stuck in France unable, for fear of arrest, to return to England and help co-ordinate Buckingham's coup. He could have been bringing about the dethronement of a king. He should have been earning himself a position right at the heart of government (what else would his reward have been if Buckingham's coup came off?). It was all he had ever lied, cheated, stolen and worked for. Instead, he was forced to stay in France. The prospect of a pivotal role diminished, then disappeared altogether. Furious and impotent, Scott learnt that the greatest opportunity of his imperfect life had been denied him by the work of a man called Samuel Pepys.

Buckingham's coup, history tells us, did not happen. When the opportunity for Scott to revenge himself on Pepys came, he grabbed it with both hands.

Ignorant of all this, Pepys lived out his last years. He had a companion, Mary Skinner, who seemed to his friends to have the status of a wife.[25] Will Hewer took good care of him. In the spring of 1700, the forty-year-old wound from the removal of Pepys's kidney stone broke open and he moved into Hewer's large house on Clapham Common to be nursed. He organised the cataloguing of his library, with his Diary and the Mornamont volumes in it. When his great friend James Houblon died in October, Pepys was too infirm to attend the funeral; his health meant he could not be away from Clapham overnight.[26] He recovered and returned to York Buildings to continue the work on the library, neatly arranged in oak presses. In June 1701, his health worsened again and he moved back to Clapham.

From there, as ever, he kept up a busy correspondence with friends. He died just before 4 a.m. on 26 May 1703, at the age of seventy.

Pepys's accumulated record of his tormentor's life lacked its final chapter. Scott's extravagant ambition, thwarted in America and Europe, shrank. He returned to the Caribbean and there, in the last years of life, unknown to Pepys, he became Speaker of the Montserrat Assembly. Finally granted a small measure of the recognition he craved, he outlived Pepys by one year.[27]

Notes

Abbreviations
PL   Pepys Library
BL   British Library
Bodl. Bodleian Library
DNB   Dictionary of National Biography
HMC Historical Manuscripts Commission

CHAPTER I INTO THE TOWER

1 The weather references throughout this book are provided by a beautifully
   bound and presented manuscript volume in the Bodleian Library
   (Rawlinson D 662). The anonymous book contains full day-by-day details of
   the weather for this period. Although it does not say where the observations
   were taken, we can be confident that it refers to London itself or to somewhere close by since it shows a close correspondence with weather references
   in Pepys's Diary.
2 Description from libel 'A Hue and Cry after P. and H.', quoted in Arthur
   Bryant, *The Years of Peril* (1948), p. 305.
3 John Field, *The Story of Parliament in the Palace of Westminster* (2002),
   pp. 14–15.
4 *Samuel Pepys's Naval Minutes*, ed. J. R. Tanner (1926), pp. 338–9.
5 Stephen Inwood, *A History of London* (1998), p. 255.
6 Adrian Tinniswood, *By Permission of Heaven: The Story of the Great Fire of
   London* (2003), pp. 194 and 243.
7 Ibid., p. 254. Inwood, p. 246. Charles II made a royal proclamation after the
   Fire for the rebuilding of a less combustible city.
8 Inwood, p. 249.
9 John Evelyn, Diary, 4 September 1666.
10 Christopher Wren's son reported that one blast shifted the masonry 'somewhat leisurely, cracking the walls to the top, lifting visibly the whole weight
   about nine inches, which suddenly jumping down, made a great heap of

ruin'. Quoted in Tinniswood, *By Permission of Heaven*, p. 258.

11 Jane Lang, *Rebuilding St Paul's after the Great Fire of London* (1956), p. 50.

12 Ibid., p. 104. The only way to undo the staining was to soak the stone in fresh water or bury it for a year.

13 Diary, 2 September 1666.

CHAPTER 2 TOYS FOR KING LOUIS

1 Diary, 22 May 1660.

2 Ibid.

3 Diary, 23 May 1660.

4 Ibid.

5 Diary, 25 May 1660.

6 Ibid.

7 On 10 July 1660, for example, Pepys expressed delight at his new silk suit, 'the first that ever I wore in my life'. On 21 August 1660 he collected a new velvet coat with equal pleasure. See Diary.

8 Diary, 6 February 1662.

9 Diary, 15 July 1663.

10 N. A. M. Roger, *The Admiralty* (1979), p. 23 cited in *The Diary of Samuel Pepys*, vol. X, *Companion*, ed. Robert Latham and William Matthews, p. 3.

11 Pepys to Commissioner Deane, 25 July 1674, *Descriptive Catalogue of the Naval Manuscripts in the Pepysian Library*, ed. J. R. Tanner (1903–23), vol. II, p. 330. 'To repair up hither to receive the king's commands touching the building of 2 yachts which the King of France desires to have built for him here in imitation of his Majesty's.'

12 Diary, 31 July 1662.

13 Diary, 12 August 1662.

14 *DNB* citing A. W. Johns in *The Mariners' Mirror*, vol. 11.

15 Pepys to Sir Joseph Williamson, 3 July 1675, *Calendar of State Papers, Domestic Series, March 1675–Feb. 1676*, p. 197, '. . . the new French yacht, which (taking in all qualities and its little depth of water) seems to outdo anything that ever swam.'

16 Ibid.

17 *Samuel Pepys's Naval Minutes*, ed. J. R. Tanner (1926), p. 195. Pepys writes as a memo, 'Look up my letter to Sir A[nthony] D[eane] prophesying beforehand the ill construction his voyage into France in the year 1675 might be subject to.'

18 *DNB*.

19 Will Hewer to Pepys, 2 August 1675, Bodl., Rawlinson MSS, A 185, f. 4.

Hewer writes, 'my dear mother . . . would very much be revived by your sending . . . to enquire after her health when you go to that end of the town which pray be pleased to do and pardon my presumption in asking it.'

20 Ibid.

21 Anthony Deane to Pepys, Paris, 18 August 1675, Bodl., Rawlinson MSS, A 185, f. 24.

22 Will Hewer to Pepys, 22 August 1675, *Letters and the Second Diary of Samuel Pepys*, ed. R. G. Howarth (1932), p. 51.

23 Joanna Richardson, *Louis XIV* (1973), p. 73.

24 Will Hewer to Pepys, 22 August 1675, *Letters*, ed. Howarth, p. 51.

25 Ibid.

26 Ibid.

27 Ibid., 12 August 1675, p. 52.

28 Sir Anthony Deane to Pepys, 18 August 1675, Bodl., Rawlinson MSS, A 185, f. 24.

29 Captain Browne's deposition, PL, Mornamont MSS, vol. I, p. 188.

30 Attestation of La Fontaine, Pellissary's Servant, ibid., p. 488.

31 Sir Anthony Deane to Joseph Williamson, 26 September 1675, *Calendar of State Papers, Domestic Series, March 1675–Feb. 1676*, p. 319.

CHAPTER 3 A SINGLE HAIR

1 J. P. Kenyon, *The Popish Plot* (1974), p. 28.

2 Anchitel Grey, *Debates of the House of Commons* (1769), vol. VII, p. 148.

3 Cited in G. P. Gooch, *English Democratic Ideas in the Seventeenth Century* (1927), p. 271.

4 Diary, 18 May 1662.

5 Diary, 28 February 1663.

6 Diary, 3 March 1663.

7 Diary, 15 April 1666.

8 For the articles of the Secret Treaty of Dover see, for example, *Crown and Parliament in Tudor–Stuart England*, ed. Paul L. Hughes and Robert F. Fries (1959).

9 John Evelyn, Diary, 2 October 1685.

10 *The Despatches of William Perwich, English Agent in Paris, 1669–77*, ed. M. Beryl Curran (1903), p. 272.

11 See Jane Lane, *Titus Oates* (1971) for Oates's career.

12 Lane, *Titus Oates*, p. 105.

13 Longleat MSS, Coventry Papers, vol. II, f. 168.

14 Ibid., f. 170.

15 Ibid.
16 *HMC Marquess of Downshire*, vol. I, part II, p. 594.
17 Lane, p. 103.
18 BL, Add. MSS, 25,124: Extraordinary Correspondence of Henry Coventry, f. 157.
19 'Junius Brutus' (pseudonym for Charles Blount), *An Appeal from the Country to the City* (1679).
20 Ibid.
21 William Bedloe, *A Narrative of the Pope's Late Fire-Works in England* (1679).
22 The ambassadors in question were Ralph Montagu and Paul Barrillon.
23 'Junius Brutus', *An Appeal*.

CHAPTER 4 GRAVESEND

1 Reports of the inquest refer to showers of hail. The weather description for the day in Rawlinson D662, f. 30r, refers to snow and freezing rain.
2 W. Stokes, Mayor of Gravesend, to Pepys, 4 November 1678, Bodl., Rawlinson MSS, A 172, f. 3.
3 Robert H. Hiscock, *A History of Gravesend* (1981), p. 38
4 Price and Gibson's information touching Scott's proceedings at Gravesend, PL, Mornamont MSS, vol. I, pp. 113–17. This five-page document provides the main evidence concerning Scott's activities at Gravesend.
5 BL, Add. MSS, 25,124: Extraordinary Correspondence of Henry Coventry, ff. 164–5.
6 Examination of James Sturgis, fisherman of Folkestone regarding the passage of a suspicious character, PL, Mornamont MSS, vol. I, p 127.
7 *Reports of the Royal Commission on Historical Manuscripts*, Report 11, Appendix, Part II (on House of Lords manuscripts), p. 16.
8 BL, Add. MSS, 25,124: Extraordinary Correspondence of Henry Coventry, f. 164.
9 Mr Price to Pepys, 6 February 1680, PL, Mornamont MSS, vol. I, p 118.
10 Diary, 24 September 1660. Pepys was later also made a JP in the City of London with limited powers to prevent fighting around navy premises, especially on pay-days (see 22 March 1663).
11 PL, Mornamont MSS, vol. I, p. 114.
12 The information of Robert Payne of Cannon Street, 'haberdasher of hats', ibid, p. 104.
13 G. W. Keeton, *Lord Chancellor Jeffreys and the Stuart Cause* (1965), p. 125.

CHAPTER 5 SAVING SAM ATKINS

1 The account of Sam Atkins's arrest, examinations and imprisonment is contained in Bodl., Rawlinson MSS, A 173, ff. 113–32, and (in a much more detailed form) in A 181, ff. 1–2, ff. 11–26.
2 John Harold Wilson, *The Ordeal of Mr Pepys's Clerk* (1972), p. 57.
3 Bodl., Rawlinson MSS, A 172, f. 132.
4 Pepys to Earl of Shaftesbury, 15 February 1673, Bodl., Rawlinson MSS, A 172, f. 135.
5 Roger North quoted in Wilson, *The Ordeal of Mr Pepys's Clerk*, p. 58.
6 For the transcription of the trial, see *State Trials*, ed. William Cobbett (1810), vol. VII, pp. 231–50.
7 Scroggs's summing-up at the trial of William Staley, quoted in J. P. Kenyon, *The Popish Plot* (1974), p. 113. 'Excuse me if I am a little warm,' Scroggs said, 'when perils are so many . . . when things are transacted so closely, and our king in so great danger, and religion at stake. It is better to be warm here than in Smithfield.' The attentive jury found Staley guilty without leaving the box.

CHAPTER 6 THE TEMPER OF THE HOUSE

1 William Cobbett, *The Parliamentary History of England* (1808), vol. IV, p. 1,126.
2 Ibid., p. 1,125.
3 Anchitel Grey, *Debates of the House of Commons* (1769), vol. VII, p. 155.
4 BL, Add. MSS, 25,124: Extraordinary Correspondence of Henry Coventry, f. 174.
5 Pepys to Captain Langley, 6 March 1679, *Further Correspondence of Samuel Pepys 1662–1679* (1929), ed. J. R. Tanner, pp. 350–1.
6 Antonia Fraser, *King Charles II* (1979), p. 369.
7 Draft of note from the King to the Duke of York, 26 February 1679, *HMC Earl of Lindsey*, p. 401.
8 Fraser, *King Charles II*, p. 369.
9 J. R. Jones, *The First Whigs: The Politics of the Exclusion Crisis 1678–1683*, (1961), p. 57 and note.
10 Jones, *The First Whigs*, p. 54.
11 Grey, *Debates*, vol. VII, p. 147.
12 Robert Southwell to the Duke of Ormonde, 29 April 1679, *HMC Ormonde*, New Series, vol. IV, p. 507.
13 Grey, vol. VII, pp. 139 and 141.
14 Ibid., p. 141.
15 Robert Southwell to the Duke of Ormonde, 29 April 1679, *HMC Ormonde*,

New Series, vol. IV, p. 507.

16 Parliament's proceedings against Deane and Pepys, PL, Mornamont MSS, vol. I, pp. 1–2.

17 Information of Atkins relating to Captain Russell, ibid., vol. II, p. 1,305.

18 Robert Southwell to the Duke of Ormonde, 29 April 1679, *HMC Ormonde*, New Series, vol. IV, p. 507.

19 The examination of Colonel John Scott before William Richards, Deputy Mayor of Dover, PL, Mornamont MSS, vol. I, p. 125.

20 The King's warrant for apprehending Scott at Dover, ibid., p. 121.

21 Bastinck's answers from Dover to Pepys's queries, ibid., p. 138.

22 Copy of Colonel John Scott's examination at Dover, 29 April 1679, ibid., p. 133.

23 Grey, vol. VII, p. 311.

24 Letter from E. R. Waley, PL, Mornamont MSS, vol. I, p. 134.

25 Ibid., p. 135.

26 Cobbett, *Parliamentary History*, vol. IV, pp. 1, 128–9.

27 Grey, vol. VII, p. 160.

28 Henry Coventry to Colonel John Strode, 1 May 1679, *Calendar of State Papers, Domestic Series, Jan. 1679 to Aug. 1680*, p. 134.

29 Henry Coventry to Henry Savile, 1 May 1679, Longleat MSS, Coventry Papers, vol. 87, f. 72b.

30 Henry Savile to Henry Coventry, 7 May 1679, ibid., vol. 34, f. 320. John Brisbane to the Earl of Danby, 19 March 1679, *HMC Earl of Lindsey*, New Series, p. 404.

31 Bastinck's answers from Dover to Pepys's queries, PL, Mornamont MSS, vol. I, p. 138.

32 Robert Southwell to the Duke of Ormonde, 3 May 1679, *HMC Ormonde*, New Series, vol. IV, p. 509.

33 Pepys to Sir John Werden, 5 May 1679, *Private Correspondence and Miscellaneous Papers of Samuel Pepys 1679–1703*, ed. J. R. Tanner, vol. I, (1926), p. 4.

34 *Samuel Pepys's Naval Minutes*, ed. J. R. Tanner (1926), pp. 71–2.

35 Pepys to Duke of York, 6 May 1679, *Letters and the Second Diary of Samuel Pepys*, ed. R. G. Howarth (1932), pp. 78–82.

36 Cobbett, vol. IV, pp. 1,130–1.

37 Cobbett, vol. IV, pp. 1,131–2. Grey, p. 243.

38 Henry Coventry to Henry Savile, 12 May 1679, Longleat MSS, Coventry Papers, vol. 87, f. 74b.

39 Cobbett, vol. IV, p. 1,133.

40 Grey, vol. VII, p. 260.

41 Ibid., p. 265.
42 Ibid., p. 285.
43 Cobbett, vol. IV, p. 1,136.
44 Duke of York to Charles II, 12 May 1679, *Memoirs of Samuel Pepys*, ed. Richard, Lord Braybrooke (1825), p. 618.
45 A— B— to the Duke of Ormonde, 13 May 1679, *HMC Ormonde*, New Series, vol. V, pp. 95–6.
46 Colonel Edward Cooke to the Duke of Ormonde, wrongly dated 19 May (actually 20 May) 1679, ibid., pp. 106–7.
47 Henry Savile to Henry Coventry, 10 May 1679, Longleat MSS, Coventry Papers, vol. 34, f. 322b.

CHAPTER 7 THROUGH PELLISSARY'S WINDOW

1 Bodl., Rawlinson MSS, D 662.
2 George Bowles's information (and subsequent notes), PL, Mornamont MSS, vol. II, p. 1,150 and pp. 1,154–5.
3 Captain Browne's deposition, ibid., vol. I, pp. 185–97.
4 Information of John James, ibid., vol. II, p. 1,247.
5 Information of James Puckle, ibid., p. 833.
6 The story Scott told is contained in Anchitel Grey, *Debates of the House of Commons* (1769), vol. VII, pp. 303–4 and PL, Mornamont MSS, vol. I, pp. 17–20. The Mornamont entry is Scott's deposition, sworn on 7 June 1679 before Justice Pemberton but making the same charges as he did in the Commons.
7 *Samuel Pepys's Naval Minutes*, ed. J. R. Tanner (1926), p. 296. This is full of naval material but also some engaging oddities, such as Sir William Dugdale's belief that parts of Lincolnshire were bounded to the north by Denmark, the question of how the herring came to be called the king of fishes and the strange case of the woman who ate for three years without ever 'going to stool'.
8 *Samuel Pepys's Naval Minutes*, p. 43. There is some evidence to suggest that Scott was lent these papers and in turn had copies made for himself. See BL Add. MSS 30,220 and the information of Giles Hancock, PL, Mornamont MSS, vol. II, pp. 1,089–92.
9 Deposition of Samuel Moone of Wimborne, mariner, PL, Mornamont MSS, vol. I, pp. 21–3.
10 Grey, *Debates*, vol. VII, pp. 304–5 and information of James to Parliament against Pepys, PL, Mornamont MSS, vol. II, pp. 1,181–5.
11 Thomas Hill to Pepys, 14 April 1673, ibid., p. 1,281.

12 Ibid., p. 1,282.
13 Thomas Hill to Pepys, 7 October 1674, ibid., p. 1,283.
14 Thomas Hill to Pepys, 1 July 1675, ibid., pp. 1,287–8.
15 Pepys to Thomas Hill, 21 November 1674, ibid., p. 1,286.
16 James Houblon to Pepys, 2 November 1678, *The Life, Journals and Correspondence of Samuel Pepys*, ed. J. Smith (1841), vol. I, pp. 190–1.
17 See Antonia Fraser, *The Gunpowder Plot* (2002), p. 238, etc.
18 Grey, vol. VII, p. 305.
19 Grey, vol. VII, pp. 305–8 for Pepys's speech.
20 Pepys thought this was 'Sir Edward (or Sir Robert) Harloe'. Tanner (*Pepys's Naval Minutes*, p. 47 and note) identifies this as Sir Edward Harley, but suggests the wrong speech. The writer then gave the speech to Pepys's lawyer John Hayes. The copy of the speech is in Bodl., Rawlinson MSS, A 173, ff. 62–4.
21 Grey, vol. VII, pp. 308–9 for Deane's speech.
22 Louise Fargo Brown, *The First Earl of Shaftesbury* (1933), p. 223.

CHAPTER 8 FAT HARRY AND THE SCOTSMAN

1 Sir Robert Southwell to Ormonde, 20 May 1679, *HMC Ormonde*, New Series, vol. IV, p. 515.
2 Col. Edward Cooke to Ormonde, 20 May 1679 (wrongly dated 19 May 1679), ibid., vol. V, p. 108.
3 Col. Edward Cooke to Ormonde, 22 May 1679, ibid., p. 111.
4 *HMC Beaufort, Donoughmore*, p. 184.
5 Sir Robert Southwell to Ormonde, 20 May 1679, *HMC Ormonde*, New Series, vol. IV, p. 515.
6 Journal of Pepys's proceedings with James and Harris, PL, Mornamont MSS, vol. II, p. 1,217.
7 Pepys to Savile, 26 May 1679, ibid., vol. I, p. 141.
8 A faint and probably unreliable oral tradition at the Tower suggests Pepys may have been imprisoned in the Beauchamp Tower.
9 Longleat MSS, Coventry Papers, vol. 11, f. 397.
10 Henry Coventry to Isaac Puller, linen draper at the sign of the Lion and Lamb, Cornhill, 8 May 1679, *Calendar of State Papers, Domestic Series, Jan. 1679 to Aug. 1680*, pp. 139–40.
11 Savile to Henry Coventry, 10 May 1679, Longleat MSS, Coventry Papers, vol. 34, f. 322b. The letter has a note written on it to say that Coventry took it to show the King.
12 Anchitel Grey, *Debates of the House of Commons* (1769), vol. VII, p. 312.

13 Pepys to John Brisbane, 26 May 1679, PL, Mornamont MSS, vol. I, p. 143. Pepys apologises to Brisbane that he has insufficient time to write him a full letter and asks him to look at the letter he has sent to his superior, Henry Savile, at the Paris embassy.

14 *DNB*.

15 *DNB* citing *Letters of John Wilmot, Earl of Rochester*, ed. J. Treglown (1980).

16 Diary, 31 July 1665.

17 Diary, 1 January 1668.

18 Pepys to Savile and Brisbane, 26 May 1679, PL, Mornamont MSS, vol. I, pp. 141–3.

19 Arthur Bryant, *The Years of Peril* (1948), p. 270, citing Roger North.

20 Anchitel Grey, *Debates*, vol. VII, p. 345 and pp. 345–6 note. Bouell to Watts, 31 May 1679, *HMC Ormonde*, New Series, vol. V, p. 119.

21 Diary, 7 November 1662.

22 Diary, 2 September 1666.

23 Diary, 4 July 1668.

24 Diary, 4 March 1669.

25 Speaker's warrant for the commitment of Pepys and Deane, PL, Mornamont MSS, vol. I, p. 13.

26 Ibid., pp. 45–77. The 'journal of the principal passages relating to the commitment of Sir Anthony Deane and Mr. Pepys and the proceedings therein', laid out by Pepys himself, provides the main framework of the legal narrative in this book. This is published in *Pepys's Later Diaries*, ed. C. S. Knighton (2004), pp. 42–60.

27 *The Stuart Constitution: Documents and Commentary*, ed. J. P. Kenyon (1986), p. 393.

28 Pepys to John Brisbane, 26 May 1679, PL, Mornamont MSS, vol. I, p. 143.

29 Morelli to Pepys, 29 May 1679, *Letters and the Second Diary of Samuel Pepys*, ed. R. G. Howarth (1932), p. 83.

30 Pepys to Will Hewer, 19 May 1682, Bodl., Rawlinson MSS, A 194, pp. 276–8.

31 *Pepys's Later Diaries*, ed. Knighton, p. 40.

32 Pepys to John Brisbane, 2 June 1679, Bodl., Rawlinson MSS, A 194, p. 5.

33 Henry Savile to Pepys, 10 June 1679, PL, Mornamont MSS, vol. I, p. 145. John Brisbane to Pepys, 31 May 1679, ibid., pp. 149–50.

CHAPTER 9 JOBS FOR THE SCOTSMAN

1 John Brisbane to Henry Thynne, 24 May 1679, Longleat MSS, Coventry Papers, vol. 36, f. 426.

2 Henry Coventry to John Brisbane, 26 May 1679, ibid., vol. 87, f. 76.

3 John Evelyn, Diary, 4 June 1679.

4 John Brisbane to Pepys, 31 May 1679, PL, Mornamont MSS, vol. I, p. 150.

5 Pepys to John Brisbane, 5 June 1679, Bodl., Rawlinson MSS, A 194, p. 6.

6 Pepys to Henry Savile, 26 May 1679, PL, Mornamont MSS, vol. I, p. 142.

7 Pepys to Sir Robert Southwell, 9 June 1679, Bodl., Rawlinson MSS, A 194, pp. 7–8.

8 Pepys to Sir John Werden, 9 June 1679, ibid., p. 10.

9 Letter from James Puckle, 13 July 1679, PL, Mornamont MSS, vol. II, p. 826.

10 Pepys to Sir John Werden, 9 June 1679, Bodl., Rawlinson MSS, A 194, p. 10.

11 Pepys to the Duke of York, 9 June 1679, *Private Correspondence and Miscellaneous Papers of Samuel Pepys, 1679–1703,* ed. J. R. Tanner (1926), vol. I, p. 11.

12 Pepys to Sir Robert Southwell, 19 August 1677, *Further Correspondence and Miscellaneous Papers of Samuel Pepys, 1662–1679,* ed. J. R. Tanner (1929), p. 304.

13 Pepys to Sir Robert Southwell, 9 June 1679, Bodl., Rawlinson MSS, A 194, p. 8.

14 Diary, 2 March 1666.

15 Diary, 9 February 1666.

16 Pepys to James Houblon, 10 June 1679, Bodl., Rawlinson MSS, A 194, p. 11. Pepys apologises for troubling Houblon with all his questions earlier in the day, then adds a further one to his list about Scott's counterfeiting a deed at The Hague and urges Houblon to 'write by this post' to add it to those already gone.

17 John Brisbane to Henry Coventry, 31 May 1679, Longleat MSS, Coventry Papers, vol. 36, f. 430.

18 Henry Coventry to Henry Savile, 2 June 1679, ibid., vol. 87, ff. 76b–77.

19 John Brisbane to Henry Coventry, 31 May 1679, ibid., vol. 36, f. 430.

20 Henry Coventry to John Brisbane, 4 June 1679, ibid., vol. 87, f. 78.

21 John Brisbane to Henry Coventry, 28 May 1679, ibid., vol. 36, f. 434.

22 John Brisbane to Pepys, 7 June 1679, PL, Mornamont MSS, vol. I, pp. 150–2. The original, complete with gold flecks, is in Bodl., Rawlinson MSS, A 188, f. 145.

23 *HMC Marquess of Downshire,* vol. I, part I, p. 206. On 8 August 1686, Sir Richard Bulstrode wrote to fellow diplomat Sir William Temple in Paris asking him for two pounds of the best French sealing wax and 'the like quantity of sand which shines like gold to throw upon letters'.

24 Henry Coventry to Henry Savile, 2 June 1679, Longleat MSS, Coventry Papers, vol. 87, f. 72b.

25 John Brisbane to Earl of Danby, in cipher, 8 January 1679, *HMC Earl of Lindsey,* pp. 396–8.

26 John Brisbane to Charles Bertie, 14 January 1679, ibid., p. 398.

27 John Brisbane to Earl of Danby, 19 March 1679, ibid., p. 404.
28 John Brisbane to Henry Coventry, 1 June 1679, Longleat MSS, Coventry Papers, vol. 36, f. 440.
29 Pepys to John Brisbane, 12 June 1679, Bodl., Rawlinson MSS, A 194, p. 12.
30 Journal of Mr Pepys's Proceedings with James and Harris, PL, Mornamont MSS, vol. II, p. 1,231.
31 Henry Coventry to John Brisbane, 4 June 1679, Longleat MSS, Coventry Papers, vol. 87, f. 79.
32 Henry Savile to Henry Coventry, undated, ibid., vol. 34, f. 349.
33 John Brisbane to Henry Coventry, 11 June 1679, ibid., vol. 36, f. 440.

CHAPTER 10 THE LIGHT AND DARKNESS

1 Richard Langhorn to William Blundell, quoted in *Cavalier: Letters of William Blundell to his Friends, 1620–1698*, ed. M. Blundell (1933), p. 102.
2 *London's Flames* (1679).
3 Richard Langhorn to William Blundell, quoted in *Cavalier*, ed. Blundell, p. 115.
4 For the events up to his trial, see Langhorn's own account, *State Trials*, ed. William Cobbett (1810), vol. VII, pp. 506–14.
5 *State Trials*, ed. Cobbett, vol. VII, p. 509.
6 For the transcription of Langhorn's trial see *State Trials*, vol. VII, pp. 417–90.
7 It still lies among the tracts of 1679 – the list of his travelling companions is item twenty-eight of his *Narrative*. Brett's name was on the list.
8 *DNB*.
9 For Langhorn's account of what happened after his trial see *State Trials*, vol. VII, pp. 516–23.
10 *State Trials*, vol. VII, p. 518. For a discussion of these estates, see Thomas M. McCoog, 'Richard Langhorne and the Popish Plot' in *Recusant History*, vol. 19, no. 4 (1989), pp. 499–508.
11 *State Trials*, vol. VII, p. 521.
12 Langhorn's speech appears in *State Trials*, vol. VII, pp. 502–6.
13 *State Trials*, vol. VII, pp. 588–90.
14 Ibid., pp. 501–2 and p. 506.

CHAPTER 11 CATASTROPHES

1 Diary, 27 August 1661.
2 Diary, 3 April 1666.
3 Pepys to John Brisbane, 19 June 1679, Bodl., Rawlinson MSS, A 194, p. 21.

4 John Brisbane to Pepys, 11 June 1679, PL, Mornamont MSS, vol. I, p. 154.

5 Pepys to John Brisbane, 19 June 1679, Bodl., Rawlinson MSS, A 194, p. 20.

6 Pepys to Captain Lovell, 17 June 1679, ibid., p. 18.

7 Ibid., p. 19. This is the accompanying letter from Pepys to Sir John Coplestone dated 19 June 1679. The list of queries on the smaller sheets following are not numbered.

8 Diary, 20 December 1665.

9 This is illustrated by a despatch from Leighton to London in December 1675 while he was serving at the Paris embassy. It described in salacious detail a court case in Paris concerning a wealthy widow, seeking to have her re-marriage annulled in front of the ecclesiastical judges on the grounds of her husband's impotence, insisting that the court should attend a special demonstration to prove whether he could 'solidly and thoroughly without lapsing, endeavour to gratify the woman'. Longleat MSS, Coventry Papers, vol. 35, f. 192.

10 Gilbert Burnet, *Bishop Burnet's History of his own Time* (1833), vol. I, pp. 246–7.

11 Order in Council, 3 October 1676, *Calendar of State Papers, Domestic Series, March 1676–Feb. 1677*, pp. 349–50.

12 John Brisbane to Henry Coventry, 8 October 1676, Longleat MSS, Coventry Papers, vol. 36, f. 8.

13 Warrant to arrest John Wickham, messenger, for allowing the escape, 21 October 1676. *Calendar of State Papers, Domestic Series, March 1676–Feb. 1677*, p. 379.

14 Sir Joseph Williamson to the Mayor of Dover, 21 October 1676, ibid.

15 *Calendar of State Papers, Domestic Series, March 1677–Feb. 1678*, pp. 294–5.

16 Sir Ellis Leighton to Henry Coventry, undated, Longleat MSS, Coventry Papers, vol. 35, f. 322.

17 Henry Coventry to John Brisbane, 8 July 1678, ibid., vol. 87, f. 51b.

18 Order in Council, 3 October 1676, and Minutes of Committee for Trade, 12 October 1676, *Calendar of State Papers, Domestic Series, March 1676–Feb. 1677*, p. 349 and p. 365. Also *DNB*.

19 Sir John Coplestone to Pepys, 21 June 1679, PL, Mornamont MSS, vol. II, p. 1,161.

20 Pepys to Balty, 29 September 1679, *The Letters of Samuel Pepys and his Family Circle*, ed. H. T. Heath (1955), p. 106.

21 A 'journal of the principal passages relating to the commitment of Sir A. D. and S. P., and the proceedings thereon', PL, Mornamont MSS, vol. I, pp. 47–8.

22 Pepys to Sir John Werden, 23 June 1679, Bodl., Rawlinson MSS, A 194, pp. 26–7.

23 The National Archives, E407/56/1, p. 155: Bill from the Lieutenant of the Tower.
24 Diary, 5 July 1660.
25 Robert Wals to Sir William Trumbull, 29 October 1685, *HMC Marquess of Downshire*, vol. 1, part 1, p. 51.
26 James Puckle to Pepys, 17/27 June 1679, PL, Mornamont MSS, vol. II, pp. 819–20.
27 Ibid.
28 For Puckle's information about Scott, see PL, Mornamont MSS, vol. II, pp. 821–4.
29 Anchitel Grey, *Debates of the House of Commons* (1769), vol. VII, p. 311.
30 Pepys to James Puckle, 23 June 1679, Bodl., Rawlinson MSS, A 194, pp. 27–8.
31 Letter from Nicholas Reeve, 17 June 1679, PL, Mornamont MSS, vol. II, pp. 701–2.
32 Evelyn, Diary, 26 March 1685.
33 Hutchinson's name had been given to Pepys by James Puckle in his paper of 17 June 1679. Scott, said Puckle, had forced Hutchinson out of his home, leaving him unable to visit his family and forced to live in Rotterdam where he had opened a pub. PL, Mornamont MSS, vol. II, pp. 825.
34 Pepys's notes for Captain Gunman, ibid., pp. 713–5.
35 Captain Gunman's Information, ibid., pp. 717–8.
36 Pepys to Sir Robert Southwell, 24 June 1679, Bodl., Rawlinson MSS, A 194, p. 29.
37 Sir Alexander Collyear to Sir John Werden, 27 June 1679, PL, Mornamont MSS, vol. II, pp. 705–6.
38 Letter from Nicholas Reeve, 20 June 1679, ibid., pp. 702–3.
39 Letter from Nicholas Reeve, 27 June 1679, ibid., p. 703.
40 Pepys to Sir Robert Southwell, 27 June 1679, Bodl., Rawlinson MSS, A 194, p. 35.
41 Letter from Nicholas Reeve, 27 June 1679, PL, Mornamont MSS, vol. II, p. 703.
42 Edmund Custis to Mr Kennedy, 2 July 1679 (NS), ibid., pp. 850–2.
43 Royal Warrant, 26 June 1679, Bodl., Rawlinson MSS, A 181, f. 116.
44 Pepys to Sir John Werden, 29 June 1679, ibid., A 194, p. 36.
45 Printed in Walter H. Whitear, *More Pepysiana* (1927), p. 105.
46 A 'journal of the principal passages relating to the commitment of Sir A. D. and S. P., and the proceedings thereon', PL, Mornamont MSS, vol. I, p. 48.
47 Samuel St Michel to Pepys, 12 June 1679, *The Letters of Samuel Pepys and his Family Circle*, ed. H. T. Heath (1955), pp. 65–6.
48 John Brisbane to Henry Coventry, 5 July 1679, Longleat MSS, Coventry Papers, vol. 36, f. 453.

49 John Brisbane to Pepys, 19 June 1679, PL, Mornamont MSS, vol. I, pp. 155–7.

50 Henry Coventry to John Brisbane, 3 July 1679, Longleat MSS, Coventry Papers, vol. 87, f. 81b.

51 A document has come to light which lays out Balty's version of the Hunter affair. In late September 1674, he was required by King Charles to write a full account of the matter. He explained in detail how the English merchants who had cargo on board the *Catherine* lied to try to recover their goods and how an ignorant English ordinary seaman tried to masquerade as the ship's commander instead of her Dutch captain. The document also reveals that when Balty went to Paris to sort out the affair, it was subsidiary to his main purpose. King Charles had sent him to see King Louis at Versailles to discuss details of the two pond yachts that Sir Anthony Deane had been instructed to build. All this is contained in Balty's 'humble representation' addressed to King Charles and the Privy Council, 27 September 1674, Bodl., Rawlinson MSS, C 384 f. 3.

52 John Brisbane to Henry Coventry, 5 July 1679 (NS), Longleat MSS, Coventry Papers, vol. 36, ff. 452–3b. Henry Coventry to John Brisbane, 30 June 1679, ibid., vol. 87, f. 80b.

53 John Brisbane to Henry Coventry, 8 July 1679, ibid., f. 457.

CHAPTER 12 THE SIGNATURE

1 Pepys to Balty, 3 July 1679, *The Letters of Samuel Pepys and his Family Circle*, ed. H. T. Heath (1955), pp. 67–9.

2 John Evelyn, Diary, 3 July 1679.

3 John Brisbane to Pepys, 2 July 1679, PL, Mornamont MSS, vol. I, pp. 157–9.

4 Pepys to Balty, 7 July 1679, *The Letters*, ed. Heath, p. 71. In this, Pepys makes it clear that this information must have been in Balty's previous letter, which is not extant.

5 Deposition of Mary Harris, the wife of Alexander Harris of Axe Yard in Westminster, PL, Mornamont MSS, vol. I, pp. 29–31.

6 Pepys to Balty, 29 September 1679, *The Letters*, ed. Heath, p. 106.

7 Using Central Statistical Office tables, this is based on a multiplier of 150.

8 *DNB* entry for Scroggs. J. P. Kenyon, *The Popish Plot* (1974), p. 194 remarks that at Wakeman's trial 'Scroggs turned.'

9 The information of John Harrison, PL, Mornamont MSS, vol. I, p. 412.

CHAPTER 13 SCOTT'S GLORY

1 The Scotts of Scot's Hall were in rapid decline, brought down by their

principled adherence to 'gavelkind', a system of inheritance once widespread in Kent, in which the wealth was divided among the children, instead of passing to the first-born son. Other Kentish families resorted to private acts of Parliament to get them out of this. The Scotts stuck to the tradition. We are indebted to Pepys Librarian, Dr Richard Luckett, for this information.

2 This account of Scott's life in America is drawn from the following sources in PL, Mornamont MSS, vol. II, unless otherwise stated: Mathias Nicolls's information (pp. 883–92); Edward Sackville's information (pp. 873–82); Jacob Milburne's information (pp. 863–6, 876–7); Richard Charlton's information (pp. 867–70); Dorothea Gotherson's information (pp. 1,046–8); William Dyer's information (p. 860); and Thomas Lovelace's information and papers (pp. 911–14 and pp. 1,011–12).

3 Lilian T. Mowrer, *The Indomitable John Scott, Citizen of Long Island* (1960), p. 63.

4 Roy Strong, *Lost Treasures of Britain* (1990), p. 150.

5 Diary, 30 June 1660.

6 Diary, 25 December 1662.

7 John Evelyn, Diary, 2 August 1663.

8 The declaration of the Scott Family, PL, Mornamont MSS, vol. II, pp. 1,101–2.

8 Dorothea Gotherson possibly to Thomas Lovelace, 9 March probably 1669, ibid., p. 1,041.

10 Lilian T. Mowrer, *The Indomitable John Scott*, pp. 82–3.

11 John Winthrop Jr to John Mason, 4 March 1663, *Collections of the Massachusetts Historical Society*, 5th Series, vol. VIII (1882), pp. 77–80. This makes it clear that Scott was representing New Haven's 'complaints' in London, and that he had been empowered by 'the proprietors about Narragansett', who were the Atherton Company, the men engaged in the land dispute. For his engagement with Southton and Southold, see PL, Mornamont MSS, vol. II, p. 886.

12 Schuyler Van Rensselaer, *History of the City of New York in the Seventeenth Century* (1909), vol. I, p. 502.

13 John Leverett to John Scott, 7 July 1663, PL, Mornamont MSS, vol. II, p. 903.

14 John Young to John Scott, 12 June 1663, ibid., p. 907.

15 John Scott to Joseph Williamson, 14 December 1663, *Documents Relative to the Colonial History of the State of New York*, ed. E. B. O'Callaghan (1853), vol. III, p. 47. In this later letter, Scott refers to 'your courteous reception of the tender of my endeavours to your service'.

16 Wilbur C. Abbott, *Colonel John Scott of Long Island* (1918), p. 15.

17 Thomas Hutchinson, *The Hutchinson Papers* (1865), vol. II, pp. 104–5.

18 Ibid., p. 105. *Documents*, ed. E. B. O'Callaghan, vol. III, p. 46.

19 The letter from Charles bore the date 21 June 1663. *Records of the Colony or Jurisdiction of New Haven*, ed. Charles J. Hoadly (1858), p. 511. See also van Rensselaer, *History of the City of New York*, p. 506.

20 *Calendar of State Papers, Colonial Series, America and the West Indies, 1661–1668*, p. 147.

21 James Renat Scott, *Memorials of the Family of Scott, of Scot's Hall, in the County of Kent* (1876), pp. 229–30.

22 Diary, 30 July 1663.

23 *Records*, ed. Charles J. Hoadly, p. 510.

24 Abbott, *Colonel John Scott of Long Island*, p. 25.

25 Hoadly, p. 541 note.

26 Van Rensselaer, *History of the City of New York*, p. 507.

27 John Romeyn Brodhead, *History of the State of New York*, vol. I (1853), p. 726.

28 Van Rensselaer, p. 507.

29 Ibid.

30 *Public Records of the Colony of Connecticut*, ed. J. Hammond Trumbell (1850), vol. I, pp. 421–2.

31 Ibid., p. 422. John Davenport to John Winthrop, 22 March 1664, *Collections of the Massachusetts Historical Society*, 4th Series, vol. VII (1865) p. 525.

32 William Leete to John Winthrop, 31 March 1664, ibid., p. 553.

33 Wilbur C. Abbott, *Conflicts with Oblivion* (1924), p. 315. Van Rensselaer, p. 518.

34 *Public Records of the Colony of Connecticut*, ed. J. Hammond Trumbell (1850), vol. I, p. 430.

35 *Records of the Colony or Jurisdiction of New Haven*, ed. Charles J. Hoadly (1858), p. 541 note.

36 Van Rensselaer, p. 518.

37 Ibid.

CHAPTER 14 NEW AMSTERDAM

1 Information of Mr Sackville, PL, Mornamont MSS, vol. II, p. 878.

2 Schuyler van Rensselaer, *History of the City of New York in the Seventeenth Century*, vol. I (1909), pp. 514–5.

3 Notes for Mr Sackville, PL, Mornamont MSS, vol. II, p. 879.

4 John Romeyn Brodhead, *History of the State of New York*, vol. I (1853), p. 737 and vol. II (1871), p. 24.

5 Van Rensselaer, *History*, p. 520.

6 Brodhead, *History*, vol. I, p. 740.

7 Quoted in Van Rensselaer, p. 524.

8 Quoted in Van Rensselaer, p. 525.

9 Wilbur C. Abbott, *Colonel John Scott of Long Island* (1918), p. 31.

10 John Underhill to John Winthrop, 23 March 1665, *Collections of the Massachusetts Historical Society*, 4th Series, vol. VII (1865), p. 190.

11 John Underhill to John Winthrop, 23 March 1665, ibid.

12 Brodhead, vol. II, p. 84.

13 Colonel Richard Nicolls to the Duke of York, November 1665, *Calendar of State Papers, Colonial Series, America and the West Indies, 1661–1668*, pp. 337–8.

14 We know this from the petition of Edward Everard of Gray's Inn 'to be granted the hundredth share of West New Jersey forfeited by Col. John Scott for a barbarous murder he has committed, and all the King's right and interest therein' dated 14 November 1687, *Calendar of State Papers, Domestic Series, June 1687–Feb. 1689*, p. 102.

15 The acquaintance's name was Colonel Morris, ibid.

16 Major Scott's relation, *Calendar, America and the West Indies*, pp. 480–1.

17 Major John Scott to Joseph Williamson, 16 July 1667, ibid., pp. 483–4.

18 A charge exhibited against Captain John Scott 'with subsequent accounts and examinations', PL, Mornamont MSS, vol. II, pp. 1,049–62.

19 Ibid., p. 1,054.

20 Sir Tobias Bridge to William Lord Willoughby, 13 July 1667, *Calendar, America and the West Indies*, p. 482. Scott also claimed that 'most of our soldiers prisoners, especially Irish, have taken up arms for the French.' John Scott to Joseph Williamson, 16 July 1667, ibid., p. 483. The freed prisoners, Scott claimed, 'give a very strange account' of relations between the Irish prisoners and their French captors.

21 Ibid., pp. 482–4, p. 499: William Lord Willoughby to Joseph Williamson, 17 September 1667.

22 Court martial of Scott at Nevis, 4 January 1667, PL, Mornamont MSS, vol. II, p. 1,049.

23 Copy of certificate from William Lord Willoughby declaring Scott's claims about the imprisoned Irish false, ibid., p. 1,061.

24 William Lord Willoughby to Joseph Williamson, 20 January 1668, *Calendar, America and the West Indies*, p. 540.

25 John Scott to Lord Arlington, 26 January 1668, *Calendar of State Papers, Domestic Series, 1667–1668*, p. 189. He was 'surprised by 4 bailiffs and their attendants, who forced him into a coach and took him prisoner to the Gatehouse on a most slender and unjust suit'.

26 John Scott to Joseph Williamson, 18 July 1668, ibid., p. 493. 'I know of no

other reason for the dislike you have taken against me than the unhappy accident in Scotland Yard, supposed to be by Andrews . . . I never heard of him after but my nephew saw him the day after the villainy was committed in Holborn . . . Attached is a scrap requesting a prayer for a troubled, sinful, and almost despairing soul.'

27 Warrant, dated 29 August 1668, apparently making Scott the King's Geographer, PL, Mornamont MSS, vol. II, p. 1,081. It is signed by Arlington at the command of the King and refers to Scott as 'our trusty and well beloved Major John Scott'. Historians have been unable to reach a consensus on the validity of the Royal Geographer warrant. Mowrer, naturally, endorses it wholeheartedly. One of Scott's stiffest critics, W. C. Abbott, was also willing to endorse it, but the coolly objective PL Catalogue describes it as 'forged'.

28 Samuel Maverick to John Winthrop, 24 February 1669, *Collections of the Massachusetts Historical Society*, 4th Series, vol. VII (1865), pp. 315–16.

29 Ibid.

CHAPTER 15 THE FALLEN MAN

1 Edmund Custis to Mr Kennedy, 2 July 1679 (NS), PL, Mornamont MSS, vol. II, p. 850.

2 Captain Platt's information, ibid., p. 842.

3 *The Diary of Samuel Pepys*, ed. Robert Latham and William Matthews, *Introduction* in vol. I (1970), p. xxxiv.

4 Attestation of Mrs Wilkes, PL, Mornamont MSS, vol. II, p. 803.

5 Captain Gunman's information, ibid., p. 717.

6 The deposition of Edmund Custis, ibid., p. 846.

7 Attestation of John Abbot, ibid., pp. 795–6.

8 The deposition of Edmund Custis, ibid., pp. 843–6. Also Custis to Kennedy, ibid., p. 851.

9 John Joyne's deposition 'on several loose particulars', ibid., vol. I, p. 254.

10 For another example of a similar cheat, see Frederick Hennick's attestation. Hennick gave Scott 200 guilders as security for a map book he borrowed, but when he returned the book he was not given the money back. Ibid., vol. II, pp. 807–8.

11 Pepys to Carr, quoting letter sent to Abraham Castelline 'the Harlem Courantier', 14 November 1679, Bodl., Rawlinson MSS, A 194, f. 111.

12 See also the information of Major Connocke, which surely relates to this incident, PL, Mornamont MSS, vol. II, p. 799.

13 Captain Gunman's information, ibid., p. 717.

14 This account of the Dispontyn affair is drawn from the following sources in PL, Mornamont MSS, vol. II: Scott's declaration against Dispontyn; William Akers's attestation; Giles Looren's information; Gerebrand Sas's attestation; Cornelia Wingarden's attestation; Richard Adams's information; William Cowley's attestation; and John Netherway's attestations, pp. 721–52. Also: Deborah Egmond 'alias Netherway's' information, pp. 761–87; attestations on pp. 791–2; and Mrs Wilkes's attestation, p. 803.

15 Letter from D'Allais, ibid., p. 588.

16 Attestation of John Lussing, shoemaker, and others, ibid., pp. 811–12.

17 Bodl., Rawlinson MSS, A 194, f. 109. This may have been Sir William Temple.

18 Letter from D'Allais, ibid., A 179, f. 57.

19 Silas Taylor to Lord Arlington from the Brill, 9 March 1672, *Calendar of State Papers, Domestic Series, Dec. 1671–May 1672*, p. 186. 'They have about 1,200 or 1,300 soldiers in this island, but expect Major Scot's regiment, he being lately made a colonel, to reinforce them.'

20 *Journal of Sir Joseph Williamson* (in *Calendar, Domestic Series, Dec. 1671–May 1672)*, p. 608.

21 Ibid.

22 March's information, PL, Mornamont MSS, vol. II, p. 815.

23 Silas Taylor to Lord Arlington, 22 March 1672, *Calendar, Domestic Series, Dec. 1671–May 1672*, p. 604.

24 Silas Taylor to Joseph Williamson, 9 April 1672, ibid., p. 296.

25 John Gelson to Joseph Williamson, 8 June 1672 (as PS to letter of 7 June), ibid., p. 175.

26 Information of Mr Page, PL, Mornamont MSS, vol. II, p. 754. This details an interview in St Bartholomew's Hospital with Captain John Netherway who was on his deathbed. Netherway revealed Scott's plan to send him from Holland 'over to the coasts to do mischief there'.

27 Silas Taylor to Lord Arlington, 22 March 1672, *Calendar, Domestic Series, Dec. 1671–May 1672*, p. 604. The reports of Williamson's agent Silas Taylor give a fascinating picture of the Low Countries at the beginning of the war. He saw the *Royal Charles*, formerly the pride of the English fleet, laid up and stripped of her bowsprit. The blackest day of Pepys's naval career had come on 12 June 1667, when the Dutch burst through the river chain at Chatham, burnt several ships and captured the *Charles* (see Diary). Taylor also saw the ship that broke the chain, a man-of-war equipped with a saw-blade keel.

28 Captain Collinson to Colonel Kennedy, 27 June 1679, PL, Mornamont MSS, vol. II, p. 709.

29 'What I can say of my own knowledge of Colonel John Scott' by James

Puckle, ibid., p. 827.

30 Letter and attestation from D'Allais about Scott, ibid., p. 588.

31 Mr Custis's note, ibid., p. 852.

32 Ibid., p. 709.

33 Ibid., p. 852.

34 The deposition of Edmund Custis, ibid., pp. 847–9.

35 Ibid., p. 849.

36 For Puckle's account, see ibid., pp. 827–32.

37 Ibid., p. 831.

38 Deposition of John Joyne, ibid., pp. 217–18.

39 *The Despatches of William Perwich, English Agent in Paris, 1669–1677*, ed. M. Beryl Curran (1903), p. 270.

40 Ibid., p. 280.

41 PL, Mornamont MSS, vol. II, p. 832.

CHAPTER 16 PELLISSARY'S HOUSEHOLD

1 Diary, 20 and 21 November 1668. Elizabeth, enraged by Pepys's affair with Deb Willet, forced him to write her a letter denouncing her as a whore. Hewer, who was to carry the letter, winked at him and brought that part of the letter back to him the next day without showing it to the girl.

2 Pepys to Balty, 14 July 1679, *The Letters of Samuel Pepys and his Family Circle*, ed. H. T. Heath (1955), p. 74.

3 K. H. D. Haley, *The First Earl of Shaftesbury* (1968), p. 537. Ambassador Barrillon to Louis XIV, 9 January 1679, Sir John Dalrymple, *Memoirs of Great Britain and Ireland* (1790), vol. I, p. 249.

4 Committee of Intelligence minutes, 3 August 1679, BL, Add MSS, 15,643.

5 Pepys to John Pepys Senior, 30 August 1679, *Letters*, ed. Heath, p. 91.

6 Attestation of Trenchepain and Pelletier 'concerning their visits to various servants of Monsieur Pellissary', PL, Mornamont MSS, vol. I, p. 164.

7 Piogerie, a commander of Marines and captain of a 32-gun ship, *L'Emerillon*, was killed in the attack on the island of Tobago on 3 March 1678. Comte D'Estrées's large fleet, of which he had been a part, was then destroyed by three small Dutch ships who lured them on to the reefs of the small island of Las Aves where shark and barracuda killed them in huge numbers as they tried to struggle ashore. For details of the wreck and modern day recovery attempts, see Barry Clifford, *The Lost Fleet* (2002).

8 Pepys to Balty, 7 July 1679, Heath, p. 71.

9 Ibid., p. 76.

10 Ibid.

11 Ibid., p. 79.
12 Ibid.
13 Ibid., p. 75.
14 Ibid., p. 79.
15 Evelyn, *Diary*, 18 July 1679.
16 For the transcription of Wakeman's trial see *State Trials*, ed. William Cobbett (1810), vol. VII, pp. 591–688.
17 J. P. Kenyon, *The Popish Plot* (1974), p. 205.
18 Information of Mr Sackville, PL, Mornamont MSS, vol. II, p. 873.
19 Wells to Pepys, 26 July 1679, ibid., p. 1,065.
20 Ibid.
21 Attestation of Paul Le Goux, ibid., vol. I, pp. 501–2.
22 Attestation of Lady Magdalen Bibaud, widow of Georges Pellissary, ibid., p. 504.

CHAPTER 17 WIND AND SMOKE

1 Sarah Barter Bailey, *Prince Rupert's Patent Guns* (2000). This excellent and detailed work also devotes some pages to a discussion of John Scott's part in the story.
2 Attestation of Edward Sherwin, PL, Mornamont MSS, vol. I, p. 396.
3 John Joyne's notes upon some papers, ibid., p. 248.
4 Scott's contract with Pellissary and company, 27 May 1675, ibid., p. 518.
5 John Joyne's notes upon some papers, ibid., p 245.
6 Tentatively identified by Sarah Barter Bailey as John Stubbs who worked with Prince Rupert at Windsor.
7 Another attestation of de La Tour's about Scott, ibid., p. 548.
8 Edward Manning's challenge to Scott, ibid., p. 393.
9 Edward Manning's letter to Scott, ibid., p. 394.
10 Manning's give-away line was 'Pellissary will never get this work going unless you give me money'.
11 Letter from de La Tour about Scott, 2 April 1680, PL, Mornamont MSS, vol. I, p. 562.
12 Bodl., Rawlinson MSS, A 188, f. 167.
13 PL, Mornamont MSS, vol. I, pp. 341 and 343. The latter is the English translation of Scott's letter to Mademoiselle des Moulins saying that his cousin, Lord Winchilsea, as Governor of Folkestone, was providing a 'pleasure boat' to bring the men over. On the reverse of the French original (p. 341) is an irritated note from Lord Winchilsea (Heneage Finch), denying any relationship to Scott who, he says, being 'presented my by his Majesty

about 8 or 9 years since for a very bad man, I have ever declined any acquaintance or correspondence with him.' It is dated 18 April 1680 from Lincoln's Inn Fields.

14 Scott to Mademoiselle des Moulins, Abbeville, 11 June 1675, PL, Mornamont MSS, vol. I, p. 344.

15 Deposition of John Joyne, ibid., p. 243.

16 Ibid., p. 221.

17 Information 'touching differences between Scott & his companions in France', ibid., p.239.

18 Ibid., p. 238.

19 Deposition of John Joyne, ibid., p. 219.

20 Scott to Mademoiselle des Moulins, 11 August 1675 (NS), ibid., p 356.

21 Scott to John Joyne, 11 August 1675 (NS), ibid., p. 353.

22 Scott to John Joyne, 14 October 1675, ibid., p. 368.

23 Attestation of John Harrison, ibid., p. 410.

24 Captain Browne's deposition 'touching Scott', ibid., pp. 187–8.

25 Deposition of Moreau, ibid., p. 478.

26 Captain Browne's deposition 'touching Scott', ibid., p. 196.

27 Scott's counterfeit letter on behalf of Sherwin to Joyne, undated but sent to Joyne 14 October 1675, ibid., pp. 369–71.

28 Deposition of John Joyne, ibid., p. 224.

29 Joyne's information touching the proof of Scott's guns, ibid., p. 277.

30 De La Tour to Pepys, ibid., pp. 564–5.

31 Further statement by Edward Manning, ibid., p. 396.

32 A memorandum 'touching the points of treason', Bodl., Rawlinson MSS, A 188, f. 195.

CHAPTER 18 THE SERPENT'S PRUDENCE

1 Pepys to Balty, 18 August 1679, *The Letters of Samuel Pepys and his Family Circle*, ed. H. T. Heath (1955), p. 85.

2 Pepys to Balty, 9 October 1679, *Letters*, ed. Heath, p. 116.

3 Pepys to Balty, 28 August 1679, Heath, p. 90.

4 Postscript to letter from Pepys to Balty, 10 November 1679, in which Pepys, expressing concern that Madame Pellissary is away and cannot give her consent, is interrupted by a letter from Balty saying she has returned to town and agreed to send her servants. Ibid., p. 130.

5 Pepys to Balty, 6 November 1679, ibid., p. 127.

6 Pepys to Balty, 2 October 1679, ibid., pp. 107–10.

7 Pepys to Denise, 29 September 1679, Bodl., Rawlinson MSS, A 194, p. 136.

8 Claude Denise to Balty, 18 September 1679, ibid., pp. 99–101.

9 For Pepys's response and inferred contents of Balty's letter, see Pepys to Balty, 2 October 1679, Heath, pp. 107–12.

10 Pepys to Balty, 29 September 1679, ibid., p. 106.

11 Attestation of Pierre Vouchard, François Trenchepain and Jean Murat, PL, Mornamont MSS, vol. I, p. 174.

12 John Joyne's deposition 'on several loose particulars', ibid., p. 254.

13 Joyne's letter from Paris, 30 September 1679, ibid., p. 178.

14 Pepys to Balty, 29 September 1679, Heath, p. 105.

15 Pepys to Balty, 18 August 1679, ibid., p. 86.

16 Deposition of John Joyne, PL, Mornamont MSS, vol. I, pp. 231–2.

17 Ibid., p. 174.

18 Pepys to Balty, 29 September 1679, Heath, p. 105.

19 Pepys to Balty, 6 October 1679, ibid., p. 114.

20 Pepys to Balty, 9 October 1679, ibid., p. 115.

21 Pepys to Balty, 11 September 1679, ibid., p. 96.

22 Pepys to Balty, 16 October 1679, ibid., p. 120.

23 Pepys to Morelli, 25 September 1679, *Letters and the Second Diary of Samuel Pepys*, ed. R. G. Howarth (1932), p. 87.

24 George Wharton to Thomas Wharton, 25 August 1679, Bodl., MS Carte 228, f. 121.

25 Extracts from *Domestick Intelligence*, PL, Mornamont MSS, vol. I, pp. 90–3.

26 *Domestick Intelligence* retraction, ibid., p. 94.

27 Mr Wright's attestation about Scott, touching the penalty of perjury, ibid., vol. II, p. 1,173.

28 'Plain Truth', Bodl., Rawlinson MSS, A 173, f. 180.

29 James Houblon to Pepys, 14 October 1679, ibid., f. 18.

30 Pepys to James Houblon, 14 October 1679, Bodl., Rawlinson MSS, A 194, p. 168.

31 The information of Phelix Donluis, PL, Mornamont MSS, vol. II, pp. 1,237–44.

32 A 'journal of the principal passages relating to the commitment of Sir Anthony Deane and Mr Pepys, and the proceedings thereon', ibid., vol. I, p. 60.

33 Pepys to Balty, 11 September 1679, Heath, p. 96.

34 Pepys to Balty, 29 September 1679, ibid., p. 103.

35 Pepys to Balty, 29 September 1679 (the second letter of that day, to be delivered together by Denise), ibid., p. 104.

36 Pepys to Balty, 11 September 1679, ibid., p. 96.

37 Pepys to Balty, 30 October 1679, ibid., p. 123.

38 Pepys to Mrs Skinner, 24 October 1679, *Letters* ed. Howarth, p. 89.
39 The information of Phelix Donluis, PL, Mornamont MSS, vol. II, pp. 1,237–44.
40 Pepys to Balty, 13 November 1679, Heath, p. 132.
41 Antonia Fraser, *King Charles II* (1979), p. 362 and p. 385.
42 Pepys to Balty, 3 November 1679, Heath, p. 124.

CHAPTER 19 JOHN JOYNE'S JOURNAL

1 The main source for this chapter is the journal 'of all that passed between myself and Col. Scott' kept by John Joyne at Pepys's instigation during his time in London. This journal, produced with the help of Paul Lorrain, is reproduced in full in PL, Mornamont MSS, vol. I, pp. 285–323.
2 Joyne's account of some passages between Scott, Manning, etc., ibid., p. 269.
3 Pepys to Balty, 8 December 1679, *The Letters of Samuel Pepys and his Family Circle*, ed. H. T. Heath (1955), p. 140.
4 Lilian T. Mowrer quotes Lady Vane's letter in *The Indomitable John Scott, Citizen of Long Island* (1960), pp. 289–91.
5 Ibid., p. 311.
6 Lady Vane to John Scott, 25 September 1678, Bodl., Rawlinson MSS, A 176, f. 107.
7 Mowrer, *The Indomitable John Scott*, p. 355.
8 Bryant, *The Years of Peril* (1948), p. 302. Bryant's account of Pepys hiding in the closet has been followed by subsequent writers and must surely be taken as correct. However, he lists as his references for this a series of Mornamont and Rawlinson folio numbers which have nothing in them concerning this aspect of the story and, in one case, is a blank page. Bryant and Mowrer go on to quote Pepys's later reactions to what he heard. Again there are no references to support that. John Joyne does not mention Pepys's presence in the Journal at all and it can only be inferred, without much substance, from his summoning Pepys to the tavern the previous day. There is no mention anywhere in Mornamont of Pepys's presence.
9 Information of Mr Wright, PL, Mornamont MSS, vol. II, p. 1,169.
10 Ibid. p. 1,171.

CHAPTER 20 HABEAS CORPUS

1 Pepys to Balty, 5 January 1680, Bodl., Rawlinson MSS, A 194, p. 52.
2 Pepys to Balty (to meet him at Dover), 26 January 1680, ibid., p. 68.
3 *Pepys's Later Diaries*, ed. C. S. Knighton (2004), pp. 50–1. This and subsequent

references to the legal proceedings in this chapter are taken from PL, Mornamont MSS, vol. I, pp. 62–77, being part of 'A journal of the principal passages relating to the commitment of Sir Anthony Deane and Mr. Pepys and the proceedings thereon'. This is printed in full in Knighton.

4 *The Stuart Constitution: Documents and Commentary*, ed. J. P. Kenyon (1986), pp. 393–4.

5 Haley points out that little is known of his direct part in what is sometimes known as the 'Shaftesbury Act' but he may have been involved behind the scenes. K. H. D. Haley, *The First Earl of Shaftesbury* (1968), p. 527.

6 *Pepys's Later Diaries*, ed. Knighton, p. 51.

7 Ibid., p. 52.

8 Ibid., pp. 52–3.

9 Ibid.

10 Ibid., p. 53.

11 Cited by Jane Lane in *Titus Oates* (1971), p. 156.

12 Knighton, p. 54.

13 Ibid., p. 54.

14 Ibid., p. 55.

15 Ibid., p. 56.

16 Ibid., p. 55.

17 Information of Mr Wright, PL, Mornamont MSS, vol. II, p. 1,170.

18 Knighton, p. 56.

19 Ibid.

20 Ibid., p. 57.

21 Ibid., p. 59.

22 Ibid., p. 58.

23 Extract from a lampoon upon Lord Chief Justice Scroggs, PL, Mornamont MSS, vol. I, p. 89.

24 Pepys to Balty at Dover, where Balty is escorting the French to their boat, 4 March 1680, Bodl., Rawlinson MSS, A 194, p. 80.

CHAPTER 21 THE CONFESSIONS OF JOHN JAMES

1 *Pepys's Later Diaries*, ed. C. S. Knighton (2004), p. 102.

2 Information of John James, PL, Mornamont MSS, vol. II, p. 1,245.

3 Ibid.

4 Ibid., p. 1,246.

5 Ibid.

6 Ibid., p. 1,248.

7 Pepys's endorsement of his copy in Rawlinson MSS, A 175, f. 236, says that

the handwriting was James's mother's. James's mother could not write but his sister could and she shared the same name.

8 William Harbord to the Earl of Essex, 25 July 1679, PL, Mornamont MSS, vol. II, p. 1,274.

9 Information of Phelix Donluis, ibid., p. 1,238.

10 Information of John James, ibid., p. 1,247.

11 *Pepys's Later Diaries*, ed. Knighton, p. 75.

12 Ibid., p. 82.

13 The declaration of Elizabeth James, widow and mother, and Elizabeth James, sister to John James, 'late of the Parish of St Margaret's, Westminster, deceased', PL, Mornamont MSS, vol. II, p. 1,275.

14 The account that follows is largely based on 'The Journal of Mr Pepys's proceedings with James and Harris', ibid., pp. 1,189–1,235. This is also reproduced in full with a useful introduction in Knighton.

15 Pepys to Lord Brouncker, 13 May 1680, Bodl., Rawlinson MSS, A 194, p. 156.

16 Journal of Pepys's proceedings with James and Harris, PL, Mornamont MSS, vol. II, p. 1,190.

17 Knighton, p. 103.

18 John James's note to Alexander Harris, 10 February 1680, PL, Mornamont MSS, vol. II, p. 1,270.

19 Knighton, p. 81.

20 PL, Mornamont MSS, vol. II, p. 1,275.

21 Knighton, p. 80.

22 Ibid., p. 81.

23 Diary, 26 March, 16 and 19 April 1664.

24 Knighton, p. 82.

25 Diary, 19 January 1663.

26 John James's unpublished libel, Bodl., Rawlinson MSS, A 173, ff. 178–9.

27 Knighton, p. 87.

28 Ibid., p. 88.

29 Ibid., p. 95.

30 Ibid., p. 91.

CHAPTER 22 THE ROAD TO OXFORD

1 Brief of the case of Sir Anthony Deane and Pepys, PL, Mornamont MSS, vol. I, pp. 78–82.

2 Scott's contract with Pellissary and company, ibid., p. 518.

3 By that curious serendipity which can make such a pleasure of research, the authors bought a copy of Lilian T. Mowrer's book on John Scott through the

internet. Mowrer, however compromised her take on Scott, was a prodigious researcher and linguist who spent more than six years on her research. She was apt to come to romantic conclusions about her hero but her endnotes show that she left no stone unturned. There was only one edition of the book, so it is hard to come by, and when it arrived in the post, the authors of this book were surprised to find a collection of typewritten letters and notes folded into the back of the book. Some were a list of errata in the book. Others formed a fascinating correspondence between Mowrer and the then Pepys librarian, Robert Latham. In one of those, dated 28 January 1975 from Wonalancet, New Hampshire, Mowrer wrote: 'Incidentally, Mornamont is not an imaginary title: it was an actual Scott estate, but sold in the sixteenth century, when, after the death of the great Sir Thomas Scott, thirty properties in Kent alone went under the hammer to provide jointures for his seventeen children. A Scott of Scot's Hall told me this some time after my book was published. I should have followed this up . . . but my informant was killed suddenly in a car accident which jolted me out of further research.'

4 Longleat MSS, Coventry Papers, vol. 11, f. 397.
5 Letters in the Coventry papers at Longleat (vol. 35, ff. 342, 350, 353 and 356) show that Renée Augier, a long-standing secret agent in Paris, had been watching John Scott's movements and reporting back to Henry Coventry during the time Scott spent there after his flight from Gravesend, passing on *inter alia* the rumour that Scott had brought a letter from the Duke of Buckingham to Paris seeking Louis's help in securing him the post of Paris Ambassador. In further ciphered letters, Augier told Coventry that Scott was attempting to subvert English soldiers in Flanders on behalf of the French.
6 Balty to Pepys, 24 September 1680, *The Letters of Samuel Pepys and his Family Circle*, ed. H. T. Heath (1955), pp. 164–8.
7 Bodl., Rawlinson MSS, A 178, f. 45.
8 Arthur Bryant, *King Charles II* (1934), p. 303.
9 Papers from Lyme, PL, Mornamont MSS, vol. II, p. 1,109.
10 Pepys to James Houblon, 2 October 1680, *Letters and the Second Diary of Samuel Pepys*, ed. R. G. Howarth (1932), p. 102.
11 Arthur Bryant, *The Years of Peril* (1948), p. 339.
12 Pepys to James Houblon, 14 November 1680, *Letters*, ed. Howarth, pp. 106–7. The portrait still exists in private hands (see plate 12). It has an inscription in gold lettering on the lower part identifying it as Pepys's gift to Houblon. This refers to the recipient as Sir Jas Houblon and must therefore have been added several years later, after he was knighted.
13 William Cobbett, *The Parliamentary History of England* (1808), vol. IV, p. 1,160. K. H. D. Haley, *The First Earl of Shaftesbury* (1968), p. 593.

14 Pepys to Will Hewer, 11 November 1680, Howarth, p. 105.
15 Sir Anthony Deane (as 'P. Bayly') to Pepys, 9 November 1680, Bodl., Rawlinson MSS, A 182, f. 138.
16 Pepys to Sir Anthony Deane, 11 November 1680, ibid., A 194, p. 229.
17 Haley, *The First Earl of Shaftesbury*, p. 602.
18 Tim Harris, *London Crowds in the Reign of Charles II* (1987), p. 112.
19 Bryant, *The Years of Peril*, p. 347.
20 Will Hewer to Pepys, 15 November 1680, Howarth, p. 108.
21 Antonia Fraser, *King Charles II* (1979), p. 400.
22 Edward Wright to Pepys, 18 December 1680, Bodl., Rawlinson MSS, A 173, f. 189.
23 Keith Feiling and F. R. D. Needham, 'The Journals of Edmund Warcup 1676–84' in *English Historical Review*, vol. XL (1925), p. 248.
24 Various letters from Pepys to John Joyne in Bodl., Rawlinson MSS, A 194, including those starting on pp. 95, 97, 124, 127 and 137.
25 Haley, p. 622.
26 Fraser, *King Charles II*, p. 405.
27 Parliament's proceedings against Deane and Pepys, PL, Mornamont MSS, vol. I, p. 4.

CHAPTER 23 THE LEMAN AND OWER

1 P. M. Cowburn, 'Christopher Gunman and the Wreck of the *Gloucester*', *The Mariners' Mirror*, vol. 42 (1956), p. 115, quoting Captain Gunman's journal.
2 Pepys to Captain Wyborne, 29 April 1682, Bodl., Rawlinson MSS, A 194, p. 272.
3 Cowburn, *The Mariners' Mirror*, vol. 42 (1956), p. 115.
4 John Charnock, *Biographia Navalis*, vol. I (1794), p. 228.
5 E. Hallam Moorhouse, ed., *Letters of the English Seaman* (1910), pp. 96–8.
6 Cowburn, p. 119, citing Sir John Berry's letter to Lord Treasurer Hyde, 8 May 1682.
7 Arthur Bryant, *The Years of Peril* (1948), p. 270.
8 Cowburn, p. 220, citing Captain Gunman's letter to his wife, written from Edinburgh, 9 May 1682.
9 Pepys to Will Hewer, 8 May 1682, *Letters and the Second Diary of Samuel Pepys*, ed. R. G. Howarth (1932), p. 135.
10 Laird Clowes, *The Royal Navy* (1897–1903), vol. 2, p. 457.
11 Pepys to Will Hewer, 8 May 1682, *Letters*, ed. Howarth, p. 134.
12 Ibid., p. 135.
13 E. Ridley to Sir Francis Radcliffe, 13 May 1682, *Calendar of State Papers*,

Domestic Series, 1682, pp. 205–6.

14 Ibid., p. 206.

15 Clowes, *The Royal Navy*, vol. 2, p. 457.

16 *Samuel Pepys's Naval Minutes*, ed. J. R. Tanner (1926), p. 147.

17 Earl of Conway to Admiralty Commissioners, 13 June 1682, *Calendar of State Papers, Domestic Series, 1682*, p. 247.

18 John Evelyn, Diary, 26 March 1685.

19 James Houblon to Pepys, 13 May 1682, Howarth, p. 127.

20 Ibid.

21 Pepys to Will Hewer, 19 May 1682, ibid., p. 139.

22 Coroner's enquiry, Bodl., Rawlinson MSS, A 173, f. 164.

23 Pepys to Will Hewer, 26 May 1682, Bodl., Rawlinson MSS, A 194, p. 277. For Hewer's information against Scott see *Calendar of State Papers, Domestic Series, 1682*, p. 211.

24 Thompson's Intelligencer, 20 May 1681, Bodl., Rawlinson MSS, A 173, f. 145.

25 Thompson's Intelligencer, 23 May 1681, ibid.

26 Papers of Col. Scott seized in his chamber in Chancery Lane on 18 May 1682 by Thomas Atterbury, messenger, *Calendar of State Papers, Domestic Series, 1682*, p. 211.

27 Forged letter nominally from Will Hewer to Pepys, 25 May 1682, Bodl., Rawlinson MSS, A 194, p. 278.

28 Ibid.

29 Ibid.

CHAPTER 24 GRAVESEND UNRAVELLED

1 Col. John Scott to Lord Arlington from Terveer in Zeeland, 26 June 1682, *Calendar of State Papers, Domestic Series, 1682*, p. 269.

2 Rupert Browne to Sir William Trumbull, 21 December 1685, *HMC Marquess of Downshire*, vol. 1, part 1, p. 77.

3 E.g., John Gelson to Joseph Williamson, 8 June (as postscript to letter of 7 June) 1672, *Calendar of State Papers, Domestic Series, May–September 1672*, p. 175.

4 *Calendar of State Papers, Domestic Series, July–September 1683*, pp. 390–1 and pp. 437–8. These last two Gelson letters which have survived in the State Papers do not have an addressee listed but in both cases they must have been sent to Sir Anthony Deane.

5 Information of Mr Wright, PL, Mornamont MSS, vol. II, p. 1,170.

6 John Gelson to Pepys, 12 July 1683, Bodl., Rawlinson MSS, A 190, f. 54. This is the original of this letter, but the following folio is the same letter, re-

written in a plainer hand.

7 Pepys to John Gelson, 11 August 1683, ibid., f. 52.

8 Pepys to Sir Anthony Deane, 23 August 1683, ibid., f. 58.

9 *Calendar of State Papers, Domestic Series, July–September 1683*, pp. 437–8.

10 *Pepys's Later Diaries*, ed. C. S. Knighton (2004), p. 131. See also *The Tangier Papers of Samuel Pepys*, ed. Edwin Chappell (1935). Chappell's edition includes Pepys's interesting loose notes.

11 Pepys to 'Gentleman', 19 May 1684, Bodl., Rawlinson MSS, A 190, f. 74.

12 John Evelyn, Diary, 25 January 1685.

13 *Private Correspondence and Miscellaneous Papers of Samuel Pepys*, ed. J. R. Tanner (1926), vol. I, pp. 27–8.

14 Pepys to his sureties, 15 October 1690, *Private Correspondence*, ed. J. R. Tanner, vol. I, p. 36.

15 Edward Wright to Pepys, 10 November 1696, *Letters and the Second Diary of Samuel Pepys*, ed. R. G. Howarth (1932), p. 263.

16 Pepys to Edward Wright, 10 November 1696, *Letters*, ed. Howarth, p. 263.

17 Edward Wright to Pepys, 12 November 1696, Howarth, pp. 263–4.

18 *Calendar of State Papers, Domestic Series, William and Mary, 1696*, p. 153 for Scott's pardon for murdering George Butler, 29 April 1696; p. 166 for his reversal of outlawry, 2 May 1696; p. 175 for signing of the Bill concerning his pardon in the minutes of the Lords Justices of England, 12 May 1696.

19 Winifred, Lady Burghclere, *George Villiers, Second Duke of Buckingham* (1903), pp. 353–4.

20 Sir John Dalrymple, *Memoirs of Great Britain and Ireland* (1790), vol. 1, p. 342.

21 Lady Burghclere, *George Villiers*, p. 354, citing French National Archives, Affaires Étrangères, 17/11/78, no. 131, f. 187.

22 Ibid., p. 353, citing Affaires Étrangères, f. 203.

23 Ibid., p. 355, citing Affaires Étrangères, f. 186.

24 Information of John Joyne, PL, Mornamont MSS, vol. I, p. 417.

25 Claire Tomalin, *Samuel Pepys: The Unequalled Self* (2002), p. 306 et passim.

26 Pepys to Wynne Houblon, 30 October 1700, Tanner, vol. II, p. 105.

27 Lilian T. Mowrer, *The Indomitable John Scott, Citizen of Long Island* (1960), p. 381.

Bibliography and Further Reading

DIARY AND BIOGRAPHIES

The manuscript of Pepys's Diary is in the Pepys Library, Magdalene College, Cambridge. The definitive transcription is the eleven-volume edition by Robert Latham and William Matthews (1970–83), which includes an encyclopaedic *Companion* on the people and places of 1660s London.

There have been a number of Pepys biographies, of which Claire Tomalin's *Samuel Pepys: The Unequalled Self* (2002) is undoubtedly the liveliest. It is a revealing analysis of Pepys's character and is the introduction of choice to his life.

Arthur Bryant's account, *Samuel Pepys,* is essential reading for Pepys's life and career up to 1688. Three volumes, subtitled *The Man in the Making* (1933), *The Years of Peril* (1935) and *The Saviour of the Navy* (1938) were produced in many editions but a planned fourth volume was never written.

Further biographies include Stephen Coote's *Samuel Pepys: A Life* (2000) and Richard Ollard's *Pepys: A Biography* (1984).

There have been two biographers of John Scott: Lilian T. Mowrer, in *The Indomitable John Scott, Citizen of Long Island* (1960), unearthed a wealth of new information about Scott's life. However, she idealises 'John', as she calls him, as an American hero whose name was quite unfairly blackened by Pepys in his own defence. Her brave revisionist argument fails to hold water. For a briefer, more objective description of Scott's life, see Wilbur C. Abbott, *Colonel John Scott of Long Island* (1918). A revised edition of this appears in his *Conflicts with Oblivion* (1924).

UNPUBLISHED PRIMARY SOURCES

The Bodleian Library
Rawlinson MSS A 172, 173, 175, 176, 178, 181, 182, 185, 188, 190, 194. Also Rawlinson MSS D 662 and MS Carte 228.

Antiquary and collector Richard Rawlinson (1690–1755) frequented booksellers and the yards of London waste-paper collectors, who bought old documents in bulk to sell on as hot-pie wrappers for food stalls. He accumulated large amounts of Pepysian material, including much of Pepys's original correspondence in the Scott case. Rawlinson A 194 is the book that was brought blank to Pepys in the Tower, into which he had his outgoing letters recorded.

Pepys Library
PL2881 and 2882: Mornamont MSS.

These are two large leather-bound volumes. They contain the neat transcriptions made for Pepys of the key documents concerning the plot against him and his investigation of John Scott. Some letters and a few other components of these long, fragmented manuscripts have been published separately. *John Joyne: A Journal* was published by the Augustan Reprint Society in 1959. *Pepys's Later Diaries*, edited by C. S. Knighton (2004) includes the 'King's Bench Journal', detailing Pepys's and Deane's court appearances, as well as their 'Proceedings with James and Harris'. Knighton's commentary on the background in each case is illuminating.

The British Library
Add MSS, 25,124, Extraordinary Correspondence of Henry Coventry.
Add MSS, 15,643, Committee of Intelligence Minutes.

Longleat Manuscripts
Coventry Papers. Archive of the correspondence of Secretary of State Henry Coventry. This is also available on microfilm at the Institute of Historical Research, London.

National Archives
Document E407/56/1. Tower of London papers.

PUBLISHED CONTEMPORARY MATERIAL

Anderson, R.C., ed., *Journals and Narratives of the Third Dutch War* (1946).
Bedloe, William, *A Narrative of the Pope's Late Fire-Works in England* (1679).
de la Bédoyère, Guy, ed., *The Letters of Samuel Pepys* (2006).
de Beer, E. S., ed., *The Diary of John Evelyn*, 6 vols (1955).
Blundell, M., ed., *Cavalier: Letters of William Blundell to his Friends, 1620–1698* (1933).
Braybrooke, Lord Richard, ed., *Memoirs of Samuel Pepys*, 2 vols (1825).

'Brutus, Junius' (pseudonym for Charles Blount), *An Appeal from the Country to the City* (1679).

Burnet, Gilbert, *Bishop Burnet's History of his own Time*, 6 vols (1833).

Calendar of State Papers: Domestic Series and *Colonial Series, America and West Indies*. By year.

Care, Henry, *English Liberties: or the Free-Born Subject's Inheritance* (1682).

Chappell, Edwin, ed., *The Tangier Papers of Samuel Pepys* (1935).

Cobbett, William, *The Parliamentary History of England*, 36 vols (1806–20). (Vol. IV (1808) covers 1660–88).

Cobbett, William and T. C. Howell, eds, *State Trials*, 33 vols and General Index (1809–1826). Vol. 7 (1810) contains the relevant Popish Plot trials.

Collections of the Massachusetts Historical Society, 4th Series, 10 vols (1852–71) and 5th Series, 10 vols (1871–88).

Curran, M. Beryl, ed., *The Despatches of William Perwich, English Agent in Paris, 1669–1677* (1903).

Dryden, John, *Absalom and Achitophel* (1681).

Grey, Anchitel, *Debates of the House of Commons from 1667 to 1694*, 10 vols (1769).

Heath, H. T., ed., *The Letters of Samuel Pepys and his Family Circle* (1955).

Historical Manuscripts Commission Reports. Various: specific volumes given in the endnotes as, for example, *HMC Ormonde*.

Hoadly, Charles J., ed., *Records of the Colony or Jurisdiction of New Haven* (1858).

Howarth, R. G., ed., *Letters and the Second Diary of Samuel Pepys* (1932).

Hutchinson, Thomas, *The Hutchinson Papers*, 2 vols (1865).

Kenyon, J. P., ed., *The Stuart Constitution: Documents and Commentary* (1986).

Lee, Nat., *To the Duke on his Return* (1682).

Lloyd, William, *A Sermon at the Funeral of Sir Edmund Berry Godfrey* (1678).

London's Flames (1679).

MacPherson, James, *Original Papers*, 2 vols (1775), containing *Extracts from the Life of James II, as written by himself*.

Moorhouse, E. Hallam, ed., *Letters of the English Seaman* (1910).

O'Callaghan, E. B., ed., *Documents Relative to the Colonial History of the State of New York*, 11 vols (1853–61).

Smith, J., ed., *The Life, Journals and Correspondence of Samuel Pepys*, 2 vols (1841).

Tanner, J. R., ed., *Private Correspondence and Miscellaneous Papers of Samuel Pepys 1679–1703*, 2 vols (1926).

Tanner, J. R., ed., *Samuel Pepys's Naval Minutes* (1926).

Tanner, J. R., ed., *Further Correspondence and Miscellaneous Papers of Samuel Pepys 1662–1679* (1929).

Trumbell, J. Hammond, and C. J. Hoadly, eds, *Public Records of the Colony of Connecticut*, 15 vols (1850–90).

SECONDARY WORKS

Abbott, Wilbur C., 'The Origin of Titus Oates' Story', *English Historical Review*, vol. xxv (1910), pp. 126–9.

Airy, Osmund, *Charles II* (1904).

Ashley, Maurice, *John Wildman, Plotter and Postmaster: A Study of the English Republican Movement in the Seventeenth Century* (1947).

Ashley, Maurice, *James II* (1977).

Baker, J. H., *The Legal Profession and the Common Law: Historical Essays* (1986).

Baker, J. H., *The Common Law Tradition: Lawyers, Books and the Law* (2000).

Barter Bailey, Sarah, *Prince Rupert's Patent Guns* (2000).

Bell, W. G., *The Great Fire of London in 1666* (1920).

Bell, W. G., *The Tower of London* (1935).

Benham, William, *The Tower of London* (1906).

Brett-James, Norman G., *The Growth of Stuart London* (1935).

Brodhead, John Romeyn, *History of the State of New York*, 2 vols (1853–71).

Brown, Louise Fargo, *The First Earl of Shaftesbury* (1933).

Bryant, Arthur, *King Charles II* (1934).

Burghclere, Lady Winifred, *George Villiers, Second Duke of Buckingham 1628–1687: A Study in the History of the Restoration* (1903).

Chapman, Hester W., *Great Villiers: A Study of George Villiers, Second Duke of Buckingham 1628–1687* (1949).

Charnock, John, *Biographia Navalis*, 6 vols (1794–98).

Christian, Edward, *A Concise Account of the Origin of the Two Houses of Parliament* (1810).

Clark, Sir George, *The Later Stuarts 1660–1714* (1955).

Clifford, Barry, *The Lost Fleet* (2002).

Clowes, Laird, *The Royal Navy*, 7 vols (1897–1903).

Cowburn, P. M., 'Christopher Gunman and the Wreck of the *Gloucester*' in two parts, *The Mariners' Mirror*, vol. 42 (1956) pp. 113–26 and pp. 219–29.

Crawford, Clarence C., 'The Writ of Habeas Corpus', *The American Law Review*, vol. xlii (July–August 1908), pp. 481–99.

Dalrymple, Sir John, *Memoirs of Great Britain and Ireland*, 3 vols (1790).

Duker, William F., *A Constitutional History of Habeas Corpus* (1980).

Edie, Carolyn Andervont, 'Succession and Monarchy: The Controversy of 1679–1681' *American Historical Review*, vol. lxx, no. 2 (January 1965), pp. 350–70.

Ellis, Markman, *The Coffee-House: A Cultural History* (2005).

Feiling, Keith and F. R. D. Needham, 'The Journals of Edmund Warcup 1676–84', *English Historical Review*, vol. xl (1925), pp. 235–60.

Feiling, Keith, *British Foreign Policy 1660–1672* (1968).

Field, John, *The Story of Parliament in the Palace of Westminster* (2002).

Fraser, Antonia, *King Charles II* (1979).

Fraser, Antonia, *The Gunpowder Plot* (2002).

Gavin, C. M., *Royal Yachts* (1932).

Geyl, Pieter, *Orange and Stuart 1641–1672* (1969).

Gooch, G. P., *English Democratic Ideas in the Seventeenth Century* (1927).

Grigsby, J. E., *Annals of our Royal Yachts, 1604–1953* (1953).

Haley, K. H. D., *The First Earl of Shaftesbury* (1968).

Harris, Tim, *London Crowds in the Reign of Charles II: Propaganda and Politics from the Restoration until the Exclusion Crisis* (1987).

Hatton, Ragnhild, ed., *Louis XIV and Europe* (1976).

Henning, Basil Duke, *The House of Commons 1660–1690*, 3 vols (1983).

Hill, Christopher, *The Century of Revolution 1603–1714* (1961).

Hiscock, Robert H., *A History of Gravesend* (1981).

Holmes, Geoffrey, *The Making of a Great Power: Late Stuart and early Georgian Britain 1660–1722* (1993).

Houblon, Lady A. Archer, *The Houblon Family: Its Story and Times*, 2 vols (1907).

Hughes, Paul L., and Robert F. Fries, eds, *Crown and Parliament in Tudor–Stuart England* (1959).

Hutton, Ronald, *Charles II* (1989).

Inwood, Stephen, *A History of London* (1998).

Jones, J. R., *The First Whigs: The Politics of the Exclusion Crisis 1678–1683* (1961).

Keeton, G. W., *Lord Chancellor Jeffreys and the Stuart Cause* (1965).

Kenyon, J. P., *The Stuarts* (1966).

Kenyon, J. P., 'The Exclusion Crisis', in Ivan Roots, ed., *Conflicts in Tudor and Stuart England* (1967), pp. 102–28.

Kenyon, J. P., *The Popish Plot* (1974).

Knight, Stephen, *The Killing of Justice Godfrey* (1986).

Lane, Jane, *Titus Oates* (1971).

Lang, Jane, *Rebuilding St Paul's After the Great Fire of London* (1956).

Marshall, Alan, *Intelligence and Espionage in the Reign of Charles II, 1660–1685* (1994).

McCoog, Thomas M., 'Richard Langhorne and the Popish Plot', *Recusant History*, vol. 19, no. 4 (1989), pp. 499–508.

Miller, John, *Bourbon and Stuart* (1987).

Mitford, Nancy, *The Sun King: Louis XIV at Versailles* (1966).

Ogg, David, *Europe in the Seventeenth Century* (1961).

Palmer, Tony, *Charles II: Portrait of an Age* (1979).

Pollock, John, *The Popish Plot: A Study in the History of the Reign of Charles II* (1903).

Richardson, Joanna, *Louis XIV* (1973).

Roberts, Clayton, *The Growth of Responsible Government in Stuart England* (1966).

Schoolcraft, Henry L., 'The Capture of New Amsterdam', *English Historical Review*, vol. XXII (1907), pp. 674–93.

Scott, James Renat, *Memorials of the Family of Scott, of Scot's Hall, in the County of Kent* (1876).

Scull, G. D., *Dorothea Scott* (1883).

Sharpe. R. J., *The Law of Habeas Corpus* (1989).

Shepherd, William R., *The Story of New Amsterdam* (1926).

Sitwell, Sir George, *The First Whig* (1894).

Strong, Roy, *Lost Treasures of Britain* (1990).

Tanner, J. R., 'Pepys and the Popish Plot', *English Historical Review*, vol. VII (1892), pp. 281–90.

Tanner, J. R., ed., *Descriptive Catalogue of the Naval Manuscripts in the Pepysian Library*, 4 vols (1903–23).

Tanner, J. R., *English Constitutional Conflicts of the Seventeenth Century 1603–1689* (1960).

Tinniswood, Adrian, *By Permission of Heaven: The Story of the Great Fire of London* (2003).

Trevelyan, G. M., *England Under The Stuarts* (2002).

Trevor, Meriol, *The Shadow of a Crown: The Life Story of James II of England and VII of Scotland* (1988).

Turberville, A. S., 'The House of Lords under Charles II', Part I, *English Historical Review*, vol. XLIV (July 1929).

Van Rensselaer, Schuyler, *History of the City of New York in the Seventeenth Century*, 2 vols (1909).

Walker, James, 'The Secret Service under Charles II and James II', *Transactions of the Royal Historical Society*, 4th Series, vol. 15 (1932), pp. 211–42.

Wilson, C. H., 'Who Captured New Amsterdam?', *English Historical Review* vol. LXXII (July 1957), pp. 469–74.

Wilson, Derek, *The Tower of London* (1989).

Wilson, Derek, *All the King's Women: Love, Sex and Politics in the Life of Charles II* (2003).

Wilson, John Harold, *The Ordeal of Mr Pepys's Clerk* (1972).

Whitear, Walter H., *More Pepysiana* (1927).

Zook, Melinda S., *Radical Whigs and Conspiratorial Politics in Late Stuart England* (1999).

Index